Upper–Intermediate

Teacher's Book

New Headway
English Course

Liz & John Soars

Oxford University Press

Oxford University Press
Great Clarendon Street, Oxford OX2 6DP

Oxford New York
Athens Auckland Bangkok Bogotá Buenos Aires
Cape Town Chennai Dar es Salaam Delhi
Florence Hong Kong Istanbul Karachi Kolkata
Kuala Lumpur Madrid Melbourne Mexico City
Mumbai Nairobi Paris São Paulo Shanghai
Singapore Taipei Tokyo Toronto Warsaw

OXFORD and OXFORD ENGLISH are trade marks of
Oxford University Press

ISBN 0 19 435803 8

First published 1998
Fifth impression 2001

Printed and bound in Hong Kong

Acknowledgements

Illustration by Tech Graphics Dept. OUP p138

The publisher would like to thank Famous Pictures and Features Agency for permission to reproduce photograph of Diana, Princess of Wales p154

Design by Fran Holdsworth Associates, Isle of Wight

Contents

Introduction

Why a new version of *Headway Upper-Intermediate*?

The main reason we have rewritten the upper-intermediate book is to make it a more compatible companion to *New Headway Intermediate Course*. In our minds, the intermediate and upper-intermediate levels are linked, just as the elementary and pre-intermediate ones are. After *New Headway Intermediate Course* appeared in 1996, it became obvious that its companion needed a similar overhaul. The two books had to tie in with each other. Hence we have produced *New Headway Upper-Intermediate Course*.

We very much wanted to rewrite the original intermediate and upper-intermediate books as there were things we wanted to change. They were our first attempts at course book writing, and over the years our ideas have developed.

How is the new version different from the old one?

The basic methodology is the same, but *all* the material is new. There is the familiar blend of the traditional and more recent developments in language teaching.

- Traditional approaches which emphasize clear focus on grammar with in-depth analysis and explanation, thorough practice activities, and the exploitation of texts for comprehension and stylistic appreciation.
- Communicative approaches which emphasize the importance of individual students' contributions to work out rules for themselves, and to express personal opinions. Tasks and topics relevant to the students, and texts with real examples of the target language.

The grammatical syllabus in *New Headway Upper-Intermediate* is similar to the old one, but extended. The vocabulary syllabus is largely new. The unit structure is different, as we explain below. The most important difference is that *all the material is new* – the presentations, the practice exercises, the topics, the reading and listening texts, the speaking and writing activities, are all new.

What are the features of *New Headway Upper-Intermediate*?

- Some of the grammar work will be familiar, for example the tense system, aspect, verb patterns, fact versus non-fact, noun phrases, participle and relative clauses, quantifiers, determiners, and conjunctions.
- There is also work on the grammar of spoken English. Of course, a lot of the grammar of the written word applies to the spoken word, too, but there are features which characterize speech. We need to signal our response to what we're hearing, and we need to convey our attitude to what we're saying. When we speak, we may exaggerate or understate our message. In the Postscript sections there are exercises on exclamations, reply questions, social expressions, soundbites, exaggeration and understatement, being polite, moans and groans, and comment adverbs.
- In the vocabulary sections, there is work on textual cohesion via synonyms and antonyms. Collocation is examined in exercises called *Hot verbs*, where high-frequency verbs such as *take*, *put*, *be*, *get*, *come*, and *go* are seen with nouns, expressions, and particles to form phrasal verbs.
- Some work on the systems of vocabulary will be familiar, such as affixes, compounds, and words with variable stress. Others will be new, for example binomials (*neat and tidy*, *give and take*) and homographs (row – /raʊ/ and /rəʊ/).

How are the units organized?

The unit structure of *New Headway Upper-Intermediate* is similar to *New Headway Intermediate*. It differs from the old upper-intermediate book in that accuracy work comes at the beginning of the unit, not at the end.

Test your grammar

This initial exercise allows students to show how much they know about the target grammar of the unit. This seems appropriate at higher levels, where the starting point is not zero. Students will already know *something* about the language being examined. *Test your grammar* also orientates students to the language work that is to come.

It is essential that the *Test your grammar* section is done briskly. You as the teacher should avoid the temptation of teaching the whole unit via this section. If students have a lot of questions, move on to the *Language in context*!

Language in context

Students see and/or hear the target language, and have tasks that prompt its analysis and use. This is the equivalent of the presentation section in lower levels of *Headway*. It ends with *Grammar questions*, which encourage students to work out rules for themselves.

PRACTICE BANK

There is a wide variety of practice exercises, ranging from controlled to free, and practising all four skills. Some are straightforward gap-fill, or put the verb in the right tense. Others are personalized activities or information gap.

The keynote of this section is *bank*. It is up to you to decide which exercises to do, and when. The idea is definitely *not* to do them one after another in the same lesson.

In the Teaching notes, we suggest which exercises can be done as homework, and which can to be done at the beginning of a lesson to act as revision.

LANGUAGE REVIEW

This section serves as a summary. It gives the essential rules of form and use, and refers students to the Grammar reference section at the back of the book. This is for home study, to consult while using the Workbook, and to refer to at any time in the future.

SKILLS WORK

There is at least one activity for the four skills of reading, listening, speaking, and writing. Reading texts come from magazines, newspapers, science journals, extracts from literature, and a biography. There is also a short story. Listening texts come from interviews with real people, and there are songs, radio programmes, and advertisements.

Speaking is threaded throughout the skills work, and there are jigsaw activities, a maze, discussions, and roleplays.

The writing syllabus includes work on correcting mistakes, formal and informal letters, note-taking, writing a review of a book or film, and joining sentences with conjunctions and adverbs.

VOCABULARY

As in all the *Headway* series, there is a strong lexical syllabus. There is at least one vocabulary input per unit in the Student's Book, and two more in the Workbook. Many of the vocabulary exercises have a pronunciation element.

We adopt three approaches to the teaching of vocabulary.

- We teach lexical sets, such as adjectives that describe character or consumer durables.
- We encourage good vocabulary learning habits, such as using a dictionary, keeping records, guessing meaning, and reading.
- We work on the systems of vocabulary, such as compounds, phrasal verbs, prefixes and suffixes, homonyms, synonyms, antonyms, and collocation.

PostScript

This section affords the teacher another opportunity to do some input of a different nature.

We present and practise survival areas such as numbers, spelling, using a phone, and understanding English signs. However, most of the work is on the grammar of spoken English – expressing interest and surprise, being polite, social expressions, and soundbites.

What's in the Workbook?

The Workbook exercises reinforce the target language of the Student's Book.

There are several other features.

- An extra input of a related grammatical area
- An exercise on phrasal verbs in every odd-numbered unit
- An exercise on prepositions in every even-numbered unit
- An exercise on pronunciation in every unit

What's in the Teacher's Book?

As well as full teaching notes, answers, and possible problems, there are extra photocopiable materials, Stop and check tests for use after every four units, two Progress tests, and a unit-by-unit word list.

Finally!

We hope that *New Headway Upper-Intermediate* helps you and your students in the whole process of language teaching and learning. And we hope that you have fun!

Liz and John Soars

There's no place like home

The tense system
Dates, numbers, spelling

Introduction to the unit

As you begin *New Headway Upper-Intermediate*, you are possibly starting a new course with a new group of students. If so, your most important aim is that everyone gets to know each other. They should learn names and find out a little about backgrounds and interests. The questions in the *Test your grammar* section which starts the unit have a dual purpose. They are designed to help students learn a little about each other as well as testing them in their use of tenses and time expressions.

The theme of this opening unit is house and home. The *Language in context* consists of three letters written to people back home. The reading texts are about two couples who decide to emigrate, one to Canada and one to Greece. The listening is a song about an American boy who goes to summer camp and suffers from homesickness.

Notes on the unit

LANGUAGE AIMS – THE TENSE SYSTEM

NB *Before beginning a unit, it might be worthwhile for you to remind yourself of the grammar by reading the Grammar Reference section at the back of the Student's Book. It is on p146.*

Unit 1 of *New Headway Upper-Intermediate* focuses on the tense system in English, so that students can begin to perceive how the elements of time and aspect combine to give us perfect and non-perfect tenses, simple and continuous tenses, and active and passive. None of these should be unfamiliar to students at this level, but it is unlikely that they will have seen the complete list of tenses as presented in the chart on page 8 of the Student's Book.

Learners will certainly be familiar with the names of the tenses (Present Simple, Past Continuous, Present Perfect Continuous, etc.), and they should *understand* their main concepts. However, you can expect there to be many problems when it comes to *producing* correct forms.

Note that all the tenses are examined in greater depth in later units. Should your students have a lot of problems with the language aims of Unit 1, you should treat this unit as orientation for later units.

Test your grammar (SB p6)

Students should find the exercises in this section quite easy and straightforward, so do them quite briskly. Listen carefully to monitor the performance of your (new) class in English. How good are they? How accurate is their grammar? What's their pronunciation like?

You should also be watching to see what sort of learners they are. Who are the dominant ones? Who are the quiet ones? Who are the ones who are happy to chatter away despite making lots of mistakes? Who are the ones who are so fearful of being seen to make a mistake that they daren't utter a sentence without five minutes to plan it first? Some upper-intermediate students can think they're pretty smart, so look out for the student who is trying to show that he/she knows more than you do.

1 Students work in pairs to put a time expression with a sentence. Check they know the word *blizzard.*

You could give an example of an *unnatural* sentence to show the kind of thing you *don't* want.
~~I'll see you for a year.~~
Ask different members of the class for their answers, and encourage the others to correct and make contributions.

Answers

a My parents met in Warsaw in the 1960s/ages ago/during a blizzard.
b My father never/rarely/always speaks Polish.
c They were working in Germany when I was born/in the 1960s/for a year/for ages/recently.
d I was born in Berlin in the 1960s/during a blizzard.

e My grandparents have never/always lived in Hong Kong/have lived in Hong Kong for a year/for ages/since I was a child.
f I never/always wrote to my grandmother/wrote to my grandmother the other day/recently.
g I'm going to work in Peru for a year.
h My brother's flying to Rome on business tonight/in a fortnight's time.
i I've been learning Spanish for a year/for ages/recently/since I was a child.
j I'll see you later/tonight.

As a quick check you could ask 'Which time expressions go with which tense? Are there some time expressions which go with several/all tenses?'

Answers

when I was born – past
never – past, present, and future
tonight – future
in the 1960s – past
rarely – present and past
for a year – past, present, and future
for ages – past, Present Perfect
ages ago – past
the other day – past
in a fortnight's time – future
recently – past and Present Perfect
during a blizzard – past
always – all tenses
later – past or future
since I was a child – Present Perfect

2 Students work on their own for a minute or two to think of similar sentences to say about themselves and their family. They then say the sentences to their partner. Encourage the pairs to correct any mistakes. Students then tell the class about their partners. This is the opportunity for the class to find out about each other, so make sure this happens. Correct students carefully at this stage.

3 Students work in pairs to think of questions to ask you about yourself. Go round the class monitoring and helping. Expect there to be problems of question formation (auxiliary verbs, word order, intonation).

Ask the students to put their questions to you. Insist on well-formed questions with suitable intonation. This could be an opportunity for the class to find out a little about you, so if a good question comes up, feel free to chat to them for a bit.

LANGUAGE IN CONTEXT (SB p6)

Letters home

BACKGROUND INFORMATION

Kate's writing is very childish. In fact she's ten.

Vicky talks about her English *department*. British universities are divided into subject departments such as maths, history, French, etc.

A *fresher* is a university student in their first year. A *freshers' ball* is a dance or disco for new students.

A *tutorial* is a lesson at university with one or two students and a tutor (teacher).

1 **T 1.1** Read the introduction as a class. Students scan the letters to answer the questions. Tell students not to worry about any unknown words at this stage. Ask them to compare their answers with a partner before you discuss them as a class.

Answers

Kate wrote the first letter to her parents. She's in Wales on an adventure holiday. In fact, it is a holiday organized by her primary school. She's been pony-trekking, and tomorrow she's going whitewater rafting. She mentions Megan, her sister. (She also mentions Eric, her horse.)

Vicky wrote the second letter to her sister. Vicky has just started at university, studying English. She mentions her room-mate, Rachel, and a boy called Luke, who she's 'sort of' going out with. Luke reminds her of Oliver, and the suggestion is that Oliver is someone that Vicky's sister likes. Vicky also mentions her mother and father.

Julie wrote the third letter probably to her parents. She is in Mombasa, a coastal town in Kenya. She is there with her husband, Martin, who is working as a teacher. She mentions her husband, and a friend in the mountains of Amani.

Now play the tape. Students read and listen at the same time.

NB The letters are on tape for several reasons.

- *Listening is a whole-class activity, where everyone is focusing on the same thing at the same time. If you are just beginning a new course, you might want to keep the whole class together for a while; if students read the letters on their own, they will all work at different speeds.*
- *The voices of the schoolgirl, the university student, and the woman in Africa add to students' understanding and appreciation of the texts.*

POSSIBLE VOCABULARY PROBLEMS

Here is a list of words and expressions you may want to check. Stop the tape at these points.

I was sick = I vomited (not 'I was ill generally')
miss you loads = miss you a lot
pony-trekking
my bum was killing me = my bottom was hurting a lot
whitewater rafting
freshers' ball
I think you'd approve The suggestion is that Luke is like Oliver, a boy who her sister likes a lot.
knackered = slang for very tired/exhausted
yonks ago = a long time ago
a.s.a.p. = as soon as possible
M. and D. = Mum and Dad
Sis = Sister
can't bear = don't like
the fan
I follow the progress of every little cloud
to head for the coolness = go towards the coolness
baboons
a log fire
steamy
sticky

2 Students work in pairs or small groups to complete the questions and answers. This exercise requires more attention, so make sure it is done carefully. It tests present, past, and future tenses, question formation, *have* and *have got*, *have to* to express obligation, and the formation of *have* in the past.

POSSIBLE LANGUAGE PROBLEMS

The verb *have* presents learners of English with many problems.

- It is a full verb (*to have breakfast*).
- It is used as *have got* to refer to the present.
- *Have to* expresses obligation.
- *Have* is an auxiliary verb in perfect tenses.

This area is explained and practised in Exercises 6 and 7 in Unit 1 of the Workbook.

Common mistakes
*~~Have you any brothers~~?
*~~What time have you got lunch~~?
*~~I got a new car~~.

You can expect many problems and mistakes with *have*. Keep correcting, and reminding students of the rules!

When getting feedback, encourage the rest of the class to contribute their suggestions.
You might well want to drill some of the questions and answers in open pairs across the room.

T 1.2 Ask students to listen and check their answers.

Answers

Kate

a How long has Kate been in Wales?
For three days.

b Is she having a good time? (Present Continuous of *have* as a full verb)
Yes, she's enjoying it a lot.

c How long did the journey take?
Twelve hours.

d What time do they have breakfast?
At 7.30.

e Why was she/did she feel nervous?
Because she had never been on/ridden a horse before. (Past Perfect)

f What's she doing/going to do tomorrow?
She's going whitewater rafting.

Vicky

a What is Vicky studying at university?
English.

b How long has she been going out with Luke? (Present Perfect Continuous)
Two weeks.

c Where did they meet?
At a dance.

d What sort of car has he got/does he have? (Both forms are possible here.)
A VW Beetle.

e Why is she/does she feel/is she feeling tired? (Both simple and continuous are possible here.)
Because she's been getting ready for a tutorial. (Present Perfect Continuous)

Julie and Martin

a How long have Julie and Martin been in Mombasa?
Since September.

b What time does Martin have to start work? (The question with *do/does* is used for repeated actions.)
At 7.00.

c Why did they decide to go to Amani?
Because it's cooler.

d Where did they have lunch? (In the past, the question is formed with *did*.)
At a friend's house.

e What has just happened?
It's started to rain.

Grammar question

Ask students to identify some of the tenses in the letters. Don't let this go on too long. It would become tedious.

Answers

Kate's letter

Past Simple got was took

Present Continuous I'm having I'm watching we're going

Present Simple miss have goes

Past Perfect I'd never been

Past Continuous was killing

Future I'll let

Vicky's letter

Present Perfect I've made I've met has happened

Present Continuous I'm sharing we're going he's going

Past Simple met left

Present Simple reminds He's got (present, although the form is Present Perfect) seems promise

Present Perfect Continuous I've been getting ready

Future we'll have I'll phone

Julie's letter

Past Simple arrived decided drove was had

Present Perfect Continuous has been getting

Present Simple is feel has to follow happens are

Past Perfect hadn't seen

Future I'll write

Present Perfect Simple I've just heard

PRACTICE BANK (SB p8)

NB *'New Headway Upper-Intermediate' contains a lot of practice activities. We call these a PRACTICE BANK because we want you to decide which ones you do and when you do them, and how many you do in one lesson. It would not be a good idea to go through all the exercises in the Practice Bank one after the other. It would be better to break them up, and intersperse them with activities of a different nature. Set one for homework, perhaps, or use one of them at the beginning of another lesson to serve as a revision exercise.*

1 Forming the tenses

Students work in small groups to complete the tense charts. Some learners may find this easy but not others, so be prepared to help. It isn't necessarily a bad thing if some students find it difficult. This is, after all, part of the learning process.
Get feedback from the class before you provide the answers.

Answers

ACTIVE

	Simple	Continuous
Present	*He works*	*We're working*
Past	*She worked*	*I was working*
Future	*They'll work*	*You'll be working*
Present Perfect	*We've worked*	*She's been working*
Past Perfect	*I'd worked*	*You'd been working*
Future Perfect	*They'll have worked*	*He will have been working*

PASSIVE

	Simple	Continuous
Present	*It is made*	*They're being made*
Past	*It was made*	*It was being made*
Future	*They'll be made*	
Present Perfect	*They've been made*	
Past Perfect	*It had been made*	
Future Perfect	*They'll have been made*	

Read the Caution Box as a class.

2 Discussing grammar

Students work in pairs to compare the verb forms. This exercise tests simple and continuous, *have* and *have got*, perfect and non-perfect, active and passive. To answer these questions requires a certain analysis. Students might be able to *feel* the difference between the tenses, but they could find it difficult to express the differences in words. Be prepared to interpret their attempts to verbalize the conceptual differences.

This type of exercise can be very beneficial as a process of consciousness-raising. We are asking students to consider the language quite analytically, and to compare it subconsciously to their own language. However, it is very important that such an analysis does not go on too long. The aim is not to have a lengthy debate, possibly in L1, about the subtle differences of meaning expressed in these sentences. It is better to get students using English purposefully, rather than talking about grammar too much.

Answers

a The Present Simple **lives** suggests Klaus lives in Berlin permanently. He comes from Berlin, and was probably born in Berlin.

The Present Continuous **is living** suggests Klaus is in London for a limited time only, perhaps a month or two.

b The Present Simple **you're very kind** suggests a permanent state. You're always kind, and you've just been kind again.
The Present Continuous **you're being very kind** suggests that this is an unusual occurrence. Usually you aren't kind, so why are you being kind now?

c In the first sentence **I've got** could also be expressed by **I have**. However, the second sentence can only be expressed by **I often have**. This is because we do not use *have got* for repeated actions.

d The Past Simple **she made** means that she started to make some coffee *after* we arrived.
The Past Continuous **she was making** means she had already started to make coffee when we arrived. We interrupted her in the middle of making coffee.

e The question in the Past Continuous **what were you doing?** asks about the activity *before* the verb action expressed by the Past Simple, in this case **you cut your finger**.
The question in the Past Simple **what did you do?** asks about the action after you cut your finger.

SUGGESTION

Ask students to look at the cartoons that go with these sentences and answer the questions.
What was she doing when she cut her finger?
She was opening a tin.
What did she do when she cut her finger?
She put a plaster on it.

f The Present Perfect **I've lived** means that I still live in Singapore.
The Past Simple **I lived** means that I live somewhere else now.

g The Past Simple **left** means Peter left the party *at the same time* as I arrived.
The Past Perfect **had left** means Peter left *before* I arrived.

h The active **didn't teach** is said by a teacher of English.
The passive **wasn't taught** is said by a student of English.

i In the first sentence, **you're annoying** is active. In the second sentence, **you're annoyed** is passive.

j The active **are you paying** means you are employing a decorator to do the job for you.
The passive **are you being paid** means you are the decorator.

3 Auxiliary verbs and pronunciation

1 **T 1.3** Students listen to the sentences and identify the auxiliary verbs and the tense. This is probably best done as a whole class.

Answers

a does	Present Simple (Not *do* – this is a full verb)
b 's been	Present Perfect Continuous
c was	Past Continuous
d had	Past Perfect (Not *been* – this is a full verb)
e won't be	Future Continuous
f 'll	Future Simple
g was	Past Simple passive
h 've	Present Perfect (Not *had* – this is a full verb)
i 's being	Present Continuous passive
j 's	Present Perfect
k had	Past Perfect
l be	Passive infinitive

2 This is a pronunciation exercise to practise contractions and weak forms. Of course students can say *I'm leaving* perfectly well, but when they say *Where* ***are*** *you going?* or *She's* ***been*** *working* or *My car* ***was*** *made*, can they say them perfectly?

Use the tape to act as a model, and drill the sentences around the class. Don't do this exercise for too long.

4 Reading

NB *You could set this exercise for homework and correct it in class.*

Focus students on the headline and picture, and ask what they think the text is about. Then ask them to read and complete the gaps.

Students might well want to argue that other tenses are possible. Answer their questions carefully, but if one tense is definitely better than another, be prepared to explain why. For example, in b, they might want to say *was situated*, but the present is better as it still *is* situated in Kew. In c, they might want to say that the Present Perfect Continuous is possible, and in a way it is, but the Present Continuous sounds better with the *Now he's very busy*. In n, the Present Perfect is much better than the Past Simple because of the present tense in *It is very solid*.

Answers

a was trying
b is situated
c is converting
d think
i has been helping
j is being decorated
k have knocked
l hadn't been used

e was telling/told	m was built
f was joking	n hasn't had
g was searching	o paid
h loves	p has spent

ADDITIONAL MATERIAL

Workbook Unit 1
Exercises 1–3 The tense system
Exercises 4–5 Passives
Exercise 6 Auxiliary verbs
Exercise 7 Forms of *have* and *have got*

LANGUAGE REVIEW (SB p9)

The tense system

Read the Language Review together as a class, and/or ask students to read it at home. If you have a monolingual class, you could use L1 and ask students to translate some of the sentences, identifying areas of similarity and difference between L1 and English.

Encourage students to ask questions if they have any queries. Upper-intermediate students tend to be aware of a lot of grammar rules, as there is little that, at some time, a teacher somewhere has not tried to teach them. Their problem lies in applying these rules accurately and consistently. As a teacher of this level, you spend a lot of time 'nudging' and reminding.

Ask students to read the Grammar Reference at home.

● READING AND SPEAKING (SB p10)

People who emigrate

Pre-reading task

You could start this activity off by asking students where people from their country traditionally emigrate to. The British, for example, emigrate to Australia, New Zealand, and Canada, in search of work, a better climate, and a new start in life.

Students work in small groups to discuss the questions. You could monitor from a distance or you could join in a group, but don't do much, if any, correcting. You might be called on for assistance, but that's different.

You decide when the discussion has gone on enough. It might be five minutes or more. Stop it before you think they've had enough. Get some feedback.

Reading

This is a jigsaw activity, so divide the class into two groups. Group A reads about the Clavy family, and group B reads about the White family.

POSSIBLE VOCABULARY PROBLEMS

There are in fact very few words that students might not know. There is a Language work exercise which comes after the Comprehension check, and this deals with the potentially unknown words and expressions.

Comprehension check

1 When you think they are ready, ask the groups to answer the Comprehension check questions a–j together. It is important that each student can answer the questions so that information can be exchanged in the jigsaw activity.

2 You need to help students find a partner from the other group. One way of doing this is to give each student in group A a number 1, 2, 3, etc., then do the same with group B, 1, 2, 3, etc. Tell the number ones to get together, the number twos, the number threes, etc. They sit down together and compare answers.

One of the advantages of a jigsaw activity is the intense exchange of information that it generates. There is a gap between what Student A and Student B knows that can only be bridged by talking. So there should be a lively buzz of conversation as students compare answers to the questions.

There is probably no need to get feedback to the questions as a class. Students have answered them twice already. If you have monitored the group and pair work carefully, you will know which, if any, of the questions caused problems.

Answers

The Clavy family

a They emigrated because they were never together as a family. Andy, the husband, worked very long hours, and when he came home, he was too tired to do anything. When he was made redundant, they decided to 'take the plunge' and move to Canada.

b They had always wanted to live in Canada, ever since they had visited cousins there.

c They live in a big house, with four acres of land, in spectacular scenery. They are much closer as a family. They do things together, like sports and visiting friends.
Andy works only eight hours a day, instead of twelve. He has more time to spend with his wife. Business is more relaxed.

d They do more things with their parents, like sport and visiting friends and sightseeing. They don't have to wear a school uniform.

e It took a long time to have their application accepted – 18 months. It cost a lot of money. At first they didn't know anybody.

They have had to get used to the way Canadian friends come into their house and use the telephone and take drinks from the fridge without asking. It took a few months for Andy to find a decent job.

f Emigrating is an expensive business. They had financial worries while Andy was finding a job. We don't know if they're better off now, but they seem to live a comfortable life.

g Much happier. Andy says it's the best thing they've ever done.

h Marion misses the castles and the greenness of the countryside. Andy misses cricket and his family.

i Very good. They have more time for each other now.

j Yes. Definitely.

The White family

a They emigrated because they wanted their daughter, Daisy, to be able to run freely as she was growing up. They felt she couldn't do this in the streets of London. They wanted her to grow up carefree and in the sunshine.

b They had had a couple of holidays on the island of Agastri, and had made some Greek friends there. They thought it was very beautiful and peaceful.

c They now live in an apartment overlooking the sea. They work in the watersports business and not hotels. They are self-employed, and have much more work in summer than in winter. Hazel has found it hard being a woman in a Greek community. Women are not treated equally.

d Daisy can run freely in the sunshine. She is more Greek than English. She goes to a Greek school. Everyone knows her. The community is like one big happy family, unlike London.

e The business was difficult to start. There was a lot of bureaucracy – a lot of forms and officials. Learning Greek was difficult for both of them. Hazel experienced a lot of culture shock. It took her a long time to get used to the Greek way of life. She used to visit women friends and understand nothing.

f Yes. The business has had some bad times, and they earn very little in winter. Money problems have caused arguments. We feel that they are worse off now than when they were in London.

g Barry is happier, and Daisy seems happy, but Hazel seems to have doubts and reservations.

h Barry misses the theatre, sausages, Stilton cheese, and white bread. Hazel misses her parents terribly.

i It doesn't seem to be very good. She says that their life on Agastri has tested their relationship, which means it is has made them question whether their relationship is good or not. They argue about money, and she is going back to London for a few months. She says she'll come back, but she's not entirely sure.

j Barry thinks it was, but Hazel has doubts about living there.

3 Students read the other text. Discuss the two questions as a class.

Language work

1 Students make guesses from context and/or use dictionaries to look up the words underlined.

Answers

a fall asleep

b He lost his job because he wasn't necessary any more.
A pay-out is a payment of a large amount of money.

c We were so worried and anxious that we bit our nails, either literally or metaphorically!

d anyone

e without care or worry

f took a bold and important decision, after thinking and worrying about it for a long time

g involving a lot of complicated official rules and processes
making you feel annoyed because you can't do what you want to

h manage to survive, but only just

i a feeling of shock and anxiety that you have when you go to another country that is very different from your own

j Money worries cause us to have arguments.

2 You might choose to do this activity and the discussion that follows on another day in order to change the topic and the focus.

Students use the words in A and B to write some questions about one of the families.

The questions are then asked and answered, either in open or closed pairs.

Discussion

Students work in small groups to list the disadvantages of emigrating. Compare points as a class, and see if they can find an advantage for every disadvantage.

● VOCABULARY AND PRONUNCIATION

(SB p12)

House and home

Compounds and dictionary work

You could lead into this activity by asking students to name various objects in the classroom that are all compound nouns, for example *tape recorder*, *briefcase*, *door handle*, *light switch*, *wristwatch*, *shoelace*. Ask if they know what sort of words these are.

Look at the headings as a class. Ask what the difference between *house* and *home* is, and whether their own language has two words or just one. (*House* is physical; *home* is more to do with feelings and belonging. For example, we can say *They live in a large house*, but not *~~They live in a large home~~. *Home* can be in a flat, or a caravan, or a tent – it doesn't have to be in a house.)

Read the Caution Box as a class. Students will almost certainly have come across compound nouns before.

In pairs, students find some compound nouns and adjectives from the texts on pages 10 and 11.

Answers

Canada	**Greece**
full-time housewife	basement flat
machine supply company	two-bedroom apartment
fir trees	hotel business
well off	watersports business
nail-biting	fishing hook
pocket-handkerchief garden	waterskiing equipment
sightseeing	speedboats
	passenger boat
	fishing trip
	culture shock
	women friends
	language barrier
	winter/summer income
	money worries

1 Students make compounds using the words *home* and *house* and a word on the right. They will need to check the spelling in a dictionary.

Answers

homework	housework	home-made
house-trained	homesick	housewife
home town	house-plant	home-coming
house-proud	homeless	housebound
home-grown	housekeeping	house-warming

2 **T1.4** Students listen and answer the two questions in pairs.

Answers

1 Two friends are talking about a puppy. It is a Labrador, just seven weeks old, so it isn't house-trained. (A Labrador is quite a large dog, usually either black or golden coloured.)

2 Two neighbours are talking. One is asking the other to look after his house-plants. The other offers to look after the whole flat.

3 Julie and her Mum are on the phone. They are talking about Julie's sister, Anna, who's coming back from the States, so they're going to give her a home-coming party. Julie isn't a career girl. She is a housewife with four children.

4 One friend is inviting another to a house-warming party.

5 Simon is phoning his Mum. He's at scout camp, and he's very homesick.

3 In pairs, students fill the gaps in the conversations.

Answers

a house-trained
b house-plants
c house-proud
d home-coming
e housewife home-made home-grown
f house-warming
g housework
h homesick

4 Students practise saying the lines of conversation in Exercise 3. Pay careful attention to all aspects of pronunciation. Students might need to go to the tapescripts to remind them of the whole conversation. When they are ready, ask some of the pairs to act out one of the dialogues.

5 This exercise is probably best set for homework. Students make compounds from the words in the two columns. They compare words with other students.

Answers

bookshop bookmaker book token bookworm
video shop video recorder
speed limit speedboat
radio-controlled
light shop light-headed light bulb
timetable time bomb time consuming time limit
remote-controlled
junk food junk mail junk shop
word perfect word processor
food processor food poisoning
air-conditioned airmail
computer shop computer software

ADDITIONAL MATERIAL

Workbook Unit 1
Exercises 8 and 9 Two vocabulary exercises connected with *house* and *home*.

● LISTENING (SB p13)

Hello Muddah, Hello Fadduh

This song was first recorded by an American comic singer called Allan Sherman. The connection with the rest of the unit is that it is about homesickness.

Pre-listening task

Read the introduction as a class. Discuss questions 1 and 2. There is a strong tradition of summer camps in some countries, but not others. They are not particularly popular in Britain, for example, but they are in France, Germany, and America.

The aim of question 3 is to pre-teach some vocabulary in preparation for the song.

Students check the verb *to disregard* in their dictionary. It means *to pay no attention to*.

Listening

BACKGROUND INFORMATION AND POSSIBLE VOCABULARY PROBLEMS

The singer has an American accent. This being a song, there is a certain amount of poetic licence in the language.

- *Poison ivy* is a bush that causes a pain on your skin if you touch it, so we cannot strictly talk about developing poison ivy, as though it were an illness.
- *Ptomaine poisoning* is another (unusual) way of referring to food poisoning.
- The song refers to *counsellors*. In British English we would probably say *supervisors*.
- The pronunciation of *Ulysses* is usually /'ju:lɪsi:z/, but in the song it changes to /ju:'lisiz/ to rhyme with *sissies*.
  Ulysses was a legendary Greek king, hero of Homer's Odyssey, who had many adventures. He was a courageous and cunning fighter.
- *You* changes to *ya* to rhyme with *malaria*.
- We usually talk about a *search party*, not a *searching party*, and *make a noise*, not *make noise*.
- *Gee* /dʒi:/ is an American expression of surprise.

T 1.5 Students listen and put the pictures in order.

Answers

Picture 1 shows the boy on his bunk-bed writing a letter. Outside it is hailing.

Picture 2 shows Joe Spivey with poison ivy.

Picture 3 shows Leonard Skinner with food poisoning after dinner.

Picture 4 shows the counsellors fighting the waiters. We can see an alligator in the lake.

Picture 5 shows a search party out looking for Jeffrey Hardy.

Picture 6 shows a bear chasing the boy.

Picture 7 shows the boy being hugged by his Aunt Bertha.

Picture 8 shows boys swimming, sailing, and playing baseball.

Ask students to describe what they can see in the pictures.

Check that students understand the last line '*Muddah, Fadduh, kindly disregard this letter.*'

Comprehension check

Students work in pairs or small groups to answer the questions.

Answers

1 At the beginning of the song, he feels fed up. The boys can't do anything at the holiday camp because of the weather. He's very homesick, and wants his parents to take him home. In the middle of the song, he sounds desperate to be home. At the end, he feels fine because the weather has changed and everybody is having a good time. He has decided that he wants to stay.

2 Joe Spivey has been poisoned by the bush poison ivy; Leonard Skinner has food poisoning; his bunk-mate has malaria; and Jeffrey Hardy has gone missing.

3 He says that the camp is dangerous, because of various kinds of poisoning and illness. The adults at the camp hate each other. There are alligators. There is a risk that children go missing. He begs to be allowed to come home, where he promises he would be well-behaved, and he would even be nice to his brother and Aunt Bertha. He says he might get eaten by a bear.

4 The head coach is trying to make the boys hard and aggressive.

5 No, he doesn't.

6 One whole day.

7 Because the weather has improved, and suddenly there are lots of fun things to do.

Language work

Students work in pairs to complete the boxes.

When getting feedback, correct any pronunciation mistakes carefully.

Answers

Adjective	Noun	Verb
enter'taining	enter'tainment	enter'tain
'funny	fun	
de'veloping/ de'veloped	de'velopment	de'velop
'poisonous	'poison	'poison
	'trainer	train
'hateful	'hatred	hate

'scary	scare	scare
'organized	organi'zation	'organize
'promising	'promise	'promise
'noisy	noise	
'messy	mess	mess
'playful	play	play

WRITING AND SPEAKING (SB p14)

Looking forward to seeing you

1 Divide the class into two groups. Each group reads one of the letters and answers the questions. Let them check their answers with a neighbour. These are actual letters written by upper-intermediate students.

Answers

Fernando's letter

a In São Paulo, Brazil.
b Fernando is the guest, Ken is the host.
c São Paulo is described. It's big, noisy, and not very suitable for tourists as it's a commercial city. There are lots of things to do, with good bars and restaurants.
d It's summer in Brazil.

Liliane's letter

a In Basle, Switzerland.
b Sophie is the guest, Liliane is the host.
c Basle is described. It's very clean, near the mountains, but rather quiet at night.
d It's summer in Switzerland.

Students pair up with someone from the other group. They go through the letters together and compare information.

2 Students work on their letter to find the mistakes. They check their answers with a partner. You might want to photocopy these answers.

Answers

Fernando's letter

Dear Ken,

In just two weeks' time I'll be with you. I cannot believe it! I'm looking forward to staying with you and your family very much, and seeing London for the first time. I'm very excited.

My city, São Paulo, is the biggest and noisiest city in Brasil. It is not very good for tourists because it's more a commercial city. Also, it has a lot of traffic and pollution. Maybe London has the same. The thing I like best here in São Paulo is the entertainment. You can find good bars and restaurants, which don't close until the last customer leaves.

My friend João went to London last year and he went to the theatre to see 'The Buddy Holly Story'. He told me it was wonderful. I'd like to see it, too.

My plane arrives at Heathrow, Terminal 3, at 6.30 am. It is very kind of you to meet me so early in the morning! Thank you.

I very much hope to improve my English when I come to London.

See you soon and Happy New Year!
Fernando

Liliane's letter

Dear Sophie,

In just one week you will be here with me in Switzerland. I want you to meet my family and I will show you my city. I hope you like it.

Basel isn't as big as London/a big city like London, but everything is very clean and very close to the mountains, which are beautiful. I am worried that you'll find Basel a little boring. It isn't as exciting as London because the streets are very quiet after six o'clock at night. The people live in flats so they can't make a lot of noise. There is a museum but perhaps that isn't very interesting to look at/see/visit.

We finished school last week and I am enjoying the holiday. My family don't speak English, so you'll practise your German a lot. I would also like to practise my English with you.

See you next week! I'll come to the airport to meet you.
Love Liliane

3 Students read the other letter to see if there are similar mistakes.

Answers

Both letters have mistakes with tenses (*you are here*; *he has gone to the theatre*), spelling (*beautifull*), punctuation (*english*), word order (*you will practise a lot your German*), grammar (*I want that you meet*), *-ed* and *-ing* adjectives (*excited, exciting*), articles (*see you the next week*), modal verbs (*can no believe*), missing words (*Is not very good for tourists*), relative pronouns (*restaurants who don't close*), and wrong word (*He say me*).

Students work as a group to write a correct version of their letter, then they take it in turns to write it on the board.

4 Students write a similar letter for homework, describing their home town briefly.

PostScript (SB p15)

POSSIBLE PROBLEMS

Upper-intermediate students will, of course, feel slightly insulted that they are being asked to work on dates, numbers, and spelling again. However, they continue to make mistakes as there are so many little bits to get wrong, for example with dates, remembering to say *the* but not to write it, and the pronunciation of the ordinals. Saying the spelling of words in three or four letter blocks is quite an advanced point. Remember there is a lot of word linking when spelling, because so many of the letters begin with a vowel sound.

Don't forget the intrusive sounds /j/ and /w/.

/j/ /j/
M-I-K-E P-R-I-N G-L-E

/w//j/
S-T-U-A-R-T

So this activity is certainly worth doing, but do it quite briskly, and correct vigilantly!

Dates

Read the introduction as a class, pointing out that when we speak we must say *the* and *of*, but we omit these when we write.

Ask the questions to elicit the use of dates, paying very careful attention to correction.

Numbers

1 **T 1.6** Students listen to the six short texts and identify the different ways of saying the number 0.

Answers

a When we say numbers one by one, for example in a phone number or an account number or a reference number, we say zero or /əʊ/ like the letter O.
b The mathematical term is **nought** or **zero.**
c In football scores we say **nil.**
d In tennis we say **love.**
e When giving the temperature we say **nought.**
f In phone numbers the British say /əʊ/, and the Americans say **zero.**

2 **T 1.7** Students listen to the news broadcasts and write down the fifteen numbers they hear.

Answers

Boeing 747 flight 409 280 passengers
10.40 in the morning

three quarters of the four thousand-mile trip

a five and a half per cent pay rise 3.2 per cent
the next sixteen months

£55,000 0151 324408.

2,876,000 32,000

seventy miles an hour minus 7 degrees Celsius.

Students practise the numbers by reading the tapescript on p128–9.

Spelling

Read the explanation as a class. Ask the students to spell their surnames for you to write on the board. Make sure that they say the letters in suitable blocks of three or four letters, with good intonation and word linking. You could play the 'silly teacher' and pretend to mishear them, so you force students to say 'No, T for television!', etc.

Students spell their surnames in pairs.

Practice

This little roleplay is like a dictation. It practises dates, numbers, and spelling. You need to photocopy the role cards (TB p123).

Read the introduction as a class. Give out the cards. Check that students know how to pronounce the money. Students work in pairs to swap the information. There are some strange words for students to spell!

Don't forget!

Workbook Unit 1

Exercise 10 Phrasal verbs, literal and idiomatic

Exercise 11 Pronunciation, vowel sounds and spelling

Been there, done that!

Present Perfect
Continuous verb forms
Exclamations

Introduction to the unit

Been there, done that, (got the T-shirt!) is the cry of bored young people. It epitomizes teenage *ennui*. The idea is that nothing about the world is of any interest because they have already been everywhere, done everything, and bought the T-shirt to prove it! It was used in an advert for Pepsi Cola, where of course the only thing which stopped terminal boredom was a can of Pepsi!

The title *Been there, done that!* illustrates succinctly both the grammar and topic of this unit. The topic is that of world travel past and present, from old-style explorers to modern-day tourism. The linguistic content includes comparison of the Present Perfect with both the Past Simple and the Present Perfect Continuous, which leads to further work on the uses of continuous forms generally.

It is worth mentioning here that it would be a good idea to ask your students to start looking for some photographs of themselves when they were young children, *not* babies. This is in preparation for a pre-listening discussion about earliest memories.

The Workbook provides practice of additional, related language areas: the Present Perfect Passive and another passive construction, *have something done*.

Notes on the unit

LANGUAGE AIMS – PRESENT PERFECT

NB See the Grammar Reference section – SB p147.

Present Perfect Simple
It is notoriously difficult for students, even at the upper-intermediate level, to be consistently correct in their use of the Present Perfect. This is because although many other European languages have a tense that is *formed* in the same way, viz the auxiliary verb *have* + past participle, its uses in English are different.

Compare the French and the German with the English:

Je l'ai vu hier (F)
Ich habe ihn gestern gesehen (G)
*~~I've seen him yesterday~~ (✘) *I saw him yesterday* (✔)

Present Perfect Continuous
Given that continuous verb forms and their associated uses do not exist in many languages, the Present Perfect Continuous presents foreign learners with even more problems of use.

Compare the French and the German with the English:

J'habite à Londres depuis deux ans. (F)
Ich wohne seit zwei Jahre in London. (G)
*~~I live in London for two years.~~ (✘)
I've been living in London for two years. (✔)

Test your grammar (SB p16)

This exercise should be done quickly and light-heartedly. If students laugh at some of the sentences it is an encouraging sign that they are developing a good 'feel' for the English language. Ask them to work in pairs. If possible, go round the class and try to follow some of the points they are making. It should not be a difficult exercise for students at this level. Bring the class together for feedback. Do not at this stage be tempted to embark on lengthy grammar explanations.

Answers

a Using the Present Perfect here suggests that this is recent news and that Columbus is still alive. The Past Simple should be used.
Columbus discovered America in 1492.
b Although the use of the Past Simple is correct here, the sentence sounds very strange and incomplete without a time reference.
Man first walked on the moon in 1969.
c My life is not finished if I am speaking about it. It sounds as if the speaker is dead, which is impossible. The Present Perfect is correct.

I've travelled/been travelling all my life. I've been everywhere.

d We need to use the Present Perfect here to relate past time to present time.
I haven't seen you for ages.

e This sounds as if the job is complete! It is much more likely that the process is still continuing so the Present Perfect Continuous sounds better: *I've been learning English for years.*

f The Present Perfect Continuous *I've been running* should be used here because the activity of running is the main focus. However, it would be fine to say *I've run all the way here* or *I've run three times round the park.* The Present Perfect Simple is used when the main focus is not on the activity in progress but on the completed event as indicated in the extra information. The simple is rarely used unqualified by further information with verbs that suggest duration. The continuous *can* be used on its own.

g Present Perfect Simple *I've lost my passport* is correct here. A verb such as *lose* is semantically impossible to spread over a period in time. If you stretch the imagination it might just be possible to say *I've been losing my passport a lot lately* meaning a repeated habit, but this still sounds very strange.

h Similarly, this sentence is strange because it suggests a repeated activity and therefore failure in many attempts to give up smoking. Much more likely is *I've given up smoking.*

i Who has done the stinging? This sentence should be in the passive. *I've been stung by a mosquito.*

LANGUAGE IN CONTEXT (SB p16)

Present Perfect

1 Ask your students for comments about the pictures of the two travellers. Use the pictures to check that they understand the words *backpacker* and *explorer*. The main differences are the dates and the reasons for travelling: the backpacker is a modern-day traveller, exploring the world for pleasure; and David Livingstone was an explorer in the 19th century, when there were still large parts of the world to be 'discovered'. Ask your class if anyone knows anything at all about him.

Encourage some brief personalized discussion about backpacking. Has anyone done this? Does anyone want to? Which countries would they like to visit?

2 Ask your students to read the paragraphs and then match the sentences with the correct person. They could work in pairs to do this. Their decisions will be governed not only by the topic but also by linguistic clues. This should provide reinforcement of their understanding of the tenses used.

POSSIBLE VOCABULARY PROBLEMS

You may need to help your students with the following words as they go through the exercise. Try to encourage them to work out the meaning from the context where feasible. Deal with problems as quickly as possible, so as to keep focused on the main aims of the activity.

vanished = disappeared
source of the Nile = where the Nile starts
remains This could be worked out from the context. In this context it means a *dead body*.
to have the travel bug This could also be worked out from the context. It is informal and means *to have a great interest in, or enthusiasm for travel.*
mugged The verb *to mug* means to attack and rob someone in the street.

Answers

a Mick Watts
b David Livingstone
c Mick Watts
d Mick Watts
e David Livingstone
f David Livingstone
g Mick Watts
h David Livingstone
i Mick Watts
j Mick Watts
k David Livingstone

T 2.1 Play the tape for students to listen and check their answers. Get feedback from the whole class, then ask them what additional information from the tape they learn about the two travellers.

Answers

David Livingstone
He was born in Scotland in 1813. He studied medicine, and in 1841 he sailed to South Africa to join a Christian mission in Botswana. He married soon after he arrived.

His second expedition was up the Zambezi River by canoe and it was a disaster. Many lives were lost as well as his wife's, who was called Mary. A few years after this he set out to discover the source of the Nile.

In 1871 the American journalist Henry Morton Stanley met him on the shores of Lake Tanganyika with the famous words 'Dr Livingstone, I presume.'

Mick Watts
He flew into Bangkok five months ago. He's met a lot of great people, but his trip has not always been easy. He was mugged once, and that was really scary. He's travelled by public transport except in Bangkok, where he got around by river taxi.

For him, the best part of the trip so far has been learning to scuba dive on the Great Barrier Reef. He is soon setting off for New Zealand.

You could photocopy the following information and give it out at the end of the lesson, or you may simply want to use it to inform yourself a little more about Livingstone, in case students ask further questions.

BIOGRAPHICAL INFORMATION

David Livingstone

Born 19 March, 1813, in Blantyre, Scotland.
Died 30 April 1873, East Africa.

David Livingstone was a Christian missionary and one of the first great explorers of Africa. He came from a very poor Scottish family and, when he was only 10, he began work in a cotton mill. However, he found time to educate himself and he saved enough money to train to be a doctor. His missionary work started in South Africa in 1841. He married in 1845 and subsequently took his wife Mary and their four children on many of his dangerous journeys. In 1851 he discovered that the slave trade, which had supposedly been abolished in 1807, was still continuing in Africa. He believed that the best way to stop this was to open Africa to trade, so he began to search for new trade routes. He began his first great expedition in 1853. He crossed Africa on foot from west to east, and was the first European to see the Victoria Falls. In 1856, back in Britain, he was hailed as a hero.

Unfortunately, his second expedition up the Zambezi River was a disaster and his wife and many others died.

He began his third expedition, to find the source of the Nile, in 1866. He disappeared for five years and many people thought he had died. He was found by Henry Stanley in 1871, with the famous words: 'Dr Livingstone, I presume.' He died two years later south of Lake Tanganyika, and loyal African servants carried his body to the coast to be shipped home to Britain.

3 This should be a quick pronunciation exercise. Even students at this level can benefit from controlled pronunciation practice.
Ask students to complete the sentences, paying particular attention to 'getting their tongues round' the contracted forms of the Present Perfect and the weak forms of the auxiliaries. *Don't* encourage detailed and lengthy recall of all the information in the text. Natural-sounding pronunciation of the contracted grammar forms is the primary aim of the exercise.

Sample answers

/hiz bɪn tə/	He's been to Java and Bali.
/hiz vɪzɪtɪd/	He's visited temples in Thailand.
/hiz siːn/	He's seen giant turtles.
/aɪv hæd/	I've had diarrhoea. /daɪə'rɪə/
/aɪv bɪn mʌgd/	I've been mugged once.
/hiz bɪn stʌŋ/	He's been stung all over.
/hiz bɪn steɪɪŋ/	He's been staying in cheap hostels.
/hiz bɪn trævlɪŋ/	He's been travelling by bus, train, and ferry.

● Grammar questions

These questions should be the means of having a quick grammar round-up. You will have already had some discussion about the tenses used. Be aware of how difficult your students find this language. You don't need to spend very long on this stage or the 'Discussing grammar' stage if they have a good understanding of the rules.

Answers

- The main tense used about David Livingstone is the Past Simple because he is dead, so all the events of his life are set firmly in past time.
- The main tenses used about Mick Watts are the Present Perfect Simple and the Present Perfect Continuous. Not only is Mick Watts still alive, but he is in the middle of his trip. He's been travelling for five months and he still is travelling, and in the course of his travels so far he's seen and done many things. The Past Simple is used about Mick's activities when they are set at a particular time: *He flew into Bangkok five months ago.*

PRACTICE BANK (SB p17)

NB Remember – you decide which of these activities to do and when.

1 Questions and answers

You could ask students to work in pairs to do these two activities. However, as the next exercise also involves pair work, it might be a good idea to do these as teacher-directed activities, asking students to ask and answer the questions across the class in open pairs and being particularly vigilant about their pronunciation.

1 Ask the students to mark the questions (DL) for David Livingstone or (MW) for Mick Watts. Ask them to ask and answer the questions across the class in open pairs.

Answers

a Where did he go? (**DL**)
He went to South Africa, Botswana, the Kalahari Desert, the Zambezi River, and the Victoria Falls.
Where has he been? (**MW**)
He's been to Bangkok, Kuala Lumpur, Singapore, Java, Bali, and Australia.

b How long has he been travelling? (**MW**)
He's been travelling for five months.
How long did he travel? (**DL**)
Thirty years.
c How did he travel? (**DL**)
He travelled by boat, canoe, and on foot.
How has he been travelling? (**MW**)
By public transport – bus, train, and ferry.
d Has he been ill? (**MW**)
He's had diarrhoea, and he's been stung a lot.
Where did he die? (**DL**)
He died in modern Zambia.
e Did he have any problems? (**DL**)
His second expedition was a disaster. Several people died, including his wife. Then he vanished whilst he was looking for the source of the Nile.
Has he had any problems? (**MW**)
He's been mugged once, but he's mainly been fine.

2 **T 2.2** Students often need practice in producing questions. Ask them to write them first in their pairs and then to ask and answer the questions across the class in open pairs. Play the tape for a final feedback, paying particular attention to the intonation.

Answers

a What did he study?
b Why did he go to South Africa?
c When did he get married?
d What did his wife die of?
e Where were his remains buried?
f How long has he been away from home?
g Which countries has he been to?
h Where has he been staying?
i How often has he had diarrhoea?
j Has he been mugged?

2 Discussing grammar

Both of the activities in this section pull together many common problems in the use of the Present Perfect.

NB *Check understanding without asking for lengthy explanations. Be satisfied with whatever way your students attempt to talk about the sentences, as long as they are on the right lines.*

1 Ask students to discuss in pairs and go round to monitor their discussion. Don't let the activity go on for more than ten minutes before you get feedback.

SUGGESTION

One way of checking understanding without wordy explanation is to ask students to continue each sentence a little further to give a wider context. Examples are given in the answers.

Answers

a The Past Simple is used, because Dickens is dead, and will not write any more novels.
He wrote 'Oliver Twist' over a hundred years ago.
The Present Perfect is used to bring past and present time together. Ken Follett is alive and may well write more novels.
– and another novel is coming out soon.
The Present Perfect Continuous is used because he is still doing the activity. He began writing eighteen months ago and he still is.
– and he hasn't finished yet.
b The Present Perfect Simple is used. The sentence means *Is this an experience you have had in your life so far?*
The Past Simple is used to refer to a particular past time when you were in Japan.
– when you were in Japan last year?
c The Present Perfect Simple is used. Kate may marry again. She is still alive.
– she's already had three husbands.
The Past Simple is used. Ken must be dead.
– his last wife died just before he did.
d The Present Perfect Simple is used. She's been to Paris at some time in her life.
– many times and she's going again next week.
The Present Perfect Simple. She's in Paris now.
– she went last week.
e Present Perfect Simple joins past and present. They still live here.
– we were born here in this house.
The Present Perfect Continuous signals that this is a temporary state.
– we're hoping to move very soon.
f The Present Perfect Simple places the focus on the result of the action.
– there are none left!
The Present Perfect Continuous places the focus on the activity.
– there are only a few left.
g The Present Perfect Continuous here focuses on the activity and its duration.
– and I'm still reading.
The Present Perfect Simple focuses on the amount read so far.
– and I've got six more to read.
h The Present Perfect Simple. This cut is a quick action event which can't have duration.
– and it's bleeding.
The Present Perfect Continuous. Cutting the grass is an activity of some duration.
– and I haven't finished yet.

2 This could be set for homework and then checked in pairs or small groups at the beginning of the next lesson. With each sentence check that your students know why it is wrong.

Answers

a He's gone to lunch. (*been* = gone and come back)
b ... have you had your car? (verbs of possession cannot be used in the continuous.)
c ... as Charlie Chaplin did. (he's dead. Tom Hanks will make more films.)
d Did you see ... (specific time past)
e Where did you buy ... (referring to a particular past time)
f I've been swimming. (focus on the action of swimming)
g She's smoked ... (focus on number of cigarettes)

3 Speaking and listening

This is an information gap activity. You will need to photocopy the Student A and Student B information (TB p124). With this type of activity it is important that your students are completely sure of what they are expected to do. Therefore you need to take sufficient time to set it up clearly. In order to do this it is necessary that you are completely sure of what is required, so spend time familiarizing yourself with the nature and mechanics of the activity as part of your lesson preparation. You may wish to check that students understand 'diversify', 'expand', and 'award'.

- Divide the class into two groups, Group A and Group B and give out the appropriate *Virgo* text.
- Read through the instructions with the whole class.
- Model the example with a student.
- Make it clear that students must take turns to ask questions to fill the gaps in the text.
- Ask students to spend a few minutes reading through their text and preparing their questions.
- Pair As with Bs. Tell your students that the As will ask all the **odd** number questions, and the Bs all the **even** numbers.
- Start the activity. Go round to monitor their efforts and check that they have understood what they have to do.
- When they have finished, conduct a full class feedback and ask for the questions again to check they have been forming them correctly.

Answers

1 A When was the company founded?
2 B Where did Jimmy Kramer open his first shop?
3 A What did he build?
4 B Where did he build a recording studio?
5 A How many bands have recorded albums there?
6 B How many copies of *Black Days, White Nights* have been sold?
7 A What did Jimmy decide to do in 1992?
8 B What did he buy?
9 A How many planes did he have in 1994?
10 B How many planes does he have now?
11 A How long has he been flying to Japan and the Far East?
12 B What has Jimmy been trying to do?
13 A How many awards has the *Virgo Group* won?
14 B How many people does the company employ?

You could photocopy the completed text below, and give students a copy at the end of the lesson.

Jimmy Kramer's VIRGO GROUP

Originally *Virgo* sold records. The company was founded in 1980. The chairman and owner of *Virgo*, Jimmy Kramer, opened his first record shop in Oxford Street, London.

He built a recording studio in the garden of his house in Cambridge, and since then more than one hundred bands have recorded albums there. One of the most successful is *Black Days, White Nights*, by Pete Moor. Over 15 million copies have been sold worldwide.

In 1992 Jimmy decided to diversify. He bought a Jumbo jet and started his own airline, *Virgo Pacific*. In 1994 he had ten planes, and now he has twenty-four planes. He has been flying to Japan and the Far East since 1996.

Jimmy has been trying to expand his business. His company now includes book publishing, film production, clubs, and hotels. The *Virgo Group* has won over twenty awards for its exports. The company employs over 22,000 people.

4 Roleplay

This is a continuation of the previous activity and cannot stand on its own. The class can stay in its two groups.

- Tell Group A that they are journalists and they are going to interview Jimmy Kramer about his *Virgo Group*. Group B are 'Jimmy Kramers'.
- You will need to photocopy the information on p124 of this Teacher's Book.
- Give out the appropriate sheet to each member of the two groups and ask them to work together to prepare for the interview.
- Allow them a few minutes to do this then ask each A to find a B and start the interview with the words suggested in the Student's Book.
- Go round and monitor how they are doing.
- Round off the activity by asking one or two 'good' pairs to act out their interviews for the rest of the class.

SUGGESTION

If you have the facilities and the time it is worthwhile to record or video some of the roleplays.

ADDITIONAL MATERIAL

Workbook Unit 2

Exercises 1 and 2 These exercises provide more practice of the Present Perfect.

Exercise 3 This provides practice of continuous forms generally.

Exercise 4 This practises the Present Perfect Passive.

Exercise 5 Explains and practises the passive construction *have something done*.

All of the above could be used in class, but given limitations of time, they will more likely be set as homework.

LANGUAGE REVIEW (SB p18)

Present Perfect and continuous verb forms

Read the Language Review together as a class and/or you could ask students to read it at home. If you have a monolingual class you could ask your students to translate some of the sentences, warning them against concentrating on form and encouraging them to consider overall meaning.

Ask students to read the Grammar Reference section at home and encourage them to use it to revise from and to consult when they are doing exercises in the Workbook.

● READING AND SPEAKING (SB p19)

Death by tourism

NB *A major aim of the choice of text is to promote discussion on the problems of tourism today. You could set your students some preparatory homework by asking them to think about themselves as tourists. Where have they been? What have they done as tourists? Where would they like to go? Also ask them to consider the effects of tourism in their own country or town. This will both set the scene for the reading text and help them organize their thoughts for the discussion tasks which accompany it.*

SUGGESTION

Read through the text and the tasks as part of your lesson preparation and if you feel there are too many unknown words for your students to be able to cope with, make a list of *some* of them, photocopy it, and give it out prior to the lesson. Ask your students to check them in their dictionaries as part of their homework. However, *don't* include in the list any words that you feel they could guess from the context (see Language work 1, SB p21).

POSSIBLE VOCABULARY PROBLEMS

ancient inscription	*grave danger*	*permit system*
ruined temple	*privileged few*	

Pre-reading task

The aim of this exercise is personalized discussion to motivate students for the text on the following page. Ask your students to work in small groups.

1 Students discuss the pictures and the questions. They will probably find some easier to identify than others. Ask for feedback on this before moving on to 2 and 3.

Answers

The pictures are:

- The ruins of the ancient city of Petra (the Greek word for *rock*) in Jordan. In Arabic BATRA.
- The Grand Canyon and the Colorado River in Arizona, USA
- Machu Picchu, the ancient fortress city of the Incas, in the Andes Mountains in Peru. (This is important because it comes up later, in the listening text on p24.)
- Prehistoric cave painting (28,000–22,000 BC) in Lascaux, Dordogne, France.

2 Give a few minutes in their groups to discuss these questions, but then try to pull the class together for a general swapping of holiday tales. If you are lucky there should be some amusing incidents related.

3 You can expect most of your students to agree with this statement. Ask them for reasons why. Then turn the page to reveal the title of the article.

Reading

NB *The first read through is not to explore the text in detail. Encourage your students not to stop at unknown words at this stage. Tell them that they should be able to get the main points without looking up lots of vocabulary.*

Before they read, ask them to tell you briefly what they think the title means. They should be able to do this and will probably say something along the lines that too many tourists spoil the places they visit. Ask them to read the entire article, set them a time limit (about 3 to 4 minutes) and encourage them to read it quite quickly. Ask them to discuss the questions in pairs and then conduct a full class feedback. Before you start the feedback ask your students to **close their books. Don't** ask for long detailed replies. Just some of the information will do to show that they have generally understood the text.

Answers

- Tourism destroys the places that tourists want to visit and the culture and way of life they want to experience. There are lots of examples of this in the text. Ask your students to recall some for you.
- Petra, the Grand Canyon, the cave paintings.
- **Petra** is being destroyed, with graffiti and thousands of tourists. (You may have to teach the word *graffiti*.) There is a description of the red rock and a bit of Petra's history: a Swiss explorer discovered the ruins and King Herod's soldiers were imprisoned there.

  The Grand Canyon is so popular there was a waiting list of eight years. Now they have a lottery.

  The cave paintings are now closed and a replica has been built because the original was being ruined by the breath of thousands of visitors.
- Lots of other places are mentioned, ask your class just to recall a bit about as many as they can.
- Pessimistic. His examples are all very depressing.

Comprehension check

Now your students are going to explore the text in more depth. Ask them to open their books and work in pairs to go through the questions.

NB *A vocabulary exercise follows the reading where students are asked to work out meanings from the context. Therefore encourage your students not to worry too much about unknown words when they tackle the comprehension tasks and only to use their dictionaries if they are really stuck.*

Answers

1

a (✗) There is some modern day graffiti at the entrance of the temple, carved by Shane and Wendy from Australia, in 1996. (l. 10)

b (✓) (l. 17)

c (✓) (l. 18)

d (✗) Tourism will *soon* be the largest industry in the world. It has grown a lot since the 1960s. (l. 28)

e (✗) It is possible to go to many places, even remote places, but not everywhere. (l. 31)

f (✗) Thomas Cook organized package tours for ordinary people, not just rich people. (l. 43)

g (✗) The number has grown very fast, especially in the last three decades of the 20th century. (l. 50)

h (✓) (l. 64)

i (✗) It is a Swiss joke that the government will have to build new mountains. (l. 73)

j (✓) (l. 85)

k (✗) The caves have already been closed and a replica has been built. (l. 106)

l (✓) (l. 121)

2 Go through this as a whole class activity, getting suggestions from round the class.

Answers

- Herod's soldiers were imprisoned in Petra in **40 BC**. (l. 7)
- Petra was discovered by a Swiss explorer in **1810**. (l. 12)
- **600 million** tourists travel the world every year. (l. 23)
- Thomas Cook organized the first package tour in **1845**. (l. 43)
- Only one million people travelled abroad in **1939**. (l. 47)
- The Mediterranean has a population of **230 million** every summer. (l. 60)
- In 1981 there was an **eight-year** waiting list to go rafting down the Colorado River in the Grand Canyon. (l. 82)
- **108** visitors enter Notre Dame in Paris every minute during opening hours. (l. 87)
- One day in **1987** Venice had to be closed. (l. 94)
- Each tourist in Barbados and Hawaii uses **ten times** as much water and electricity as a local inhabitant. (l. 97)

Language work

You could set both these exercises for homework and move straight on to the discussion at this point. If you do them in class do the first exercise as a teacher-directed activity and the second in pairs or small groups.

1 Ask students to find the word and then suggest alternatives. Here are some ideas.

Sample answers

chiselled = cut, carved (*carved* is used in l. 6 so as not to repeat *chiselled*.)

tramp = march, walk in a heavy or tired way (*tramp* is used so as not to repeat *march*)

treasured = valuable and loved

swells = grows, increases, gets bigger

clicking = the noise made by your camera when you take a photograph.

whirring = the noise made by a camera or camcorder when you film a scene.

2 Get feedback after the pair or group work.

Answers

shows – reveals (l. 8)

reached a decision – concluded (l. 14)

serious – grave (l. 15)
hardly – barely (l. 30)
distant and far away – remote (l. 32)
having special rights and advantages – privileged (l. 40)
unbelievable – incredible (l. 58)
defeated and controlled – conquered (l. 73)
choose – select (l. 86)
extremely beautiful or delicate – exquisite (l. 93)
admit, accept – acknowledge (l. 101)
left – abandoned (l. 121)

Discussion

- Put students in small groups.
- Ask them to discuss the questions within their groups. (Appoint one student to read out the questions, and one to take notes.)
- Monitor carefully.

The answers as to which activities are most 'green' in question 3 are not as straightforward as you might first think.

- Ask a spokesperson from each group to report back and then encourage comment from everyone else.
- The leaflet below states the views of Green Tourism. Put the main points up on the blackboard, or photocopy it and give it out after the discussion to see if it causes any surprises and further debate.

What does GREEN TOURISM approve of?

- It approves more of package tourists than backpackers because they spend more money and stay on designated routes. It favours backpackers less because not only do they help ruin famous places, but they also contribute less to the local economy than the richer package tourists.
- 'Green tourism' approves more of special tourist coaches because this frees public transport for the local people, and the cost is less likely to rise.
- It approves more of wildlife safaris because these are well-organized and interfere less with the natural habitats of the animals. Too many trekkers (walkers) in the Himalayas are polluting the area with litter.
- It approves more of five-star hotels because these bring employment. Wealthy tourists spend money and help the local economy.

ADDITIONAL MATERIAL

Workbook Unit 2

Exercise 6 There are various vocabulary exercises on the theme of transport.

● VOCABULARY (SB p22)

Hot Verbs (1) : *take* and *put*

NB This is the first of a series of exercises in both the Student's Book and Workbook on Hot Verbs. These are verbs which are much used in English, both in expressions and in phrasal verbs.

Don't ask students to open their books yet. Begin the lesson by writing some common 'hot verbs' on the board: *take*, *put*, *have*, *make*, *do*, *go*, *come*. Ask students to write down *any* words that go with these verbs. Then get the class to swap ideas. Now ask them to open their books and read through the introduction and the examples with the class.

Expressions with *take* and *put*

1 This first exercise practises a variety of common expressions. You can help them a bit by saying that there are more *take* expressions than *put*.
You could just ask your students to do it then check their answers with a partner, but there are more interesting approaches if you have time and space.

SUGGESTIONS

Here are two alternative approaches. You could choose one of them (but not both).

1 Divide the blackboard into two columns. Write *take* above one column, and *put* above the other. Invite the students to the board to discuss where the expressions should go. Appoint one student to respond to the suggestions of the others and write the expressions in the correct columns.

2 Write each expression on a separate piece of paper or card and lay them on the floor.
Write *take* and *put* on two more cards and lay each at opposite ends of the room with the expressions in the middle. Invite students to stand up and discuss which verb the expressions go with and to lay them next to the appropriate one.

When they have finished stand back to survey their work and check that they all have agreed, before going through it with them.

Answers

TAKE	PUT
three hours to get there	my arm round sb
sb/sth for granted	sb in charge of
responsibility for sth	a plan into practice
drugs	pressure on sb
no notice	his work first
part a risk	
place my advice	

2 Students could do this exercise in pairs. Go through it with the whole class.

Answers

a Have you ever taken drugs?
b The wedding took place in an old country church. It took three hours to get there.
c I put my arm round her…
d … you have to learn to take responsibility for your own life.
e You should have taken my advice …
f The police put a very good plan into practice …
g He's taking a very big risk.
h Two thousand people took part in a demonstration …
i My boss has been putting a lot of pressure on me …
j … she took no notice of me …
k They just take their parents for granted.
l He always puts his work first.
m I was delighted to be put in charge of the under-fives …

Phrasal verbs with *take* and *put*

1 Ask students to close their books. Write the examples on the blackboard, and after each discuss the meaning as a class. Ask them to tell you what these kind of verbs are called. They will most likely have come across phrasal/multi-word verbs before. Now let them see that the examples are in their books.

Answers

took off his coat = removed
took a day *off* = had a one-day holiday
was *taken off* = substituted by another player
The plane *took off* = left the ground
The business *took off* = became successful very quickly
put it down = stop reading it
Put it down in your diary = write it
she *puts me down* = criticizes me

2 This exercise could be set for homework or done in pairs in class.

Answers

put on your make-up in the morning
take off your make-up at night
take after your father in looks
take over a company by buying most of its shares
put off a meeting until next week
put someone down by saying something cruel or unkind
put on a CD so we can listen to some music
take something back to a shop because it's faulty
put on weight
put somebody up for a couple of nights
put out a fire/a cigarette
take somebody out to the cinema/for a meal
put away your clean clothes in the cupboard
put up with noisy neighbours without complaining

SUGGESTION

As a follow-on activity you can give some personalized oral prompts to the class which are designed to lead to the natural production of one of the phrasal verbs in context. Do it quickly round the class encouraging responses from different students and focusing on some of the better replies. Try to make the exercise *topical*, *personalized*, and *amusing*. Here are some examples.

	Sample teacher prompts	Sample student answers
a	I'm really cold/hot in this room.	Why don't you **put on/ take off** your sweater?
b	I don't think you're ready for the test next week.	Can we **put it off** until the week after?
c	I've just bought this pen and it doesn't work.	You should **take it back** to the shop.
d	Luis, are you like your mother or your father?	I definitely **take after** my mother. I've got curly hair and I'm very talkative.
e	All the dictionaries were left on the desks after the last lesson.	Don't worry, we'll **put them away** after this lesson.
f	Did you read about the Rolls-Royce company?	Yes, it's been **taken over** by BMW.
g	Listen to that terrible noise coming from the classroom next door!	I don't think we should **put up with** it any longer. Let's go and complain.
h	I've heard that Maria's got a very rich boyfriend.	Yes. He **took her out** for a meal at the Ritz last night.

● LISTENING AND WRITING **(SB p23)**

Memories

PRE-LESSON SUGGESTION

Photographs of earliest memories
Prior to the lesson ask your students to bring in one or two photographs of themselves as young children. Stress that these should *not* be of themselves as babies, because you want them to be able to *remember* where the picture was taken and what was happening at the time.

Pre-listening task

If students have brought in photographs of themselves ask them to tell the others in the group about them. What was happening? Where? How old were they? This can generate a great deal of amusement and interest. If it is not possible for your students to bring in photos encourage discussion by writing some specific questions on the board. *What is your earliest memory? Where/When was it? Why do you remember it?*

Ask students to look at the photos on p23 and compare with their own memories. What is the memory for each photo?

Listening and note-taking

World traveller and lavender farmer

Ask students to look at the photographs from the photo album of a lady called Natalie Hodgson. They should motivate students to want to listen to Natalie talking about her very rich and interesting life. Ask them how old they think she is in each photo. Discuss the photos a little before you give them the actual facts about them.

FACTS ABOUT THE PHOTOS

They are all of Natalie Hodgson.

- In one of the fields on her lavender farm, aged 80.
- Aged three in 1918.
- Water-skiing in the Lake District aged 83. This is the most recent picture.
- Getting married, aged twenty-five, in 1939.
- Aged 73, in 1988, in Jerusalem with her husband, not long before he died.

Part One Childhood

NB *The tape is divided into three sections with different tasks for each. The tasks are staged, going from a simple listen and underline activity to more challenging note-taking activities. The aim is to ease students into the listening process, and let them gradually become more familiar with Natalie's voice.*

T 2.3 Play part one. Ask students to underline the correct answers. Make clear that sometimes more than one is correct. Get feedback before moving on to part two.

Answers

1. Natalie was born just before the First World War.
2. Her earliest memory is her third birthday party. (The cake *did* have candles on it. She had a beautiful cake despite wartime shortages. She says *'Everything was very short.'*)
3. When she was a child she wanted to fly the Atlantic, become a Member of Parliament.
4. In her life she has been a librarian, a glider pilot, a lavender farmer.
5. During her life, she has lived in Paris, Dresden, Wolverhampton, Shropshire.
6. She went abroad to learn foreign languages.

BACKGROUND INFORMATION

- The First World War began in 1914 and ended in 1918.
- Shropshire is a county in the west of England.
- An MP is a Member of Parliament. MPs work in the Houses of Parliament in Westminster, London.
- Dresden is a town in Germany.
- Schalliapin /ʃælɪjæpɪn/ was a Russian opera singer (1873–1938). *Boris Godunov* was his most famous operatic role.
- Wagner /vaːgnə/ (1813–1883) was a German composer of operas. Major works: *Tannhäuser*, *The Flying Dutchman*, *Tristan and Isolde*, *The Ring of the Nibelung*.

Part Two The war years

Read aloud the introduction to the whole class. Read the questions aloud also. You could ask students to do this. Play part two and ask your students to take notes to answer the questions. Make clear that you don't want full sentences, just words to jog their memories. The words in bold show the key words that students should have noted down.

Answers

1. Natalie was in **Germany** immediately before the Second World War.
   She was **too young** to understand but she remembers **days when** she was **not allowed to go out, torchlight processions**, the **Jews' shop windows** being **broken.**
2. During the war she was involved in **political warfare,** and sent **misinformation to** the **enemy.** After the war she worked in **naval intelligence.** It was **secret** work.
   It was difficult to **keep secrets from her husband** when she **wrote letters.**

Ask individual students to construct full sentences from their notes. Be quite exacting in the level of intelligibility you accept. Make sure that answers are really understandable even if there are small grammatical mistakes.

Part Three The best is yet to come

This last part is the longest. It reveals how Natalie loves life and looks forward to the future despite her great age.

POSSIBLE VOCABULARY PROBLEMS

cedar tree = tall evergreen tree
hives of bees = 'houses' for bees
step-grandchild = one of Natalie's children married someone who already had a child.
lemurs /li:məz/ = animals like monkeys
two-seater = plane with two seats
golden age = best part of your life

Read aloud the introduction to the whole class. You could ask a student to do this. Play part three and ask your students to take notes again, but this time under the headings given. You could write these on the board in columns and then students can come up to the board after discussing their answers in groups and fill out the columns with their ideas.

Sample answer notes

Natalie's life:

Home and family
- 1953 bought lovely house and gardens in Shropshire
- 8 grandchildren, one step-grandchild

Travel and places visited
- travelled a lot
- Machu Picchu a favourite place
- helicopter to see Grand Canyon
- also been to India, the Great Wall of China, Madagascar, Jerusalem
- *not* been to Egypt

Work
- grows lavender and keeps bees
- works most of the time

Pastimes and hobbies
- goes waterskiing and gliding

The future
- interested in the future
- wants to know if life in outer space
- lots to look forward to

Language work

This could be set for homework or done in groups in class. There should be a general feedback session with the whole class sharing ideas. The gaps cover a wide range of words, both grammatical and lexical, giving students challenging practice in many areas of English.

Answers

a eighties
b just/immediately
c still
d where
e be
f spent
g got/was
h had
i who
j until
k During
l had
m moved
n up
o didn't
p been
q successful
r keeps/has
s deal
t goes

Writing

A biography

Use these exercises to set up the final writing activity, which can be given for homework.

1 Ask students to work in pairs. However, if they have been working a lot in pairs or groups recently, you could do this as a full class activity. This should mean that it takes less time. Often there are a few possibilities, the most natural are given below.

Answers

a She frequently goes waterskiing in summer.
In summer she frequently goes waterskiing.
b She likes her garden very much, especially in summer.
c She works hard with her bees in the gardens every day.
Every day she works hard with her bees in the gardens.
d Nowadays she only goes gliding occasionally.
She only goes gliding occasionally nowadays.
e When she was in Dresden in 1934, she often used to go to the opera.
In 1934, when she was in Dresden, she often used to go to the opera.
f Ten years ago she thoroughly enjoyed visiting the Grand Canyon.
She thoroughly enjoyed visiting the Grand Canyon ten years ago.
g Unfortunately her husband died suddenly in 1989.
Unfortunately, in 1989, her husband died suddenly.
h She really enjoys looking after her grandchildren during their school holidays.
i She's travelled abroad to many countries throughout her life.
Throughout her life, she's travelled abroad to many countries.
j Fortunately she's still fit enough to keep travelling.

2 Ask your students to think of someone who is still alive that they want to write about. Get them to write a few notes about the person using the headings as a guide. Share ideas round the class. *Who did you choose? Why?*

If you have time it is sometimes worthwhile to work on pieces of writing in class, or at least work on a rough draft in class before doing it in neat for homework. Allocate class time for going through it so that everyone ends up with a good piece of writing. (You could ask students to bring in photographs to accompany their biographies, if it is possible for them to do so.)

PostScript (SB p26)

Exclamations!

NB An area of focus in 'New Headway Upper-Intermediate' is work on the grammar of spoken English. These are aspects of the language such as social expressions, exaggerating and understatements, being polite, and reply questions to express interest and surprise. This exercise on exclamations is the first of these. It should be fun as well as useful. There is a lot of pronunciation practice, particularly of stress and intonation.

1 **T 2.4** Write a huge exclamation mark (!) on the board to launch the lesson. Ask students which words in English come to mind. *Before* you play the tape, ask students to open their books and look at columns A and B. Can they make any matches at this stage? Play the tape and stop after each one to ask for suggestions.

Answers

1 d Yuk! How disgusting!
2 f Ah! What a shame!
3 b Wow! Triplets! How amazing!
4 g Ouch! I've just cut my finger.
5 e Whoops! I've dropped it!
6 a Mmm! It's absolutely delicious!
7 c Hey, Peter! Come over here and sit with us.
8 h Uh? That's crazy! What a stupid thing to say!
9 i Uh-huh. Of course I'm listening to you.

Before you move on, check these dialogues by reading aloud the first lines yourself from the tapescript and asking students for the right responses. Be strenuous in encouraging good stress and intonation all the while.

2 Ask students to work in pairs to choose the next line for each dialogue.

Answers

e b f a i d g c h

T 2.5 Play the tape for students to listen and check. After playing *each* dialogue, practise it in open pairs (student to student across the class). Use the tape as a model for your students' stress and intonation.

3 This should be a quick, snappy exercise. Ask students to work in pairs to complete the exclamations. Then go round the class, calling out the letters at random and nominating a student to produce the correct exclamation.
Example T: *g!* S: *What a mess!*
Be sure to encourage wide voice range and good stress and intonation.

Answers (p = positive reaction n = negative)

a What a silly mistake! (n)
b What a brilliant idea! (p)
c What ghastly weather! (n)
d How utterly ridiculous! (n)
e How terrific! (p)
f What rubbish! (n)
g What a mess! (n)
h How dreadful! (n)
i How absolutely fabulous! (p)
j What appalling behaviour! (n)
k What a hell of a journey! (n)
l What a terrible thing to happen! (n)

Ask your students: *What are the rules?*

Answers

- *What* + uncountable nouns and plurals.
- *What a* + singular nouns
- *How* + adjective

4 The situations you read out should be *personalized*, i.e. about your students and yourself. They should also be amusing, if possible. You could either address the whole class and encourage general responses, or you could write the situations on separate pieces of card, give one to each student and ask them to read it aloud for others to respond. This could be done in groups.

Sample situations and answers

1 I've just won $5,000 in the lottery! *How terrific/wonderful/fantastic!*
2 You have to learn the whole dictionary for homework! *How utterly ridiculous!*
3 We drove to the beach last Sunday. I was in a traffic jam for four hours and by the time we arrived it was time to come back. *What a hell of a journey!/What a terrible thing to happen!*
4 Maria, you've written *arrive at Rome* instead of *arrive in Rome*! *What a silly mistake!*
5 Look at George's homework! I can hardly read it. *What a mess!/How dreadful!*
6 Let's have a long coffee break! *What a brilliant idea!*

5 This exercise may require too much imagination for some students. You could prompt them with an example.

What was the party like? Well, it was really boring!
What a shame! Yes. Nobody enjoyed it.

You could ask students to write a few dialogues for homework if there is no time in class.

Don't forget!

Workbook Unit 2
Exercise 7 Prepositions of movement
Exercise 8 Pronunciation – word stress

What happened was this ...

Narrative tenses
Expressing interest and surprise

Introduction to the unit

What happened was this ... is all about telling stories. This is the obvious theme for a unit covering the major narrative tenses: the Past Simple, Past Continuous, Past Perfect Simple, Past Perfect Continuous, and Present Simple (for dramatic effect). There are different types of story in the unit. The first is an oral anecdote told by a flight attendant; the second a newspaper article; and the third a literary extract which is introduced by a short radio dramatization. The listening and writing sections involve book reviews.

The Workbook has exercises on all past passives and various kinds of time expressions, as well as providing additional practice of the narrative tenses.

Notes on the unit

LANGUAGE AIMS – NARRATIVE TENSES

NB See the Grammar Reference section – SB p148.

Narrative tenses

Students at this level will of course be familiar with the Past Simple, Past Continuous, and Past Perfect Simple, but they will still be making many mistakes when attempting to use them correctly, and may not have practised the latter two in the passive.

They will be less familiar with the Past Perfect Continuous and may not have been made aware of the dramatic or historic use of the Present Simple: *Then the police arrive and try to arrest him but he runs away and jumps into his car*. This is dealt with in the writing section of the unit. It doesn't usually cause problems, as it is a common feature of many languages.

Test your grammar (SB p27)

This *Test your grammar* is designed not only as a grammar check but also as a direct introduction to the *Language in context* to motivate the students to listen to the story which follows.

Begin by focusing your students' attention on the cartoon. Encourage comment: *Who are the people? Where are they? What has happened?*

1 Read the situation aloud. Ask students to name the two tenses used. Ask why they are used. Do **not** be tempted to embark on lengthy grammar explanations. Keep it brief.

Answer

The two tenses used are the Past Continuous and Past Simple. The continuous action or the action in progress *was travelling* is interrupted by two consecutive short actions *stood up, fell over.*

2 Ask individual students to read aloud the questions about the situation. Ask what they think the answers are. They can only guess at this stage. Tell them that soon they will hear the full story. Now ask them to name the tenses in the questions.

Answers

Where was the plane flying to? = Past Continuous
Did the man have food poisoning? = Past Simple
What had he eaten? = Past Perfect
Had he been drinking? = Past Perfect Continuous

3 Ask students to write more questions, individually or in pairs. This requires some imagination from your students, which can be difficult. Be prepared for few contributions and be grateful for any, especially because most of the more obvious questions have already been asked. Possible suggestions might be: *Did anyone help the man? Was the plane flying through a storm? Had he drunk too much whisky/champagne? Had he seen someone with a gun? Had he been sleeping and had a bad dream?*

Lead the questions directly into the *Language in context*. Tell your students that they are now going to hear the story of what actually did happen.

LANGUAGE IN CONTEXT (SB p27)

Narrative tenses

NB *The story is completely true. Two friends Laura and John are talking about it. The story happened to Laura's friend Mandy, who is an air hostess.*

1 **T 3.1** Focus the students on the questions, then ask them to listen to the story. Students then work in pairs to answer not only the questions in this exercise, but any other ones they may have thought of. It can be interesting to see which of their questions are actually answered.

POSSIBLE VOCABULARY PROBLEMS

These could be researched by your students for homework prior to the lesson.
Check them before the listening.

aisle (you could check this from the cartoon.)
resuscitate /rɪˈsʌsɪteɪt/ = bring back to consciousness
duty-frees (short for *duty-free goods*. In this case it refers to alcoholic drinks only.)
leaking = losing water through a hole
dripping = liquid falling drop by drop
off balance = in danger of falling
cramped = narrow, restricted, not enough space

Answers

- Mandy's an air hostess (now called *flight attendant* because this term covers both men and women. *Steward* and *stewardess* are also used.)
- The flight attendants thought at first that he'd had a heart attack. Then they smelled alcohol and thought he'd been drinking, possibly that he'd drunk too many duty-free whiskies.
- He'd taken off his wooden leg to go to sleep. When the whisky had started to drip onto his head, he'd stood up, forgetting about his leg, and fallen over.

Bring the whole class together to discuss the answers.

NB *These questions have been designed to prompt students' use of some of the narrative tenses. Listen carefully when they answer and try to assess their ability to use them correctly. Make sure that you encourage good, not unclear or one-word, replies.*

2 Ask students to work in pairs again to do this. Point out that the first sentence comes exactly halfway through the story, and it has been numbered for them.

Answers

1 The man took off his wooden leg.
2 The man fell asleep.
3 A bottle started leaking onto the man's head.
4 The man woke up.
5 The man stood up and fell over.
6 The flight attendants ran to help him.
7 They smelled alcohol on him.
8 The flight attendants helped him back into his seat.
9 The man explained what had happened.

Get feedback by asking one or two students to retell the story from their answers. Encourage them to make it sound more natural by using linking words and personal pronouns. *The man took off his wooden leg and he fell asleep but a bottle … so he woke up …*, etc.

SUGGESTION

At this point write on the board. *A man was travelling on a plane, when suddenly he stood up and fell over …* ask students to continue the story from this middle point and push them to use the narrative tenses correctly, especially when giving the man's explanation of what happened. This is more or less what you want:

'A man was travelling on a plane, when suddenly he stood up and fell over. The flight attendants ran to help him but they were not very sympathetic when they smelled alcohol on his breath. However, they helped him back to his seat. Then the man explained what had happened. He said that he had a wooden leg, which he had taken off before he fell asleep. He said he hadn't been drinking, but while he was sleeping, a bottle of whisky in the overhead compartment had started leaking onto his head. This had woken him up and he'd stood up quickly, forgetting about his leg, and had fallen over.'

Or you could ask them to write the story for homework.

3 This exercise has the double aim of pronunciation practice and recalling parts of the story. Do it with the whole class and nominate individual students to continue the sentences. Correct vigilantly. This is controlled practice, not free speaking.

NB *Remember that a weak form is either a contracted form: he'd, or a weak vowel sound: was* /wəz/ *not* /wɒz/ *and were* /wə/ *not* /wɜː/.

Answers

it was /wəz/ in the night-time and most people were sleeping.
they were /wə/ trying to find out what was wrong.
he managed to tell them what 'd /wɒtəd/ happened.

He'd been fast asleep, and a bottle of whisky or gin ... had started leaking.

he'd forgotten that he'd taken off his false/wooden leg.

I've no idea why he'd taken it off.

Grammar question

You will have already had some discussion about the tenses used, so this section should be done quite quickly. It would be a good idea to read the Language Review on p29 with your class at this stage. Students could give examples from the story to illustrate the points being made in the review.

Answer

- The past tenses used are the Past Simple, Past Continuous, Past Perfect Simple, because these are the main tenses used in storytelling. (See Language Review p29 for a more detailed account.)

PRACTICE BANK **(SB p28)**

NB Remember – you decide which of these activities to do, and when.

1 Discussing grammar

The first exercise should be done in class. The second could be set for homework.

1 Students could work alone and then check each other's ideas in pairs or groups before you have a full class feedback. Alternatively, they could work in pairs from the start. Ask students to discuss reasons for their decisions and to check their ideas with the explanation given in the Language Review on p29.

Answers

a wasn't wearing (activity in progress)
b ran (one action following another)
c was reading (didn't finish it, it's too long)
d had seen (past action before another past action)
e had been flying (long past activity before another) happened (interrupted activity)
f had been drinking (continuous long activity before another)
g had done (past action before another past action)

2 Books closed. Write the example on the board. Write *When Peter got home ...* beneath it. Then discuss with the class how to rewrite the sentence and build it up on the board. This can be a more impactful introduction to the activity than simply reading it aloud from the book. Students open their books and do the exercise.

Answers

a Last night Sally was celebrating because she had received a letter saying that she had won £2,000 in a competition.
b When I got home from work I found that my flat had been burgled and someone had stolen my TV.
c Mick was a homeless beggar but he hadn't always been poor. Once he had had a successful business, which unfortunately had gone bust.
d When Jane and Peter arrived home they were broke because they'd been shopping all day and had spent all their money on clothes.
e John decided to emigrate to Australia because his parents had died and he had no relatives left in the UK.

2 Gilly's story

Exercise 3 of this activity could be set for homework, after doing Exercises 1 and 2 in class in preparation.

1 Ask students to look at the pictures and encourage comment. *Have you heard of Harrods? What do you know about it? Do you like what Gilly is wearing?*, etc. Ask a student to read aloud the photograph caption.

BACKGROUND INFORMATION

Harrods is probably Britain's most famous and exclusive department store. It is very big and beautiful, famed for its amazing food halls, which are elaborately decorated. It is said that you can buy everything in Harrods, even an elephant! It is owned by a rich Egyptian called Mohammed al Fayed.

2 Encourage your students to think why Gilly wasn't allowed in the store on Saturday, even though she'd been shopping there the day before. Do this quickly as a class activity. They may well guess correctly that she was barred because of the clothes she was wearing: *She was wearing old, torn jeans.* Be prepared to teach the word *torn*.

3 Check that your students understand the meaning of *barred* in the headline: *bar someone from doing = not allow someone to do*. Students could work in pairs to do the exercise. Emphasize that passive as well as active forms are required. Afterwards, conduct a feedback session with the whole class.

Answers

a had just bought	j were torn
b returned	k had bought

c was barred	l didn't listen (*wouldn't listen = refused to listen* is also correct)
d was wearing	m had gathered
e had been staying	n left
f had happened	o had never felt
g was walking	p was introduced
h was stopped	
i pointed	

You could round off the session by inviting your students' opinion on a store that has such a dress code. Do they know any stores, restaurants, or any public places where there is any kind of dress code?

3 Listening to the news

This activity comprises three news stories, each with a different kind of controlled practice task.

NB *In the development of the skill of listening, it is, of course, beneficial for students to have listening activities where they listen for general or gist information. However, it is also beneficial for them to listen for more detailed information. This series of activities is designed to do this, whilst also giving controlled practice of various aspects of past tenses.*

1 **T 3.2** Students close their books. Play the first news item. Ask a few check questions about the content of the story. *What's the item about? Is it good news or bad news? Where does it happen? What happened last month?*
Students open their books. Ask them to look quickly through the phrases. Can they identify any words that they did not hear? (This is just to 'tune them into' the activity.) Now play the item again, warning students they will have to listen very carefully indeed to find the small differences.

Answers

a (✔)
b (✘) who are all from Glasgow
c (✘) had been climbing
d (✘) were forced
e (✔)
f (✘) They are recovering in hospital
g (✘) are said
h (✘) have been warning walkers

If you have time, check the exercise by playing the tape (SB p131) once more and asking students to listen and read at the same time.

2 **T 3.3** Ask students to read through the answers before you play the tape. This will help prepare them for the content. Now ask them to listen and then work in pairs to write the questions.

NB *Students often have problems with forming questions correctly. This exercise practices this.*

Answers

a Who has died?
b When did she die?
c Who found her?
d Where did he find her?
e How did she die?
f How long had she been depressed?
g When was her last novel published?
h How many times had she been married?
i How many children did she have?

Check the answers by nominating pairs of students: one to ask and the other to answer the questions in open pair practice.

3 **T 3.4** Read out the instructions. Stress that the first time they just listen for the overall content. The next time they start to write. Ask them to check in pairs before going through the tapescript (SB p131).

NB *This is a dictation activity. Unfashionable as it has been for many years to do this, it provides excellent listening practice if done occasionally as part of a varied listening syllabus. Students may find it quite challenging and it can be illuminating to find out what they think they are hearing.*

Answers

Passives: was stolen, were fired, was hurt, were given, had been pulled off, is believed

ADDITIONAL MATERIAL

Workbook Unit 3
Exercises 1 and 3 Past Simple and Past Perfect
Exercise 2 Past Simple and Past Continuous
Exercise 4 Time expressions with all past tenses
Exercise 5 All past tenses
Exercises 6 and 7 Past passives

All of the above could be used in class. Exercises 5 and 7 are especially suitable for classroom use. However, given limitations of time, they will more likely be set as homework.

LANGUAGE REVIEW (SB p29)

Narrative tenses

You may well have incorporated the Language Review already into your lessons, encouraging your students to use it whilst working on some of the exercises. If not, read it together as a class and/or ask students to read it at home.

Ask students to read the Grammar Reference section at the back of the book at home. Suggest that they use it to revise from or when they are doing Workbook exercises.

● READING AND LISTENING (SB p30)

The man who sold his wife

NB *This is one of two places where we include extracts from literature. This piece is from a very famous 19th century novel, whereas later, in Unit 11, we include a modern short story.*

Pre-reading task

1 Before students open their books, ask them if they can name any famous English writers. They will probably manage at least Shakespeare and Dickens. Write their suggestions on the board and then write up Thomas Hardy. *Has anyone heard of him? Is he still alive? When did he live?*

Students open their books. Invite comments on the pictures and the dates. Now ask them to read the biographical information. You may need to teach *stonemason* and *gloomy*, but otherwise there should be little difficulty with the vocabulary.

2 Ask them to work with a partner to form the questions and answer them. Go round the pairs and monitor their efforts, helping them form the questions where necessary.

NB *When describing the scenes and events from a book it is usual to use the Present Simple tense*. This is called the dramatic or historic use of this tense. Point this out to your students when going through the answers.*

Answers

When/where was Thomas Hardy born?
On 2 June 1840, near Dorchester, in Dorset.

When/where did he die?
On 11 January 1928, in Dorchester.

What did his father do?
He was a stonemason.

What did he do after he left school?
He became an architect and went to work in London.

Why did he return to Dorset?
Because he missed the countryside.

When did he begin writing novels?
In 1867.

What *does *Under the Greenwood Tree* describe?
Characters and scenes from country life.

When was his first big success?
In 1874. A book called *Far from the Madding Crowd*.

*Are his stories optimistic or pessimistic?
They're pessimistic – gloomy and tragic.

Who *is Michael Henchard? What *does he do?
He is the main character in *The Mayor of Casterbridge*.
He sells his wife and child to another man.

* Does *The Mayor of Casterbridge* have a happy ending?
No, it doesn't. Michael Henchard is destroyed.

Go through the questions and answers quickly with the whole class.

Reading (1)

Students have already learnt a little about *The Mayor of Casterbridge* from Thomas Hardy's biographical information. Ask them to look at the picture and nominate a student to read the caption underneath aloud to the rest of the class. Now ask some questions about the picture.

Who is the man holding the bottle? Michael Henchard.
Who are the two people standing next to him? His wife and child.
Who are the people listening to him? Other people at the fair.
What is happening in the background? A horse auction.

Ask your students to read Extract 1 and point out the glossary at the side.

NB *Although the language used is a little old-fashioned, it is fairly simple and should not be difficult for your students to understand with the help of the glossary. In the early 19th century, wife-selling was not uncommon in rural areas of England.*

Comprehension check

Do this quite quickly as a class activity.

Answers

1 Michael and some other men are talking about marriage, or more particularly how good men can be ruined by marrying the wrong woman.
2 He regrets having married too early, at eighteen, and now has a wife and child.
3 His wife is clearly not surprised at Michael's behaviour, and 'seemed accustomed to such remarks.' He probably gets drunk quite often.
4 In the field outside, a horse auction is going on and this gives Michael the idea that men can sell their wives just as they sell their horses, to the highest bidder.

Listening and speaking

Divide the class into small groups (if possible).

1 Tell them that they are going to hear a short play about what happens next in the story, but before they

do this, you want them to predict what happens. Give them a few minutes to discuss the list and choose their three ideas. Then have a full class feedback where the groups compare what they think. Ask them which ideas they think are most unlikely.

2 **T 3.5** Ask students to listen and tick the sentences that are correct in Exercise 1.

Answers

The auctioneer agrees to auction Susan like the horses.
A sailor buys Susan and the child for five guineas.
Susan believes that she and the child will be better off without Michael.

NB Five guineas is the modern equivalent of £5,000.

3 Ask: *What noises did you hear on the tape?* Have a general discussion about it.

Answers

The noises are:

- the horse auction in the background.
- Michael's fist coming down angrily on a table.
- coughs, laughs, gasps of amazement from the people around.
- the notes and coins being counted out by the sailor to pay for Susan.
- the notes and coins being picked up by Michael.
- the child crying.
- Susan throwing her wedding ring at her husband as she leaves the tent. He shouts out with pain as it hits his face.

SUGGESTION

Students can be allocated the different parts in the drama and act out the scene themselves, reading from the tapescript on p131.

Reading (2)

Students read Extract 2. The biographical information, radio play, and discussion should have prepared them well for this.

POSSIBLE VOCABULARY PROBLEMS

There are a few words of old English that your students may query:

I be = I am (this is still part of west country dialect in England today – *be* is used with all persons: *you be, he be, we be*, etc.)

ye = you *thee* = you (informal)

Comprehension check

Students could work in pairs to do these exercises.

Answers

1 There is not in fact a lot extra learnt from the reading. The sound effects and various noises in the radio play illustrate many of the written words. We learn that:

- the auctioneer is a short man.
- the sailor has been watching the proceedings from the door of the tent for a while.
- he paid with five new Bank of England pound notes.
- the people watching became seriously interested at the sight of the money.

2 Ask students to underline the adjectives that describe Michael Henchard. Then divide the board into three columns. Ask a few of them up to the board to fill in the columns with appropriate adjectives. Invite the others to comment and give reasons for their choices.

Answers

Michael	Susan	The sailor
unhappily married	unhappily married	polite
disloyal	polite	sensible
immature	sensible	thoughtful
insensitive	thoughtful	sober
belligerent	pitiable	kind-hearted
unreliable	sober	
irresponsible	long-suffering	
self-pitying		
reckless		

3 First allow a little time for discussion in pairs. Then ask for suggestions for paraphrasing the quotations from the whole class.

Sample answers

She doesn't like her husband. (In those days married women were considered to be their husband's possession.)

Saying you will do something is not the same as actually doing it. Michael wants the sailor to put his words into action.

chink is the noise of the coins going down on top of the notes. The sailor puts them down one after the other (= *severally*).

The chief actors are the main characters in the drama: Michael, the sailor, and Susan. The bystanders couldn't take their eyes off them because they were so interested in the scene.

The sailor invites the child too, and in a very kindly way. If taking one person is good (*merry*) then more than one is even better. *Let's invite everyone to the party, the more the merrier!*

Susan says that she will try for better luck in life with someone else. (It can't be worse than with Michael.)

What do you think?

Perhaps by now your students would like to know what happens to all these characters in the complete novel. These questions are designed to help them predict what might happen. Conduct a class discussion on these questions and try to get some consensus about the outcome of the story. Then photocopy and give out the synopsis of what actually happens (TB p125).

In our experience students are really surprised to learn how the story unfolds, and a few are actually motivated to read *The Mayor of Casterbridge* and other books by Thomas Hardy as a result. There is an abridged adaptation of *The Mayor of Casterbridge* in the *Oxford Progressive English Readers* series.

● VOCABULARY (SB p33)

Suffixes and prefixes

***NB** This is a self-contained vocabulary activity. However, it does have links with the previous reading activity and therefore is best done following it, though not necessarily in the same lesson. Make sure that there are monolingual dictionaries in the class for your students to consult.*

1 Books closed. Write the verb *to respond* on the board. Ask if they know the noun and adjective forms, write up *response* and *responsible*. Open books. Now read through this section with the whole class. Point out that suffixes go after the base words and prefixes go before.

2 Students work in pairs. Ask them to make new words as you did in Exercise 1.
Allocate a fixed time, about ten minutes, then collate ideas from the whole class.

Answers

Prefixes	**Suffixes**
unconscious	consciousness
unhelpful	helpful helpless
	helpfulness helplessness
unkind	kindness unkindness
illiterate	literacy illiteracy
disloyal	loyalty disloyalty
immature	maturity immaturity
immeasurable	measurable
impolite	politeness
unpopular	popularity unpopularity
irrelevant	
unreliable	reliable reliability
disrespect	respectful disrespectful
	sensible senseless(ness)
insensitive	sensitive sensitivity
unsuccessful	successful
	thoughtful
	thoughtless(ness)
misunderstand	understandable
disuse misuse	useful useless
(unused)	usefulness uselessness

3 Space permitting, you could invite a few students up to the board to fill in columns, asking the others to comment. Photocopy the complete set of answers to give out at the end. The base word which can form the most new words is *use*.

4 This exercise could be set for homework and you could move directly to Exercise 5.

Answers

a sensible helpful
b immature insensitive
c senseless unconscious
d helpless
e disused useless
f unhappiness illiteracy
g impolite disrespectful
h immeasurable

5 Do this with the whole class. A few common examples are given next to each one, but there are many more in the dictionary. However, ask students to think of some for themselves. (They can consult the dictionary after the lesson if they want to.)

Answers

a	**self-** = of, to, or by oneself	*self-confident self-employed*
b	**anti-** = against	*anti-smoking*
	pro- = for/in favour of	*pro-government forces*
c	**non-** = not	*non-smoking compartment*
		non-profit-making
d	**pre-** = before	*preview*
	post- = after	*post-mortem*
e	**re-** = again	*recycle rewind*
f	**ex-** = former	*ex-wife ex-convict*
g	**over-** = too much	*overwork*
	under- = too little	*underachieve*
h	**fore-** = before	*forename forecast*
i	**ante-** = before	*ante-room antecedent*
j	**sub-** = below	*subtitle subconscious*
k	**co-** = with	*co-star cooperate*
l	**bi-** = two	*biannual bisexual*

● SPEAKING AND LISTENING (SB p34)

Talking about books

SUGGESTION

It would be a good idea prior to this lesson to ask your students to think about one of their favourite books and make a few notes about it.

1 Tell your students a bit about when and what you like to read. Now ask them about themselves. This should be just a few minutes of introductory discussion with the whole class to set up the activity.

2 Read through the introduction and example. Ask students to work in pairs to write the questions. Go through the answers with the whole class.

Answers

a When was it written?
b What kind/type of book is it?
c What's it about?
d Who are the main characters?
e Has it been made into a film?
f How does it end?
g What did you think of it?
h Would you recommend it?

3 Focus your students' attention onto the cover. *Have any of you heard of this author or the book?* Ask them to read it and work in pairs to go through the questions. Make it clear that they will *not* be able to answer all the questions.

Answers

Who wrote it? Ken Follett.

a When was it written?
Don't know exactly, but it seems modern.
b What kind/type of book is it? A thriller.
c What's it about? A beautiful scientist who discovers a mystery to do with identical twins.
d Who are the main characters?
Jeannie Ferrami and Steve.
e Has it been made into a film? Don't know.
f How does it end? Don't know.
g What did you think of it?
Don't know but the cover looks interesting.
h Would you recommend it?
I haven't read it so I don't know.

Go through the questions with your students. Ask them if they think they would like to read the book, having read the cover. Tell them a bit more about it.

NB *The following background information will help you answer some of the questions your students have not been able to answer from the cover.*

BACKGROUND INFORMATION

Ken Follett is an English thriller writer who lives in Chelsea, in London. He has so far written nine best-sellers. His first, *Eye of the Needle*, won an award and was made into a film. His most successful book so far is *The Pillars of the Earth*.

This book, *The Third Twin*, was first published by Pan in 1997. It is, in fact, not a story about twins, but a story about cloning, hence the *third* twin. It is set in Baltimore on the east coast of the United States. Twenty-two years ago some evil scientists made eight male clones. All the clones, except for the hero, Steve, grow up to be criminals. Jeannie Ferrami, the heroine and a *good* scientist, discovers the truth and her life is in danger. In the end Jeannie and Steve solve the mystery together, the evil scientists are punished and Jeannie and Steve fall in love and live happily ever after! The book may soon be made into a film.

Now students ask and answer questions in pairs about a book they have read. (This will go more smoothly if you have set the suggested homework.) Ask for some feedback on their choices.

Listening and note-taking

POSSIBLE VOCABULARY PROBLEMS

This is just for your information. The texts are not difficult to follow and these words should not need pre-teaching, but only you can be the final judge of this for your students. You may want to draw students' attention to them after the listening and note-taking, either by playing the tape and stopping at the relevant points or by looking at the tapescripts (SB p131).

Joey
prolific
to pinpoint
threads
mistaken identity
asylum
bump into
sticky end
I couldn't put it down

Ken
what makes a person tick
acute observations
a little encounter with Rosie

Kate
cave
treasure map
it kept you on the edge of your seat

T 3.6 Ask students to copy the headings onto a separate piece of paper. Stress that they just take notes, they don't write long sentences. Stop after each person and ask students to discuss their notes.

Answers

Joey

Title and author *The Woman in White* by Wilkie Collins.

Type of book A detective story (the first one) and romance.
Setting 19th century London and the north of England.
Who and what it is about The woman in white and Walter Hartwright, a young artist. He falls in love with a young lady, Miss Fairlie, who looks like the identical twin of the woman in white. So when one dies, who is it?
Personal opinion Joey enjoyed it very much. She couldn't put it down.

Ken
Title and author *Cider with Rosie* by Laurie Lee.
Type of book An autobiography.
Setting A little village in the Cotswolds (in rural England).
Who and what it is about The author's childhood in the village. How the village society works, the village characters. Especially an incident with Rosie in the bushes with some cider!
Personal opinion Recommends it to students. Likes the poetry and humour of it.

Kate
Title and author *The Valley of Adventure* by Enid Blyton.
Type of book An adventure story.
Setting A deserted valley or island.
Who and what it is about Four children and a parrot who get on the wrong plane and end up looking for treasure in a deserted valley.
Personal opinion Very exciting (she was on the edge of her seat), and funny because of the parrot.

SUGGESTION

If you have sufficient space and tape recorders, this could be done as a jigsaw activity.

ADDITIONAL MATERIAL

Workbook Unit 3
Exercise 8 This is a vocabulary exercise on words related to literature.

● WRITING AND SPEAKING (SB p36)

A review of a book or film

SUGGESTIONS

1 This activity could be set for homework. However, it is worthwhile to do some work on developing the writing skill in class. In this instance a good approach might be as follows:
- discuss Exercise 1 in class
- set the note-making in Exercise 2 for homework. (Your students may already have a first draft of this if you followed the suggestion prior to the speaking and listening activity.)
- discuss the notes back in class and then start doing Exercise 3 (writing the review) in class.
- encourage students to swap ideas and read each other's work.
- finish the review for homework.
- mark work.
- write on the board some of the incorrect sentences from various pieces of homework.
- invite students to correct.
- students correct their individual work.
- pin up and/or read out some of the final reviews.

2 It can be a good idea (if possible in your particular teaching situation) to have a class library of English books. Encourage students to borrow books on a regular basis and exchange views about what they have read. There are many major books adapted for foreign learners, such as in the Oxford *Bookworms* series.

1 Ask your class these questions. You could remind them of how the people on the tapes told the stories of their chosen books. *Which tense did they use to tell the story? Why?*

Answer
The Present Simple is used to give life and colour to the telling of a story. The Past Simple does not have the same dramatic effect. Jokes often are told in the present because of this: *A man goes into a pub and asks for a glass of water* ... is much more dramatic than *A man went into* ... etc.

NB This use of the Present Simple does not usually cause many problems as it is a common feature of many languages.

2 Your students should have done some preparation before beginning this exercise in class. They may already have made a few notes. These headings and questions should provide a prompt for them to make more detailed notes. After they have done this, either in class or at home, get them to use the notes as a basis for talking to a partner about their book. You can lead this to an open class exchange of information.

3 These expressions are intended to give some concrete help in the full writing of the review. Everyone should be able to incorporate a few of them. This exercise can obviously be completed for homework.

NB It is important to mark and return homework and give feedback as soon as possible. It is very demotivating for students if there is a delay. Your use of class time in going over it will encourage students to take their written work seriously in future.

PostScript (SB p37)
Expressing interest and surprise

NB *One of the aims of this PostScript is to give useful pronunciation practice of stress and intonation. Some foreign learners find the wide voice range used in English rather embarrassing for them to imitate. However, if the exercise is fun they are more likely to attempt it.*

- *Remember that reply questions are not the same as question tags (see 2 below).*
- *This activity can be done at any stage, for example as a warmer at the start of a lesson.*

1 **T 3.7** Books closed. This short dialogue is simply a fun way of introducing the fact that repeating the information is a simple way of showing surprise. It paves the way for the introduction of reply questions in Exercise 2.

Answer

The man shows surprise by repeating the information which surprises him.

2 **T 3.8** Ask students to listen and complete the dialogue.

Answers

Has she? Does he? Did she?

Now practise it, first in open pairs so that you can encourage a wide voice range, then in closed pairs. Focus students' attention on the language and put one or two other examples of question tags and reply questions on the board to show the difference.

POSSIBLE EXAMPLES FOR THE BOARD

He works in New York, doesn't he? = question tag

A *He works in New York.*
B *Does he?* = reply question

It's raining isn't it? = question tag.

A *It's raining.*
B *Is it?* = reply question.

Ask your students: *What are the differences?*

Answer

The auxiliary verb is used both in question tags and reply questions. However, in reply questions it does not change positive to negative, negative to positive as it does in question tags. Also, the question tag is added by the speaker, but a reply question comes in response from another speaker.

3 Ask students to work in pairs. Tell them to make the dialogues sound as natural as possible by varying the use of direct echo and reply question. Ask them to practise saying them as they go through the exercise.

POSSIBLE VOCABULARY PROBLEMS

What a drag! = How awful and boring! (colloquial)
chap = man (informal/affectionate), e.g. *He's a nice chap.*
Blimey! = expressing surprise or annoyance (slang)

Answers

(The more natural answers are given. Where there are two suggestions the first is possibly more natural.)

a Does he?/ Apologize?
My mother's Chinese vase?/Has he?
b Did you?
Did it?
Was it?
c Is he?
Six glasses of whisky?/Has he?
Doesn't he?
Can't he?
Don't you?/Never?
d Did it?/Three hours?
Ten miles long?/Was there?
Have you?
e Have you?
Next Saturday? In Barbados?/Are you?
Have you?/Concorde?
f Are you?
Have you?
Marry me?/Would you?

T 3.9 Play the tape for students to listen and compare. Use the tape as a model for your students' stress and intonation. Ask some pairs of students to act out the dialogues to the rest of the class. Keep exhorting good stress and intonation. This can add to the fun.

4 Round off the lesson by saying some surprising things about yourself. Of course they need not be true, but it is more fun if you pretend they are.
Examples
I've been married five times.
I came to school in a Rolls Royce today.
I'm not going to give you any homework ever again.

You could ask students to make similar surprising statements about themselves.

Don't forget!

Workbook Unit 3
Exercise 9 Words commonly confused
Exercise 10 Phrasal verbs type 1
Exercise 11 Pronunciation – diphthongs

4 It's a deal!

Expressing quantity
Social expressions

Introduction to the unit

This is the first unit in *New Headway Upper-Intermediate* where the main grammatical focus shifts from the verb phrase to the noun phrase. Noun phrases are further dealt with in Units 6 and 12.

There is a considerable amount of skills work in this unit. The *Language in context* section consists of a jigsaw reading activity; the main reading text about the history of world trade is quite challenging; the speaking activity is a business maze, which involves a lot of interaction; and the listening exercise is an interview with an English couple who opened a restaurant in France. So make sure you allocate your time appropriately.

The writing activity consists of preparing a report on trade, past and present, in the student's own country. You could ask them early on to start thinking about this, and to discuss where they might get the information from.

Explain to students what *It's a deal* means. You could say the following.
Imagine a person, A, is trying to buy a car from B. They are talking about the price. 'One thousand pounds,' says A. 'No,' says B. 'One thousand five hundred.' 'Mmm,' says A. 'What about £1,250?' 'OK,' says B. 'It's a deal.' *It's a deal* means *we agree to do something*.

Explain that the topic of this unit is business and trade.

Notes on the unit

LANGUAGE AIMS – EXPRESSING QUANTITY

NB See the Grammar Reference section – SB p149.

The grammatical area of quantifiers seems very 'bitty' compared to the substance of the perfect aspect or narrative tenses. There are so many little areas to understand. Is the quantifier used with a countable noun only? Uncountable only? Both? Singular nouns only? Can the quantifier be used without a noun? When do we need *of*? Is *none* followed by a singular or plural verb? What's the difference between *not … anyone* and *no one*? Can we use *much* and *many* in affirmative sentences? Is it correct to say *less* people? How is *all* used?

Students will be familiar with the concepts of countable and uncountable nouns, and the use of *some* and *any* in affirmative, negative, and questions. They will probably recognize a lot of the other quantifiers, but it is unlikely that they can produce them accurately and appropriately. There will not be a breakdown in communication if and when students make mistakes in this area. Nevertheless, it is an area that needs to be confronted.

Test your grammar (SB p38)

1 This exercise is probably more difficult than it looks, especially as students aren't allowed to use *some*. They need to decide if the noun is singular or plural, countable or uncountable, and then choose an appropriate quantifier. Students may want to use *a lot of*, which is fine.

You might decide to do this exercise as a class, so that you can monitor, correct, and drill. There is a risk that errors would be compounded if it was done in pairs.

This exercise might well prompt students to ask questions about quantifiers, how they are used, and what they mean, so be prepared to explain.

Sample answers

She's got lots of/several pens.
There are a few stamps.
She hasn't got many cigarettes left.
I can see a couple of photos.
She's got hardly any money.
There are no hankies.
There isn't much perfume.
She's got lots of credit cards.
There isn't much chocolate.
She's got lots of make-up.
There are lots of keys.

She hasn't got any matches left.
There's no aspirin.
There are a couple of receipts.
She's got a few phone cards.

2 Students can now work in pairs or small groups to say what's in *their* bag. Give help with vocabulary. Ask a few students to feedback to the class. Encourage use of all the quantifiers, not just *some* and *any*.

LANGUAGE IN CONTEXT (SB p38)

Expressing quantity

You will need to photocopy the reading exercise (TB p125).

1 Read the instructions as a class. Emphasize to students that a lot of the information in the two texts is the same. Students are used to doing jigsaw activities where they are given totally different information.

- Direct them to the newspaper article in the Student's Book and read out the headline *Woman who left England penniless is now worth £20m.* Then hold up the other article and point out the headline *I left England with £5 and now I'm a multi-millionaire!*
- Ask the questions *How much money did she have when she left England?* and *How much money has she got now?* This should make the point to students that the articles are very similar, but with different detail.
- Divide students into two groups.
- Give out the photocopied articles to Group B. Ask them to close their Student's Books, so they only look at their article. The questions are reproduced next to their article.
- Ask Group A to read the article in the Student's Book.
- When they have finished reading, they discuss their answers with a partner from their group.

Answers

Group A

a Very little.
b Four years ago.
c £20 million.
d Because there wasn't much employment.
e No, none.
f Only very few.
g We don't know exactly, but it cost all the money she had.
h Not much.
i Over A$200,000 a year.
j Three weeks.
k She had hardly any work experience.

Group B

a Five pounds.
b A few years ago.
c A huge amount of money.
d Because there weren't many jobs.
e No, she didn't have any.
f Just two.
g £1,500, which is all the money she had.
h A$10,000 a year.
i A great deal of money.
j Several weeks.
k She had very little work experience.

2 Read the instructions and the example as a class. Students find a partner from the other group. They sit down together and compare answers.

3 Draw two columns on the board, and write the headings and examples as shown in the Student's Book. Give out a few board pens for the students to come up and write on the board.

Answers

Expressions of quantity	Actual quantity
very little money	just £5
a few years	four years
all of her fortune	...
a huge amount of money	£20 million
not much unemployment	...
not many jobs	...
with no qualifications	...
without any qualifications	...
very few friends	Two friends
every penny	...
wasn't earning much	just A$10,000
a great deal of money	over A$200,000
several weeks	three weeks
very little work experience	...
hardly any work experience	...

When the students have finished writing on the board, ask them to discuss the two questions in small groups. Get some feedback.

Answers

not ... any is the same as *no ...*, but *no ...* is more emphatic. *not ... any* is neutral.
very little ... and *very few ...* are similar to *hardly any ...* .
several is similar to *some. Several* means more than a few but not a lot. *Some* means a certain number or amount.
a great deal is the same as *a great amount.*
a lot is the same as *lots of.*
all is similar to *every,* but *every* is used with a singular noun only. Compare *all the people here are wearing ...* and *every person here is wearing ...* .

Don't expect to get this depth of analysis from students, and don't necessarily go into all the above areas with your class. Avoid weighing them down with too much information that they can't absorb.

Grammar questions

Answer these questions as a class. Don't worry if all the students don't seem to understand everything. These questions are a teaching tool, not a testing mechanism.

Answers

- *Very little* and *not much* are used with uncountable nouns.
  A few and *not many* are used with countable nouns.
- Yes, this rule is generally correct.
- B is happier. *A few* is positive, *few* is negative.
- *Hardly any work experience* is similar to *little work experience.*

4 Students close their books and retell the story. This is simply to get some immediate practice of the expressions of quantity.

SUGGESTION

You will need to prompt. You could put notes such as the following on the board.

… British woman … Australia … very little money … sold her business … huge amount … Cherry Haines … market stallholder … made all of her fortune … left England … jobs … arrived … qualifications … friends, etc.

You could even ask students to retell the story for a second time at the beginning of the next lesson.

PRACTICE BANK (SB p40)

1 Countable or uncountable?

1 The aim of this exercise is to get some quick personalized question and answer practice.
You might decide to do it first in open pairs, so that you can establish the correct questions, then ask students to do it again in closed pairs. Encourage the use of a variety of expressions of quantity in the answers.

NB *The questions test the very basic area of countable and uncountable, which students will have a certain familiarity with. Note, however, that 'homework' in English is uncountable, unlike other European languages. Students also have to realize that some nouns, for example 'time', can be both countable and uncountable, which is the focus of the next exercise.*

Sample answers

a How much money have you got?
Not a lot/not much/very little/not a penny/loads/quite a lot/not enough.

b How many pairs of jeans do you have?
Just a couple/quite a few/none.

c How much coffee do you drink a day?
Three or four cups/not much/none.

d How many times have you flown on a plane?
Loads/lots/very few/never.

e How much homework do you do a night?
Too much/about an hour a night.

f How much time do you spend watching TV?
A couple of hours a night.

g How much sugar/how many sugars do you take in coffee?
Two/just a little/none.

2 Read the instructions as a class. Students work in pairs to do the exercise.

Answers

a money **U** dollar **C**
b beggar **C** poverty **U**
c traffic **U** lorry/van **C**
d travel in general **U** *Travel broadens the mind.*
travel = one particular journey **C** *My travels in Africa.*
journey **C**
e job **C**
work in general **U** *I hate work.*
collection of art **C** *The works of William Shakespeare.*
f glass = the material **U**
glass = the receptacle **C**
g coffee **U** *I like coffee.*
coffee **C** *Three coffees, please.*
h time **C** *How many times … ?*
time **U** *I haven't got much time.*
i gold **U**
j experience **U** *I have a lot of experience of working abroad.*
experience **C** *We had some strange experiences while travelling through China.*
k apple **C**
fruit **U**
l qualification **C**

2 Expressing quantity

1 This is an old-fashioned substitution drill, so be prepared for your students not to know what to do! This exercise is best done as a class activity, and quite briskly. No one is pretending that this is a communicative activity. It is an exercise in manipulating forms.
Read the instructions and the examples as a class. Having established the right answer, drill it around the class a few times.

Answers

a She hasn't got many friends.
She hasn't got a lot of friends.
She's got hardly any friends.

b There are some eggs in the fridge.
There are a few eggs in the fridge.
There are enough eggs in the fridge.

c There aren't many eggs in the fridge.
There aren't enough eggs in the fridge.

d There are no eggs.
There isn't a single egg.
There are none.

e Did you spend much time in France?
Did you spend a lot of time in France?

f I don't have much holiday a year.
I have hardly any holiday a year.

g I've put on a huge amount of weight!
I've put on far too much weight!

h Nearly all of my friends have a car.
Most of my friends have a car.
The majority of my friends have a car.

i Very few of them smoke.
Hardly any of them smoke.

j None of my friends takes/take drugs.
Not one of my friends takes drugs.

k Ken works all (of) the time.
Ken works the whole of the time.

l Yesterday I didn't eat (very) much at all.
Yesterday I ate very little.
Yesterday I didn't eat a lot.

2 Read the introduction as a class. Students work in pairs to choose the correct alternative.

Answers

a a few	f Everything
b very little	g All
c less	h his whole life
d Fewer	i Everyone (*People* is plural.)
e Everyone	j Any

SUGGESTION

After doing this exercise and coming up against problems with *all* and *everything*, direct students to the Workbook Unit 4 Exercise 8.

3 A class survey

This speaking exercise will work best if you personalize it to *your* students in *your* town. It could take just ten minutes, or you could make it last thirty minutes or more, depending on how you set it up and keep it going.

Read the introduction as a class. Look at the sample answers. Ask students to work in groups to think of similar questions, about shopping in general, and for particular things such as food, clothes, books, etc. Basically, each student needs to have at least one question (but it could be two or three) to ask every other member of the class. This is a mingle activity. Having asked everybody, the results of the survey are expressed using an expression of quantity, as in the examples. Prompt with ideas such as the following: *… favourite clothes shop? What … buy there? How much … jeans? … shop at (the most expensive shop in your town)? … second-hand shops? … designer clothes?*
When students are ready, and you are sure that their questions are correctly formed, ask students to stand up and ask everyone in the room. You could make this more elaborate by asking your students to ask the members of another class, rather than just asking each other. Make sure the students express the results of the survey using an expression of quantity.

ADDITIONAL MATERIAL

Workbook Unit 4
Exercise 1 Countable and uncountable nouns
Exercises 2–6 Expressing quantity
Exercise 7 Compounds with *some*, *any*, *no*, and *every*
Exercise 8 *All* and *every*

LANGUAGE REVIEW (SB p41)

Expressing quantity

Read the Language Review as a class, and/or ask students to read it at home. Refer students to the Grammar Reference at the back of the Student's Book, and encourage them to ask questions if they have any queries.

● READING AND NOTE-TAKING (SB p41)

Three thousand years of world trade

SUGGESTIONS

1 This is quite a long activity, so allow adequate time for it. It is probably best to defer the final *Note-taking and report writing* to a later lesson.
2 You could set the vocabulary in Exercise 2 of the Pre-reading task for homework prior to this lesson.

Pre-reading task

1 Students work in small groups to discuss what they can see in the pictures.
After a while, get some feedback.

Answers

They are all engaged in doing business of some sort.

1 A big harbour (in fact Rotterdam, Europe's largest port). Cargo is being loaded and unloaded.
2 An Arab open-air market. People are buying and selling fruit and vegetables.
3 The New York stock exchange. Dealers are buying and selling shares.

2 Read the introduction as a class. It would be a good idea to set this exercise for homework prior to the lesson, as there are a lot of words, some quite difficult. This is an occasion when translation can be the best and quickest form of checking meaning. All the words are concrete nouns, presumably with an equivalent in L1. If you had to take responsibility for teaching, explaining, and testing each of the items, it would occupy an inordinate amount of classroom time. So bilingual dictionaries are best for this activity. You could also ask students to translate the items in class to serve as a check.

3 You might decide to do this exercise as a class, so that it is done more quickly. It doesn't matter if there is a degree of disagreement over what is still traded today and what isn't, and what is a luxury and what is a necessity. Students will inevitably have different opinions on this.

Don't let this exercise go on too long. You could easily get bogged down with any of the questions. It really isn't necessary to answer every question in detail. Get a general response to each question, then move on to the actual reading.

Sample answers

Items no longer traded
flint tools slaves fodder armour

Luxuries
gold silver silk wine

Necessities
metalware copper tin fodder glassware textiles grain olive oil corn drugs clothes cars

Raw materials
copper gold silver tin

Manufactured goods
flint tools metalware pottery soft drinks cars clothes glassware leatherwork armour

Reading

SUGGESTION

You might like to read the text aloud, while students listen and read at the same time. This has the advantage that you can stop to examine a vocabulary item, or ask one or two comprehension questions to check they're following. It also forces students to read more quickly, and not stop whenever they come across an unknown word.

POSSIBLE PRONUNCIATION PROBLEMS

Whether you read aloud or not, there are some words and proper nouns in the text that students might have difficulty saying.

Rhodes /rəʊdz/	Egyptians /ɪ'dʒɪpʃnz/
Zambezi /zæm'bi:zɪ/	Mesopotamia /mesəpə'teɪmɪə/
Athens /'æθɪnz/	Byzantium /baɪ'zæntɪəm/
ancient /'eɪnʃnt/	Byzantine /bai'zænti:n/
Asia /'eɪʒə/	Phoenicians /fə'ni:ʃnz/
Genoa /'ʤenəʊə/	Venetian /və'ni:ʃn/
Syria /'sɪriə/	homogeneous /hɒmə'dʒi:nɪəs/
Cyprus /'saɪprəs/	

Direct students to the map on p42. Ask them to say what they can see.

If you want students to read silently, set them a time limit of, say, five minutes.

Comprehension check

Students work in small groups to answer the questions.

Answers

1 So they could have more varied goods.
2 Very little. Maybe it was English flint, or maybe it was the Egyptians.
3 The goods had to be small, light, and valuable.
4 They developed commerce by sea. They imported raw materials such as tin, copper, and silver.
5 Athens was the first big commercial city in Europe, and it was the first to import and export necessities such as grain. They imported grain because of their increasing population.
6 No, but it imported a lot. They didn't pay, because all the imported goods were seen as a tax.
7 It was the first single currency of European business.
8 They divided up the world to explore and exploit.
9 1000 BC The Phoenician ports in Syria, because the Phoenicians developed commerce by sea.
8th century AD Byzantium, because it was the political capital of the Roman Empire.
13th century AD Venice and Genoa, because they are beside the sea, and as goods arrived by sea from the East, they were re-exported to Europe.
17th century AD Holland, France, and England, because they opened up many distant lands and brought back new products.
10 Imports used to bring diversity. Now imports bring the same things to all of us.

There will undoubtedly be a lot of words that students don't know in this text. You could ask them to go through it again for homework, checking any words they don't know. This would be better than doing it in class.

Discussion

These two questions could be discussed in small groups, or as a class. You decide.

Note-taking and report writing

Hopefully, students will already have started doing some research into trade in their country.

1 Students read the text again and make notes. Naturally, they will have to reproduce the chart in their own note-books, allowing for a lot more space to write in. Tell them to write the main ideas, not every single detail for every single column.

Answers

	DATES	PLACES	PEOPLE	GOODS
In the beginning	Thousands of years BC	Europe	English and Europeans	Flint
	3000 BC	Egypt and the Zambezi River	Egyptians	Gold, silver, and slaves
The Ancient World BC	2500 BC	Across the deserts of Asia	Arabs	Gold and precious stones
	1000 BC	Syria, Cyprus, Rhodes, Africa	Phoenicians	Metalware, glassware, textiles, tin, copper, silver
	1000 BC	Athens imported from the Black Sea, Persia, Central Asia, and India	Greeks	Grain, food and wine, pottery, metalware, textiles, spices, drugs, silk
The Ancient World AD	27 BC–476 AD	Roman Empire	Romans	Tin, slaves, cloth, jewels, silk
	Fifth century AD	Byzantium	Romans	Textiles, leatherwork, armour, pottery, metalwork
The Middle Ages	12th and 13th century	Venice and Genoa	Venetians and Genoans	Spices, silks
		China Europe	Marco Polo	
The Modern World	15th and 16th century	Spain and Portugal	Columbus, da Gama, Magellan	Tomatoes, potatoes, cocoa, beans, corn
		Americas, Africa, India		
	17th century	Holland, France, England East and West Indies	Dutch, French, English	Sugar, tobacco, tea, coffee

2 Students discuss their notes with a partner and find the places on the map on p42.

3 This needs to be set up for homework. Students will undoubtedly have to do some research, using reference sources such as encyclopaedias, and they will need time to do this properly.
You might allow at least a week between setting this for homework and doing the activity in class. If you see your students in the meantime, ask how their research is going. You will no doubt need to feed in suggestions and keep motivation going.
When you feel they are ready, do the group work.

4 Students write a report based on their notes.

● VOCABULARY AND PRONUNCIATION

(SB p44)

1 export: /ˈekspɔːt/ or /ɪkˈspɔːt/?

1 Read the introduction as a class. Students decide where the stress is when the word is a noun, and when it's a verb. This is something they might know already, or they might never have considered it. The problem might have arisen during the reading about world trade.

Answer

The stress is on the first syllable when it's a noun, and on the second syllable when it's a verb.

2 This is a simple opportunity for practice of stress. Do it first in open pairs, so students get the idea, then in closed pairs. Expect students to find this exercise quite tricky. It requires good control over word stress, and you will need to exaggerate the stress pattern for students to get the idea.

3 Students work in pairs to fill the gaps.

Answers

a im'ports 'exports
b 'progress
c 'increase
d de'creased
e 'insult
f pro'testing
g 'records
h re'cording
i pro'duces

T 4.1 Students listen and check their answers.

2 refuse: /'refju:s/ or /rɪ'fju:z/?

1 Read the introduction as a class. Students use their dictionary to check the two meanings. Expect students to know one of the meanings, but not both.

Answers

a 'refuse /'refju:s/ the things we throw away
re'fuse /rɪ'fju:z/ to say no

b 'present /'presənt/ there in person; a gift
pre'sent /prɪ'zent/ to give somebody something

c 'minute /'mɪnɪt/ 60 minutes in an hour
mi'nute /maɪ'nju:t/ very small

d 'desert /'dezət/ The Sahara Desert
de'sert /dɪ'zɜ:t/ to abandon

e 'content /'kɒntent/ the contents of a box
con'tent /kən'tent/ happy

f 'object /'ɒbdʒekt/ thing
ob'ject /əb'dʒekt/ to protest about something

g 'invalid /'ɪnvəlɪd/ a person made weak because of illness
in'valid /ɪn'vælɪd/ an invalid passport

h 'contract /'kɒntrækt/ a legal document
con'tract /kən'trækt/ to get smaller; to get an illness

2 Students practise saying the words. Again, you can expect there to be problems, so give exaggerated models yourself.

3 This exercise is perhaps best done as a class. Establish the correct answer, then drill it around the class.

Answers

a He takes away our 'refuse.
b An unidentified flying 'object.
c A 'desert.
d 'Presents!
e The 'contents pages.
f con'tent a 'contract in'valid (passport) mi'nute ob'ject to re'fuse to

T 4.2 Students listen and check their answers.

3 row: /rɑʊ/ or /rəʊ/?

1 Read the introduction as a class. Students check the meaning and pronunciation in their dictionary. Again, this might be more difficult than you expect. Students will need to be very precise in their pronunciation for the difference to be clear.

Answers

/rɑʊ/ an argument
/rəʊ/ a row of seats; to row a boat
/tɪə/ in your eye when you cry
/tɜə/ your shirt on a nail; a page out of a magazine
/ju:st/ When I was young, we used to go on holiday to the sea-side.
/ju:zd/ A pen is used for writing with.
/lɪv/ Where do you live?
/laɪv/ A live (music) band; a live (electric) wire
/li:d/ to show someone the way
/led/ a heavy grey soft metal
/wɪnd/ Did you hear the wind last night?
/waɪnd/ rewind a tape
/ju:s/ noun – What's the use of worrying?
/ju:z/ verb – You use a cloth to clean the sink.

2 Students work out the pronunciation from the phonetic symbols.

T 4.3 They listen and check their answers.

3 In pairs, they think of a sentence that illustrates the other meaning.

● SPEAKING (SB p45)

A business maze

BACKGROUND INFORMATION

A maze can be an excellent activity to provoke lots of animated discussion in class, and students often have lots of fun doing it.

The task consists of an initial situation with a menu of choices as to what to do next. Students work in small groups to decide what is best to do. Four per group is a nice number – it is small enough for everyone to participate, and large enough for there to be a variety of opinions. Hopefully, they will rarely agree on the best course of action, so they need to persuade the others in their group. When finally a decision has been made, they tell you which number they want to go to.

Often, the groups take a very long time over their first three or four decisions, then make subsequent decisions with less argument. They will come to an end of the maze after about eight or nine decisions. Obviously, you have no way of knowing just how long this activity will take, but you can expect the actual maze to last about 30 minutes minimum.

There are 23 different endings to the maze, 11 of them successful, and 12 ending in failure.

SUGGESTION

Photocopy the role cards (TB p126–137). You need one complete set of all 72 cards for each group, so your initial preparation for this class will take a long time. We suggest you stick the cards onto different coloured stiff cardboard. That way, the cards will last a lot longer, and you can easily put the sets of cards back together – all the red cards go together, the blue cards, the green cards, etc.

Write the word *Maze* on the board. Ask what it means. Then read the introduction to the activity as a class.

It might be best if you think about the groupings of your students whilst preparing this lesson, rather than leaving to chance who works with who. You need to avoid groups of quiet students together – the talkative ones need to be distributed. Allocate the groups, and ask students to consider Situation 1 in the Student's Book.

Meanwhile, you need to arrange the piles of role cards very carefully, one for each group. You need to be VERY organized! Be careful not to mix up the cards for the different groups.

As the groups decide which situation they want to move to, find their appropriate card and give it to them. You could try to give the card to a different member of the group each time, so everyone has a chance of reading out the next situation.

This process continues until the various groups come to the end of the maze. If one group finishes very early, you can ask them if they want to go back and try again.

Inevitably, they will finish at different times. Ask the groups to consider their performance. Where did they go wrong? What should they have done? What shouldn't they have done? What did they do right? If they do this, they are in fact beginning to work on the Post-maze activity which follows.

Post-maze activity

1 The groups appoint a spokesperson to tell the rest of the class how they did. This might need a few minutes' preparation. See the questions eight lines above.

2 Students consider question 2.

Answer

Activities such as these are used for management training exercises because they practise the process of decision-making and groups co-operating together. It is important that everyone has their say, and everyone listens to each other. It is no good if one person dominates.

● LISTENING (SB p45)

'An English restaurant in France? You must be joking!'

This activity should follow on well from the maze, where students were considering how to manage their own restaurant.

Ask students to comment on the title *'An English restaurant in France? You must be joking!'*

T 4.4 Read the introduction as a class.

1 Students listen to the interviewer's introduction. In pairs they answer the questions.

Answers

a Lyon is the gastronomic paradise of France, and it has hundreds of fine restaurants.
b English food is inedible.
c Mister Higgins.
d How did they get the idea?
Why did they do it?

2 Students work in pairs or small groups to think of other questions they would like answered. If they have recently done the maze, the topic of opening restaurants and its inherent problems should be quite fresh in their minds.

Go round the groups checking their questions. Remember that learners always have problems forming questions, so take this opportunity to help.

Encourage students to write their questions on the board.

3 Students listen to the rest of the interview and answer the questions on the board. If some of the questions remain unanswered, it doesn't actually matter.

Discussion

These topics will only really take off if you happen to have one or two students who are interested in starting a business. If not, don't labour too long trying to make it work.

PostScript (SB p46)

Social expressions

INTRODUCTION

These two exercises teach or revise 16 social expressions, some of which could well be used in a business context. If students start to use these items, that is wonderful and a credit to them. Generally speaking, however, these expressions are introduced here for recognition purposes only, rather than language to go into students' immediate productive repertoire.

Such expressions, like any idiomatic language, are extremely context sensitive. It would be so easy for a student to attempt to use one of these expressions in a real situation, and for any number of reasons it would be inappropriate. Maybe the expression is fixed, and the component parts can't change. We can't say *~~Hang on an hour~~, or *~~By some means~~ or *~~When come?~~

Native speakers don't expect to hear idiomatic English coming out of the mouth of foreign learners. If students try to be idiomatic and make a mistake of any kind – grammatical, word order, pronunciation – it can be impossible to understand what they are trying to say. So don't discourage your students from trying to use these expressions. But equally don't expect to hear them being used spontaneously from now on.

1 Students work in pairs and match a line in A with a line in B. Some pairs might do this very quickly with insufficient attention. Correct their work, and say how many they have right, but don't say which ones are wrong. Let them think again.

Answers

a 6 b 5 c 4 d 8 e 7 f 2 g 1 h 3

T 4.5 Students listen and check their answers. You now need to make sure students understand the expressions.
You could ask students to translate them.

We say *Let me see* when we need a pause in order to think.
Point out the use of *have* and the use of the noun in *have a look*.
Hang on a sec means *Wait a moment*.
I don't care and *I don't mind* need to be compared and contrasted. Again, translation is the best tool. *I don't mind* means *I have no strong feelings; I don't object*. The tone of *I don't care* is one of defiance and rejection – *it is of no importance to me, it doesn't worry or upset me*.
I bet means *I'm sure*.
It's a deal is said when two people agree to do something. This could be in a business context, agreeing a price, for instance.

2 Students again match a line in A with a line in B.

Answers

a 5 b 8 c 4 d 7 e 3 f 6 g 1 h 2

T 4.6 Students listen and check their answers.
Again, you need to check meaning very carefully.
How come? means *How is this situation possible?*
I was kidding means *I was joking*.
I can't be bothered means *I don't want to do it because I'm not interested and I don't have the energy*. It is the cry of the bored teenager.
For goodness' sake is an expression of mild annoyance.
Never mind means *Let's not worry about it*.
I see what you mean means *I understand what you're saying*.
Point means *aim* or *purpose* or *reason*.
I wouldn't stand a chance means *I have no hope of succeeding*.
I don't blame you means *I think what you did was right and reasonable*.

3 In pairs, students try to think of ideas that will prompt the use of some of the expressions in B. Be prepared for students to find this very difficult. They might well have a good feel for what one of these expressions means, and when to use it, but trying to think of a prompt sentence is the job of a teacher or a writer, not necessarily a student.

You will probably have to help an awful lot with this exercise. Beware of accepting a prompt and a response that doesn't really work. With an exercise that students are having difficulty with, it is tempting for the teacher to give praise and encouragement even when it is not deserved.

4 Students read out their prompts, and others respond with one of the expressions.

Don't forget!

Workbook Unit 4
Exercise 9 Food
Exercise 10 Prepositions + nouns
Exercises 11 and 12 Pronunciation – sentence stress and phonetics

5 Whatever will be, will be

Future forms
Telephone conversations

Introduction to the unit

In this unit, the grammatical focus shifts back to verb forms. Future verb forms present students with quite a few problems in English, for the reasons outlined below.

The reading text is a true story about a couple who, before they decide to marry, draw up a very detailed pre-nuptial agreement in the hope of ensuring the success of the marriage.

The listening activity is a jigsaw. Three friends phone each other to arrange to meet. This practises listening and speaking, and of course it revises future forms.

The PostScript section practises ways of beginning and ending telephone conversations.

Notes on the unit

LANGUAGE AIMS – FUTURE FORMS

NB See the Grammar Reference section – SB p150.

You can be sure that your students will have come across and will have a certain familiarity with the three main future forms – *will*, *going to*, and the Present Continuous. This unit also introduces and practises the Present Simple, the Future Continuous, and the Future Perfect.

There are two main reasons why students have problems with this area. Firstly, English has more forms to refer to future time than many other languages; and secondly, the choice of future form depends on aspect (that is, how the speaker sees the event) and collocation, and not on time, nearness to present, or certainty.

Students may have some of the following problems.

- They over-use *will*, seeing it as the standard future tense. English doesn't have a standard future tense. They don't see that the pre-arranged nature of the verb action requires the Present Continuous or *going to*.
  * What time ~~will you meet~~ your friends?
  * ~~Will you go~~ to the cinema tonight?
  * ~~We'll go~~ on holiday to Greece.
- They resort to a ubiquitous Present Simple/verb stem 'tense' to refer to all time.
  * ~~I go~~ to Paris this weekend.
  * ~~What you do~~ tonight?
  * ~~When you go~~ on holiday?

  This mistake is common in the spontaneous use of *will*.
  * ~~I open~~ the door for you.
  * It's very nice. ~~I buy~~ it.
- The Present Continuous is very common to refer to arrangements between people. It *cannot* be used where human arrangement is not possible.
  * ~~It's raining~~ tomorrow.
- Students need to perceive the relatively few common collocations of noun + Present Simple.
  The match/term/film starts at …
  The train/plane/bus leaves at …
  My birthday/wedding/party is on Saturday.

The Future Perfect is rarely used, and is not worth a lot of classroom time. However, the Future Continuous has one very subtle meaning, which is to refer to an event that will happen as a matter of course. It is estimated that this use is on the increase. It is by no means an easy concept to convey to your students. Nevertheless, a start must be made somewhere.

The first three sections of this unit are staged very carefully. In the *Test your grammar*, students are asked to recognize the different future forms, with large hints from contextual and lexical clues. In the Presentation, they hear a variety of people referring to future events, and answer questions. In the first Practice exercise, *will*, *going to*, and the present tenses are revised, before moving on to the other future forms.

There is little free practice of future forms in the Practice section. This is because we want students to think very carefully about the six or seven future forms, where their meanings overlap, and where one form rather than another would be favoured by a native speaker.

Ask students what they understand by the title of the unit, *Whatever will be, will be*. It suggests a fatalistic attitude to life, but not necessarily pessimistic.

Test your grammar (SB p47)

NB Remember to keep this section brief.

Ask students as a class what they can see in the pictures. This is to establish what the rather small cartoons are illustrating.

Answers

1 It's 6.00 in the evening in an office. They're saying goodbye.
2 A futuristic car.
3 A man is leaving prison.
4 A man and a woman are looking at a lot of travel brochures.
5 She's inviting someone to her party.
6 They are at a train station.
7 It's the TV weather forecast.
8 The builders are having a cup of tea.

1 In pairs, students match a line of dialogue a–h with a cartoon 1–8. Note that all seven future forms are included (*will* is used twice, once as an auxiliary verb to express future time, and once as a modal auxiliary to express willingness or intention). Students are given large visual and semantic clues to help them match a line with a picture.

Answers

1 a 2 g 3 f 4 e 5 c 6 b 7 d 8 h

2 Students identify and underline the future forms in the dialogues.

Answers

a I'll see you tomorrow. Bye!
b The train to Dover leaves at ten past ten.
c We're having a party next Saturday. Can you come?
d Tomorrow's weather will be warm and sunny.
e Where shall we go on holiday this year?
f I'm going to lead an honest life from now on.
g In a hundred years' time, we'll all be driving solar-powered cars.
h The builders say they'll have finished by the end of the month.

LANGUAGE IN CONTEXT (SB p47)

Future forms

Ask students to look at the pictures. How old are the people? What are their jobs?

1 **T 5.1** Students listen to the people talking about the future and try to guess who says what.
Ask them to check their answers in pairs before you give the answers.

POSSIBLE VOCABULARY PROBLEMS

Joan talks about *the little 'uns*. These are *the little ones*, her grandchildren. *A good old chat* is just a chat. *Old* is used as a familiar expression.
'A' levels = exams that school-children take at 17. They need good 'A' level results to go to university.
Arsenal = a London football team.
Eurostar = the train that goes in the tunnel under the sea to France.

Answers

4 Ellen	1 Joan	7 Alex	6 Tony and Marie
8 Penny	2 Amy	5 Mike	3 Simon

SUGGESTION

Play the tape again, and stop it after each person. Ask students to repeat the sentence or part sentence that contains a future form. Drill this around the class, paying careful attention to pronunciation.

2 Students work in pairs to answer the questions. Get some feedback as a class before you give the answers.

Students will probably reproduce the future form used by the speakers. However, it is possible in some cases to use a different form.

Answers

a She's going to Hawaii because her mother's a marine in the US Navy, so they move every couple of years.
b Her daughter and grandchildren will be visiting/are going to visit. They'll have a cup of tea and some cake, and they'll chat.
c He says he'll have finished school in ten years' time. He's going to have a toy factory.
d Because Marie's having/Marie's going to have a baby.
e She's going to France for the day. Her dad's giving her a lift. The train leaves at 9.30.
f She hopes she'll be earning a lot of money.

g He's going to study medicine at university. If he doesn't get good results, he doesn't know what he'll do/he's going to do.
h He's going to see/he's seeing a football match.

3 Students work in pairs to write the questions. Monitor carefully and help with problems, then get some feedback.

POSSIBLE PROBLEM

Forming questions to refer to the future is quite difficult. The form used in the answer is not necessarily the best form to ask the question. For example, Joan says *I'll bake a cake, a ginger cake.* This could be an example of *will* to refer to future time or *will* to express intention. The question, however, is best expressed by *going to*, not *will* – *What sort of cake is she going to bake?* By asking someone about the future, there is the implicit suggestion that a decision has already been reached. *What will you do when you arrive?* can suggest that you have not yet considered this question.

For these reasons you might decide to do Exercise 3 as a whole class, so you can explore this area together. Otherwise students might make all sorts of mistakes that could have been prevented.

Answers

a What sort of cake is she going to bake?
b Where will Amy be living/where does Amy hope she'll be living in the next few years?
c Which university is Simon going to?
d How long will Ellen be/be staying/stay in Hawaii?
e Who is Mike going to the football match with?
f Who's playing/who's playing who/who's the match between?
g When is Marie's baby due?
h What time does Penny's train leave?

● Grammar questions

Answer these as a class.

Answers

– *I'm waiting* present
We're moving future
The train leaves future
We move present/all time
– *What do you do ... ?* asks about all time generally.
What are you doing ... ? asks about this evening only.
I'll help ... is an offer thought about at the moment of speaking. *I'm going to help ...* is an intention thought about before the moment of speaking.
We'll have supper at 8.00 means we will start to eat at 8.00. *We'll be having supper at 8.00* means we will be in the middle of eating at 8.00.
I'll write the report tonight means I will start it and finish it tonight. *I'll have written the report by tonight* means I will finish writing *before* tonight.

PRACTICE BANK (SB p48)

NB Exercises 1 and 3 in this Practice section ask students to discriminate between two or three future forms. The idea is to try to make students perceive the differences between the various forms rather than the areas of overlap, where two or more forms are possible. You might want students to read the Language Review on p51 before you begin these Practice exercises.

1 Choosing future forms

Students work in pairs or small groups. Notice that there are some sentences where both forms are possible, but by a process of elimination, there is one best answer.

Answers

a	I'll get	(an offer)
	I get	(a habit)
b	I'm going to see	(It's planned.)
	I'll see	(I'm deciding now.)
c	are you going to do	(I presume you've made some plans.)
	will you do	(This is the first time you've considered this.)
d	I'll come	(a spontaneous offer)
	I'm coming	(I've already made up my mind.)
e	are you going to do	(What is your intention?)
	are you doing	(What have you arranged?)
f	It's going to rain	(The Present Continuous is not possible with inanimate subjects.)
	It's raining	(Now.)
g	I'm getting	(It's all arranged for Monday, a definite time.)
	I'm going to get	(I intend to do this at some indefinite time.)
h	He's going to crash!	(We can see it happening.)
	He'll crash it.	(A future prediction)
i	programme starts	(Future as fact)
	husband is starting	(A future arrangement. The answer could also be *My husband starts a new job*, a more impersonal future fact.)

2 *We'll be flying at 35,000 feet ...*

NB The Caution Box serves as a sort of presentation for a use of the Future Continuous that has not yet been dealt with in this unit. This use is the action that will take place in the normal course of events.
This use is increasingly common but quite subtle and could be difficult for students to understand, let alone produce. They will need to see this tense many, many times before they understand quite when it is and is not used.

Read the Caution Box as a class. The information in 1 will very probably be new. The information in 2 and 3 should be reminders.

Before you read the instructions, ask students to look at the heading *This is your captain speaking* ... and the two cartoons. Ask 'How does the captain of a plane usually sound? Calm and confident? Or mad and indecisive? Does he/she want to reassure passengers, or make them think that the pilot doesn't know what he/she is doing?'

Look at the captions. If students laugh, then they are beginning to understand the difference between the Future Simple and the Future Continuous.

Now read the instructions as a class. This exercise could well be done for homework, but it still needs to be set up very carefully in class. There is a danger that students would not understand what they have to do and then do it all wrongly, which would be counterproductive.

Ask students in pairs or small groups to do the first paragraph together. Check this first. Then students can either do the exercise for homework (but remember the answers are in the tapescripts) or finish it in class.

Answers

a have received (*receive* is possible)
b we'll be taking (*we'll take* is possible)
c have reached (*reach* is possible)
d we'll be flying
e we'll be
f will be serving
g you enjoy (*you'll enjoy* is possible)
h need
i will come
j look
k you'll see
l will be coming
m We'll also be giving out
n you've filled
o They'll be collected
p go
q we'll be landing
r has come (*comes* is possible)
s you leave
t you haven't left
u you'll fly

T 5.2 This text can be played as a check if you want.

3 Discussing grammar

NB This exercise aims to explore the difference between three future forms, the Future Simple with 'will', the Future Continuous, and the Future Perfect. There are sentences where other future forms, especially 'going to', would be perfectly acceptable, but that is not relevant to this exercise. You might want to direct your students to the Language Review on p51 whilst doing this exercise.

1 Read the introduction as a class. Stress that only the three tenses should be used (even though sometimes another future form may be possible).
Do the first three together so students see what they have to do. Then they work in pairs to complete the exercise.

Answers

make
a I'll make
b We'll be making
c I'll have made

see
a I'll have seen
b You'll see
c I'll be seeing

have
a I'll have had
b She'll have
c I'll be having

2 This exercise is perhaps best done as a class. It is short, and there is quite a lot of room for error.

Here are the 'best' answers. Hopefully, your students will be developing a feel for which future form is most appropriate, even though several might be possible.

Answers

a What time does your plane arrive?
b Which hotel are you staying in?
c What are you going to do while you're on holiday?
d How long are you/ will you be away for?
e What will you do if you don't like the hotel?

4 *I hope so/I don't think so*

1 **T 5.3** Students listen to the dialogues and fill in the gaps. This is like a dictation.
You could give the answers, or ask them to refer to the tapescripts at the back of the book.

Answers

a
Do you think you'll ever be rich?
I hope so.
I might one day.
It's possible, but I doubt it.
I'm sure I will.
I'm sure I won't.

b
Are you going out tonight?
Yes, I am.
I think so, but I'm not sure.
I might be.

c
Do you think the world's climate will change dramatically in the next fifty years?
I don't think so.
I hope not.
Who knows? Maybe.

Point out to students the following sentences.
I hope so and *I think so*.
I hope not and *I don't think so*.

2 In pairs, students ask and answer the questions about themselves. Try to personalize these questions to your students and their own interests and ambitions.

Notice that the questions a, b, and c match the questions and answers in Exercise 1: a is about their possible future life, b is about the immediate future, and c is about the world.

Before you sense that students have had enough of this activity, get some feedback as a class.

ADDITIONAL MATERIAL

Workbook Unit 5
Exercise 1 A recognition exercise on all the future forms
Exercises 2–6 All future forms practised and contrasted
Exercise 7 Future time clauses

LANGUAGE REVIEW (SB p51)

Future forms

Read the Language Review together as a class, and/or ask students to read it at home. We sometimes suggest asking students to translate some of the sentences into L1 at this stage, but we don't feel that this would be appropriate with this language area. It is unlikely that the future forms of English will translate easily into L1. If students are beginning to understand the seven future forms explained in the Language Review, asking them to compare English and L1 could result in chaos. Ask students to read the Grammar Reference at home.

● READING AND SPEAKING (SB p51)

I'll marry you, but only if…

SUGGESTION

Bring in pictures from newspapers and magazines of couples who have recently married or divorced for the nth time.

Pre-reading task

You might decide to discuss these three questions in groups or as a class. Ask students to look at the picture and say what they can see. Why are these images associated with romance?

BACKGROUND INFORMATION

- St Valentine was a Roman priest. He is known as the patron of lovers. The customs practised on his feast day, 14 February, have no connection with his life.
- It is tradition on 14 February to send a Valentine card as a declaration of love to the person you love. The cards are usually unsigned. Red roses are the flowers of romance.
- In Britain the marriage vows are as follows: *'I (A) take you (B) to be my wife/husband, to have and to hold from this day forward, for better for worse, for richer for poorer, in sickness and in health, to love and to cherish, till death us do part, according to God's holy law, and this is my solemn vow.'*
- In Britain, approximately one in three marriages ends in divorce.
- Prenuptial agreements (literally *agreements before marriage*) stipulate what happens to a couple in the event of their separation. This is usually to do with money and divorce settlements. If one of the couple is very wealthy, he or she does not want to lose half his/her fortune if they divorce.

Reading

Students read the text quickly and answer the questions.

POSSIBLE VOCABULARY PROBLEMS

NB *This list does not contain the vocabulary items that are tested in Language work 1 on p54.*

We are not suggesting that you need to pre-teach all these items before students read. This list is for your information only. You might decide to do nothing with them, or you might want to go through the text as a class once the Comprehension check questions have been answered. An important part of the reading skill is the ability to extract the main points despite the presence of some unknown words.

spontaneous	*smooth*	*goal setters*
ultimate	*aspect*	*fundamental*
itemize	*allowance*	*enterprise*
significant	*unleaded fuel*	*probing*
witnessed	*fuel gauge*	*fondness*
regulate	*tank*	*intensity*
chaotic	*saviours*	

Students work in small groups to compare their answers to the questions.

Answers

There are no set answers to these questions.

1 Many students find Clifford and Annie weird (/wɪəd/), ridiculous, and cold and calculating. Their whole relationship seems unbelievable.
Some students might argue that they are sensible having had such bad previous experiences.

2 Who knows if their marriage will last? Maybe it stands as good a chance as any other marriage.

3 The rules are:

- We will have healthy sex 3 to 5 times per week.
- We will spend $400 a month.
- The ceremony will last twenty minutes. The reception will be held in a restaurant on Miami beach. We will invite a total of twenty guests each, who will be served two drinks, one of which may be alcoholic.
- Once we are married, we will receive an allowance of $70 per week.
- We won't raise our voices. If we get angry, we will count to ten and take a deep breath.
- We will not smoke.
- We will go to bed and turn out the lights by 11.30.
- Clifford will make the main decisions. Annie will make decisions when Clifford isn't there.
- We will buy unleaded fuel, and will always keep the petrol tank at least half full.
- We will provide unconditional love and fulfil each other's basic needs.
- In five years' time we will have moved from our present address, and we will be living in a beach house overlooking the ocean.
- We will not start a family for the first two years of our marriage.

If they break a rule, they have to pay a fine.

Comprehension check

Students read the text more carefully and answer the questions. Ask them to check their answers in pairs or small groups.

Answers

1 **Things they have in common**
They both love lists, cook, drink coffee. They both wanted a prenuptial agreement. They have both been married before. They have their own marketing business. They are both goal setters.

Things they don't have in common
He's older than her. He has children, she doesn't. She saw the prenuptial contract as a way of getting to know each other, not just as a long list of rules. She wants to have children, but he has problems with the idea of more children and more expenses.

2 **Rules about money**
We will spend $400 a month.
Once we are married, we will receive an allowance of $70 per week.

Rules about behaviour
We won't raise our voices. If we get angry, we will count to ten and take a deep breath.
Clifford will make the main decisions. Annie will make decisions when Clifford isn't there.

Rules about sex
We will have healthy sex 3 to 5 times per week.

Rules about children
We will not start a family for the first two years of our marriage.

3 a (✗) It is his turn to cook today, so she must also cook.
b (✓) All the ingredients are prepared and weighed and waiting in a line.
c (✗) The living room is neat and tidy. The kitchen bar is pristine.
d (✓) She thinks he is telling her off for saying something wrong. In fact, he was just showing affection.
e (✗) They want the contract to ensure that their marriage works.
f (✗) Everyone can have one alcoholic drink.
g (✗) If a rule is broken, they have to pay a fine.
h (✓)
i (✗) They met at a dance. On their first date, he took her to a movie and dinner.
j (✗) Her perfect man was a younger version of her father.

SUGGESTION

At this point, you might want to go through the text as a class, so you can explore some of the vocabulary and check further items of comprehension.

It is interesting to see the occasions when the opinion of the journalist comes through. Timothy Laurence makes certain asides which make clear exactly what he thinks of Clifford and Annie. For example:
Clifford explains ponderously.
… spontaneity is not at the heart of this marriage.
Oh, good. So that's all right then.
With so much romance in the air …
Such is the wild intensity of passion in the heat of Florida.

It is apparent that he thinks they're crazy. Love for him should be more to do with the heart and less to do with the head.

Language work

1 Students work in pairs to find a word in the text with a similar meaning.

Answers

lines 9–23 chatting pristine ponderously
lines 39–55 bliss fine

lines 71–81 budget
lines 90–105 courtship

2 The aim of this short exercise is to revise future forms.

Answers

They're getting married in six months' time. The ceremony will last twenty minutes. The reception will be held in a restaurant on Miami beach. There will be forty guests.
He's going to write a book about their experience, which will be a bestseller.
They're going to move to a beach house overlooking the ocean.
They aren't going to have children until they've been married for two years.

What do you think?

Students discuss the three questions in groups. Have some class feedback.

● VOCABULARY (SB p54)

Word pairs

NB *This activity is carefully staged to help students with a language area that is slightly more complex than it looks. These word pairs, also known as binomials, are very idiomatic. They have precise meanings and only a limited application.*
Exercise 1 prepares students for Exercise 2. It may seem unnecessary to first identify the concept, then match the word pair, but in our experience it was too much for students to do at once.

Read the Caution Box as a class, and the examples. The first three examples of word pairs are easy to explain. *Touch and go* refers to a situation with an uncertain result.

1 Students complete the sentences with words from the box.

Answers

a compromise/be flexible
b things
c the wrong way round
d exact details
e be patient and find out later
f put up with it
g advantages and disadvantages
h generally speaking

2 Students do Exercise 1 again, this time using a word pair.

Answers

e wait and see
c back to front
a give and take
h by and large
d ins and outs
b odds and ends
f grin and bear it
g pros and cons

3 This exercise is perhaps best set for homework. Tell students not to spend too long on it. They could drive themselves crazy looking up endless word pairs that don't exist.

Answers

now and then = occasionally
more or less = approximately
safe and sound = safely
peace and quiet
sooner or later = some time
slowly but surely = gradually
sick and tired = fed up
law and order

4 This is quite difficult, so don't expect too much from your students. Just one or two sentences with gaps would be enough.

● WRITING (SB p55)

Formal and informal letters

1 Read the introduction as a class. Have a short discussion on the organization and content of a formal and informal letter in students' own language. There are wide divergences in different languages.

Answers

The characteristics of a formal letter in English are as follows:
- The writer's address comes at the top. If it is handwritten, it appears at the top right. The number of the street comes before the name of the street. The sender's name does NOT appear at the top of the letter.
- The date comes below the address on the right.
- In typewritten letters, the name and address of the person or organization you're writing to goes on the left, with the date underneath.
- All letters, both formal and informal, begin with *Dear ...* . If you know the person's name, you can begin *Dear Mr Smith.* If you don't know who you're writing to, begin *Dear Sir or Madam.*
- In formal style, we avoid contractions, slang, certain phrasal verbs, and language that sounds spoken rather than written. We use the passive more, and we use longer words rather than shorter ones.
- *I look forward to ...* is formal.
- End the letter with *Yours faithfully* if you begin with *Dear Sir* or *Dear Madam.* End with *Yours sincerely* if you begin with the person's name. If you know the

person well, you can put *With best wishes* before *Yours sincerely*.
- Sign and print your name at the bottom of the letter.

Informal letters are more often handwritten.
- The sender's address still appears on the right with the date.
- We begin with *Dear Robert*, or *Dear Ann and David*.
- There can be contractions, and the style can sound quite conversational.
- *I'm looking forward to ...* is informal.
- End by writing *With best wishes* or *Love*.

2 In groups, students choose the words that are more formal or appropriate in the letter.

Answers

Dear Sir or Madam

I am writing to confirm a reservation that was made this morning by telephone. The reservation, for two nights, is for myself, David Cook.

I would like a room with a bathroom, from 12–14 July inclusive. I will be attending the Trade Fair that is being held in Bristol that week.

Would it be possible for me to have a room at the back of the hotel? I am afraid that the room I was given last year was rather noisy.

Thank you for sending me the brochure regarding your conference facilities, which I received this morning. They look most interesting. Unfortunately I am unable to provide you with any definite dates at the moment, as we have yet to finalize the details of our sales conference. However, I will contact you as soon as possible.

I look forward to meeting you on 12 July.

Yours faithfully

David Cook

For the answers to *What makes a letter more or less formal?*, see above.

3 Students write an informal letter for homework. Discuss in class how they might open and close the letter, and generate some ideas as to why they want to be put up for a few nights.

Here are some addresses for students to write on the envelopes. They will need to invent a name.

36, Bath Road, Bridgeport, Somerset TA6 3GP
117, Harbour Way, Plymouth, Devon PT8 9OR
36b, Finchley Road East, London NW3 4HA

● LISTENING AND SPEAKING (SB p56)

The reunion

NB This is a jigsaw listening activity. You will need two tape recorders, and ideally two rooms. The whole activity takes about 30–40 minutes.
You also need to photocopy the map of Durham (TB p138) for students to complete as they listen.

Read the introduction as a class. Point out that the three students in the picture are wearing their gowns and mortar boards, which have to be worn on graduation day.

The picture at the bottom of the page is of Durham (/ˈdʌrəm/) Cathedral on the right. The Castle, on the left, is part of the university.

Tell students that it is common in Britain for students to go to university away from their parents and their home town. This is the opportunity for many children to 'leave home'.

1 **T 5.4** and **T 5.5** Divide students into two groups.
Group A hears Alan phoning Sarah.
Group B hears Sarah phoning James.
Give out the map of Durham.
Point out the various proper names in the box. This is to help students with spelling.
Lead one group to a separate room, and leave the students in charge of their tape recorders. It shouldn't be necessary for you to intervene for the next 5–10 minutes. Your students should be able to organize themselves on their own, filling in the chart and completing the map of Durham.

POSSIBLE VOCABULARY PROBLEMS

We aren't suggesting that you pre-teach these items before students listen. This list is for your information. Students might ask about these words as they are listening. You might choose to do some work on them after the whole activity.
tough = difficult
You're not kidding = you're absolutely right
things are looking up = the situation is improving
I've got a lot on = I've got a lot of work/I'm very busy
snowed under = having too many things to do
a bar meal = a small meal/snack in a pub
bang opposite = right opposite

2 Students check their answers with the others in their group. This is a very important stage. If they aren't sure of their answers, the jigsaw activity in Exercise 3 won't work. While they are in their initial groups, allocate each student a number, 1 to however many students there are in the group. Do the same with the other group. Then, when the groups come together, you can say 'Number ones, sit here. Number twos, sit here.' etc.

Answers

Group A's answers

	Alan	Sarah	James
Travelling from?	The Midlands		
How?	By car	By train	
Leaving at what time?	About 3.00	Don't know, but the journey takes less than an hour	
Arriving in Durham at?	Between 5.00 and 6.00		
Staying where?	The County	The Three Tuns	
Going to which restaurant?	The Lotus Garden		
Where is it?	Clay Path		
Where are they going to meet? What time?	In the bar of The County at about 6.30	In the bar of The County at about 6.30	

Group B's answers

	Alan	Sarah	James
Travelling from?		Leeds	Sunderland
How?		By train	By bus
Leaving at what time?		5.00	6.30
Arriving in Durham at?		Some time before 7.00	About 7.00
Staying where?			With a friend
Going to which restaurant?		The Kwai Lam	The Kwai Lam
Where is it?		On the corner of Saddler Street and North Bailey	On the corner of Saddler Street and North Bailey
Where are they going to meet? What time?		The Kwai Lam at about 7.15	The Kwai Lam at about 7.15

3 Bring students back in the same room. Students find a partner from the other group. They swap information to complete the chart and the map.
Students also discuss what might go wrong with their arrangements. Who is going to meet who where at what time?

Answers

The two groups will swap a lot of information, but there are a few contradictions. When Alan spoke to Sarah, they didn't know that the The Lotus Garden closed three years ago. So the arrangements that Sarah made with James are more recent and more accurate. However, Alan and Sarah are still going to meet in the bar of The County at 6.30.

James said that he was going to phone Alan, anyway. In that conversation, he would surely mention that The Lotus Garden was closed, and that they were now going to meet in the Kwai Lam. So everything should work out all right.

Completed map of Durham
Map with places named.

Questions for Group A

1 What's this building?
The Sports Centre.

2 What's this road?
Hallgarth Street.

3 What's this building?
The Police Station.

4 What's this building?
St Bede's College.

5 What's this?
The Lotus Garden Restaurant.

Questions for Group B

6 What's this road?
North Street.

7 What's this shop?
Fairbrother's jeweller's.

8 What's this building?
The Town Hall.

9 What's this bridge?
Elvet Bridge.

10 What's this?
The Kwai Lam Restaurant.

Language work: Hot Verbs (2): *to be*

This exercise could be set up in class and given for homework.

1 Read the introduction as a class. Ask students what the three sentences mean.

Answers

away = not at home
back = back home
up to = a familiar way of asking *What have you been doing?*

2 Students complete the sentences with words from the box. This is more difficult than it looks. Students are sometimes tempted to underestimate this exercise, and do it quickly without using dictionaries, with inevitable consequences.

Answers

a up with	e out of	i on
b off	f for	j down
c into	g around	k over
d out	h up	l up to

PostScript (SB p57)

NB *You will need to photocopy the list of expressions to use on the phone (TB p139), and the role cards (TB p140).*

Beginning a telephone conversation

Ask students if they have used a telephone in English, and how they got on. Using a phone in a foreign language is quite difficult, for obvious reasons. You can't see the other person, so you can't see their lips, and you have to listen very carefully. Also, in all languages there is a certain amount of ritual and formulaic exchange when using a phone.

1 Read the introduction and the two telephone conversations as a class. Ask students what the differences are between them.

Answers

The first is business-like, between two people who don't know each other.
The second is informal, between friends. They ask about how each other is, and work, and give news of family members.

2 Students work in pairs to put the lines of dialogue in order. This looks more complicated than it in fact is. As was said above, there is a lot of ritual and turn-taking in such conversations.

T 5.6 Students listen and check their answers.

Answers

A Hello. TVS Computer Services. Darren speaking. How can I help you?
B Good morning. Could I speak to your customer services department, please?
A Certainly. Who's calling, please?
B This is Keith Jones.
A One moment, Mr Jones. I'm trying to connect you.
B Thank you.
A I'm afraid the line's busy at the moment. Will you hold?
B Yes, please.
A OK. You're through now. Go ahead.
B Hello. Is that customer services? I was wondering if you could tell me ...

Ending a telephone conversation

1 Students again work in pairs to put the lines of dialogue in order. This time, students need to pay attention to who is speaking, Andy or Barry. Both have similar roles, unlike the previous dialogue where one was the customer and one the telephonist.

T 5.7 Students listen and check their answers.

Answers

A So, Barry. It was good to talk to you. Thanks very much for phoning.
B My pleasure. By the way, how's your golf these days? Still playing?
A No, not much. I just don't seem to find the time these days. Anyway, Barry ...
B What a shame! You used to enjoy it so much.
A It's true. Right, Barry. I must fly. I'm late for a meeting.
B OK. I don't want to keep you. So, you'll give me a ring when you're back, right?
A I certainly will. And you'll send me a copy of the report?
B It'll be in the post tonight.
A That's great, Barry. Have a good weekend!
B Same to you, too! Bye, Andy.
A Bye, Barry.

2 Discuss these questions as a class. It probably isn't worth asking students to work on them in pairs.

Answers

Andy is trying to end the conversation. Barry wants to chat.

Andy tries all sorts of ways to bring the conversation to a close. He says 'So, Barry. It was good to talk to you,' but Barry doesn't get the hint. Next he says 'Anyway, Barry', which again signals the end of a conversation, but Barry just keeps going. Finally, Andy is more direct, and says 'Right, Barry. I must fly. I'm late for a meeting.' Barry eventually gets the message.

They confirm arrangements by repeating them. 'You'll give me a ring when you're back, right?' 'I certainly will. And you'll send me a copy of the report?'

Practice

Hand out the list of expressions to use on a phone. You need to photocopy them (TB p139).

Students will undoubtedly be familiar with the concept of small talk, which presumably is a language universal. We have small talk to show we care, and to lead up to the main reason for phoning without being abrupt. It can be about health, family, work, the news – anything that the two people know about each other.

Students work in pairs. Give them a role card. They need to prepare on their own. When they are ready, they sit back to back and have their conversation. If you don't have a large class, you could do this with the rest of the class listening. Otherwise, all the conversations will have to take place at the same time.

You could ask two or three of the students to have their conversation again so that everyone can listen.

Don't forget!

Workbook Unit 5
Exercise 8 Health vocabulary
Exercise 9 Hot Verbs *be* and *have*
Exercise 10 Phrasal verbs types 2 and 3
Exercise 11 Pronunciation – sounds and spelling

People, places, and things

Relative clauses
Participles and infinitives
English signs

Introduction to the unit

In this unit, the grammatical focus shifts to clauses – relative clauses, participle clauses, and infinitive clauses. The topic is description, so there are readings about the richest man in the world, Bill Gates, who owns *Microsoft*; an eccentric Englishman; Antarctica; and the aircraft flight recorder known as the 'black box'.

Students are invited to talk about their favourite advert, and they listen to a selection of radio adverts. In preparation for this, you could ask students now to start looking for adverts they like in magazines, and to look out for a advert on TV that appeals to them. The writing exercise is about *My favourite part of town*, and the PostScript practises comprehension of everyday signs.

Notes on the unit

LANGUAGE AIMS – RELATIVE CLAUSES, PARTICIPLE CLAUSES, INFINITIVE CLAUSES

NB See the Grammar Reference section – SB p152.

Relative clauses and participle clauses are quite easy to recognize and understand, but learners at this level don't always find it easy to produce the correct forms in their speaking, and certainly not in their writing.

Students will undoubtedly have been introduced to relative clauses some time in their learning before, and have a certain understanding of them. It is unlikely that they are aware of the difference between defining relatives clauses (DRC) and non-defining relative clauses (NDRC). An understanding of this difference is essential, however, for correct usage, and this is one of the main grammatical aims of the unit.

Your students will probably also have come across participles and infinitive clauses in their reading, but they will benefit from controlled practice in both areas.

Both relative clauses and participles as adjectives are used to build information onto a noun phrase. Nouns can be added to both before and after.

- *a* [*thirteen-year-old*] [*schoolgirl*] [*from Liverpool*] [*who won first prize in a competition*]
  (thirteen-year-old: number + noun; schoolgirl: noun + noun; from Liverpool: prepositional phrase; who won first prize in a competition: relative clause)
- *a* [*fascinating*] [*love story*] [*set in Africa*] [*during the Second World War*]
  (fascinating: adjective; love story: noun + noun; set in Africa: participle clause; during the Second World War: prepositional phrase)
- *a* [*depressed*] *man* [*sitting in the corner*]
  (depressed: adjective; sitting in the corner: participle clause)

There are exercises throughout the Student's Book and the Workbook that aim to develop students' awareness and production of noun phrases.

Test your grammar (SB p58)

1 Students work in pairs to discuss the difference between the pairs of sentences. Don't let this go on too long. Keep the *Test your grammar* section brief. Don't fall into the trap of giving too much explanation, or you run the risk of pre-empting the *Language in context* section.

Answers

a In the first sentence, there is only one son.
In the second sentence there is more than one son – my son in Manchester, as opposed to my son in Paris.

b In the first sentence, it is only that limited number of politicians who tell lies that are to be despised.
In the second sentence, it is all politicians who are to be despised, since, by their very nature, they all tell lies.

c In the first sentence, it is the very fact of my having a cocktail that was unusual – I never usually have cocktails.

In the second sentence, it was the cocktail itself that was unusual. Perhaps it had some strange ingredients.

d There is no difference in meaning between the two sentences. English can drop the relative pronoun completely in some sentences.

e In the first sentence, the person is driving round looking for a parking space.
In the second sentence, the person is looking for the car. She has forgotten where she parked. (See the cartoon.)

2 Students correct the mistakes. You might choose to do this as a class activity, in order to use time economically.

Answers

a I was fascinat**ed** ...
The film was horrify**ing**.

b ... there were people dancing and chatting.
... people injur**ed** in the accident ...

c My grandfather, **who's** 75 ...
... a dog **whose** name is ...

LANGUAGE IN CONTEXT **(SB p58)**

Relative clauses, participles, infinitives

SUGGESTION

Have a brief discussion about computers.
Who uses computers at home? What for?
What kind of computer have you got?
What do you know about Bill Gates and Microsoft? (a software manufacturer)
What is Windows? (an operating system)

1 Ask students to look at the pictures and describe what they can see.

Answers

The man is Bill Gates, the director of *Microsoft*. We can see the mansion he has had built in Seattle, Washington.

SUGGESTION

You might want students to read the text briefly and answer the questions a–g at the top of p59 before they do the gap-filling exercise. This would provide some gist comprehension work before students work intensively on the grammar.

Students work in pairs to read the text about Bill Gates and fill the gaps with one of the clauses. They write a number 1–16 in the gaps in the text.

POSSIBLE VOCABULARY PROBLEMS

We are not suggesting that you pre-teach all these words. The list is here for your information.

software = the program that makes a computer work; not the hardware
tycoon = wealthy and powerful business person
shares in a company = equal parts into which the money of a company is divided, giving the holder a right to a portion of the profits
output = production
packed with = full of
high-tech = high technology
gadgetry Gadgets are small, useful, cleverly-designed machines or tools.
smart card = a small plastic card, like a credit card, with information stored electronically
cold-blooded = without pity or emotion
mobiles = mobile phones
nerd = a boring person with no character or interests other than one particular hobby
fancied If you fancy someone, you are attracted to them sexually.
clicking onto icons with a mouse These are all computer terms. An icon is a small sign or picture on the screen. You click on it with a hand-held object called a mouse.

Answers

a	8	he can't afford
b	4	of which he owns 39% of the shares
c	6	estimated at £18 billion
d	7	overlooking Lake Washington
e	11	that he's packed with high-tech gadgetry
f	13	encoded with their personal preferences
g	14	who is now a very successful businesswoman
h	1	discussing the plots and swapping opinions
i	15	that allows him
j	9	leaving his wife behind
k	16	which put him among the top ten students
l	3	he fancied
m	10	what to do
n	2	why *Microsoft* has been so successful
o	12	that can be run by clicking on icons
p	5	whose software is used

2 Students answer the questions. This could be done as a class activity. The aim of the questions is to exploit the text for reading comprehension as well as a way of testing clauses. Bill Gates' story is a fascinating one.

Answers

a He is the richest private citizen in the world. His wealth is estimated at £18 billion, but it is going up all the time.

b $20 million.

c There is a lot of electronic gadgetry in it. Visitors are given a smart card which lets them into certain rooms but not others. As they go into a room, their favourite music plays and their favourite pictures appear on the screens.
d They seem a little cold-blooded. When he was going out with Ann Winblad, they didn't even go to the same cinema together. As part of his prenuptial agreement with his wife, he is allowed to go on an annual holiday with his ex-lover.
e He inserted a piece of software which put all the girls he fancied into his class.
f He saw that his future and fortune was in software, not hardware.
g Windows is an operating system which runs by clicking on icons on the screen with a mouse.

SUGGESTION

Ask students to close their books, and in pairs try to retell the story of Bill Gates and *Microsoft*. Then do this again briefly as a class, with you designating two or three students to speak. See how much, if at all, they manage to use relative clauses.

● Grammar questions

Discuss these as a class. Don't expect any great detail in answer to the first of these Grammar questions. Listen carefully to see how much students might be able to tell you about the rules, but it would be most unusual if they were able to quote accurate grammar rules.

Answers

- We use *who* for people. We use *that* for people and things. We use *whose* for possession. We use *which* for things.
- There is nothing ___ he can't afford.
  the music ___ they like
  the girls ___ he fancied
- *leaving* is active.
  left is passive.

PRACTICE BANK (SB p59)

1 Pronunciation and punctuation

NB *This might seem a rather dry way of approaching the first practice of relative clauses, but it is fundamental to an understanding of the difference between defining relative clauses (DRC) and non-defining relative clauses (NDRC). The pronunciation of them is different when we speak, and the punctuation is different when we write. By pointing this out, it should help students perceive the subtle but significant difference between the use of the two clauses.*
You might choose to ask students to read the Language Review on p61 before beginning these Practice activities.

1 **T 6.1** Students listen to the six sentences and answer the three questions. These are perhaps best answered as a class. It is important that these answers are established very firmly before you move on to the next exercise.

Answers

There is no pause in DRC. In NDRC there is a pause before the clause, and after it as well if the sentence continues.
There is no pause in DRC because the extra information is essential to the sentence. It cannot be left out. In NDRC there is a pause because the information is not essential. It is additional information that can be left out.
In writing the pauses are expressed with commas.

2 **T 6.2** Students listen and write D or ND. Again, this is perhaps best done as a class, in order to establish the answers clearly and quickly. There is plenty of opportunity for pair work later.

Answers

a D b D c ND d ND e ND f D g ND h D

2 Relative clauses

1 Read the introduction as a class.

NB *It is essential that students understand the point that is being made here. They need to perceive that the distinction between DRC and NDRC is not random, but is to do with how clearly we know which person or thing is being referred to.*
To get the point across to students, you could say the following: When we hear 'My youngest daughter Kate', we know there can be only one. Similarly, there is only one Channel Tunnel. We don't need any more information to know what is being talked about. But 'Police are looking for a man' is silly. Which man? What was he doing?

Students look at the sentences and decide if the gaps are more likely to be filled with a D or an ND relative clause. Do the first couple as a class, then ask students to do the rest in pairs.

Answers

a ND b D c D d ND e D f ND g D h D
i ND j ND k D l ND

2 Students insert the correct sentence as a relative clause. They put commas where necessary, and leave out the relative if possible. This exercise should be done in pairs.

Answers

a The apple tree at the end of our garden, which my grandfather planted seventy years ago, needs to be chopped down.
b People who do regular exercise live longer.
c She married a man she met on holiday in Turkey.
d Let me introduce you to Peter James, who works in our Paris office.
e Did I show you the photographs I took in Barbados last month?
f We saw *West Side Story* last night, which is one of the best musicals I've ever seen.
g Jane's the sort of person you can always go to with a problem.
h I'm looking for a book that has information about tropical fish in it.
i The Great Barrier Reef, which is situated off the north-east coast of Australia, is the largest coral reef in the world.
j My great aunt Freda, who I was telling you about last night, is coming to lunch.
k I was speaking to someone you went to school with.
l Our house in the country, which we bought as a weekend retreat, is much used by all the family.

SUGGESTION

Ask students to practise reading the completed sentences out loud, paying careful attention to pauses and lack of pauses. Do this as a class.

3 *-ed* or *-ing* participles

NB *Students will have come across '-ed' and '-ing' adjectives many times, but even at this level mistakes are very common.*

1 **T 6.3** Read the instructions as a class. Students look at the cartoon and caption. Draw their attention to the words *depressed* and *depressing*. Ask *Which is active? Which is passive? How does she feel? Why?*

Students listen to the dialogues. Nominate individual students to respond orally, making two sentences for each, saying how the woman feels and why. They should know all of the adjectives in the box.

Answers

a She's fascinated.
The gossip is fascinating.
b She's disappointed.
Her exam results were disappointing.
c She's relaxed.
The holiday was relaxing.
d She was frightened.
Seeing the ghost was frightening.
e She's tired.
The journey was tiring.
f She's excited.
The job's exciting.
g She's amused.
The story's amusing.
h She's bored.
The documentary's boring.
i She was annoyed.
The children's behaviour was annoying.
j She's embarrassed.
The situation's embarrassing.

2 Read the introduction as a class. Students work in pairs to decide what the missing word is, then write it in the gaps in either the *-ing* form or *-ed* form.

Answers

a playing
played
b *Made*
making
c writing
written
d bought
buying
e breaking
broken
f taken
taking

4 Describing

NB *You will need to photocopy and cut up the sentences (TB p139).*

SUGGESTION

Before you read the instructions, ask students to describe what they can see in the picture. Don't give any further instruction or help. They will inevitably produce a series of sentences, not just one.

1 Read the instructions as a class. Students work in pairs to add the words and phrases from the box to make one long sentence.

Answer

There are no doubt several possibilities.

Exhausted after a hard day's work, the middle-aged man, wearing a crumpled suit and carrying a briefcase, walked slowly along the road that led from the station to his home, pausing only to look up at the night sky.

2 Students work in pairs. Give out a short sentence (TB p139) for them to make as long as possible. Get some feedback.

3 This exercise will have to be done in a later lesson. Students find a picture in a magazine and describe it to a partner. The partner has to draw it.

5 *I didn't know what to do*

Students work in pairs to complete the sentences. This is a very straightforward exercise.

Answers

a I don't know what to wear.
b I can't decide which restaurant to go to.
c Could someone show me how to put paper in the photocopier?
d I'm not sure whether to phone the police or not.
e Can you tell me how to get to the station?
f I don't understand what to do with this exercise.

ADDITIONAL MATERIAL

Workbook Unit 6
Exercise 1 A general knowledge quiz on Britain
Exercises 2 and 3 Defining and non-defining relative clauses
Exercise 4 All relatives
Exercise 5 Prepositions in relative clauses
Exercises 6 and 7 Participles
Exercise 8 Infinitives
Exercise 9 Revision text

LANGUAGE REVIEW (SB p61)

Relative clauses, participles, infinitive clauses

Read the Language Review carefully as a class, and/or ask students to read it at home. If you have a monolingual class, you might choose to compare the use of relative clauses and participles in L1 and English.

Students read the Grammar Reference at home. Encourage students to study this carefully whilst doing the exercises in the Workbook.

● READING AND SPEAKING (SB p62)

I've never seen anything like it!

Pre-reading task

1 Students look at the photographs, the captions, and the titles of the articles to find some strange facts about the person, the place, and the thing.

Answers

Professor Mangle-Wurzle sleeps in a bath. He collects toilets.
Antarctica is the coldest, highest, driest place on earth.
The black box isn't black. It's orange. There are two of them, not one.

2 Students find other words for *mad* and *strange*.

Answers

mad – crazy
strange – eccentric, weird, mysterious

Reading

POSSIBLE VOCABULARY PROBLEMS

This list is here for your information. We are not suggesting that you need to pre-teach all these words.

King of the eccentrics
striking = remarkable
curious = wanting to know about everything
displays
obstinate
outskirts
ventures out = dares to go out
convert
ahead of their time

Antarctica
abounds
seals
penguin
snowblindness
unremitting
barometer
impact
species /spi:ʃi:z/

The orange black box
legendary
invincibility
fluorescent
flight recorder
in the event of
stored
fuselage
tail fin
indestructible
withstand
impact
strain
encased
titanium
heat-absorbing
memory chips

1 Students decide which article they want to read. It would be helpful if they then moved to sit with others who want to read the same article.
Together, they write some questions they'd like answered. Go round the groups checking that the questions are well-formed.

2 Students read their chosen article.

Comprehension check

1 Students answer their own questions.

2 Students decide which of the questions a–o relate to their article, then answer them.
They check their answers in groups.

Answers

King of the eccentrics
c He's obstinate, non-conformist, and creative.
e He gives guided tours to people from all over the world, and he preaches to his sheep.

g He's delighted. It's the best Christmas present he's ever had.
l They are curious about everything, so they have a goal in life.
n They think the rest of the world is insane.

Antarctica
b The Greek word for bear, 'arktos'.
d Because it is isolated from the rest of the world, and it has avoided industrial pollution.
i There is very little plant life, and almost no flying insects. However, there are over 12 million penguins.
j Whales and seals and lots of living creatures.
m Because the ice retains ancient atmospheric samples and meteorites, so scientists can see what the air was like many years ago. Also, the skies are clear, so telescopes can see clearly into space.

The orange black box
a The story is 'If the aircraft were made of the same strong material as the black box, people would survive an air crash'.
f They are stored in the rear of the aircraft, because that part of the plane has the best survival record.
h No, it isn't impossible.
k They are encased in two layers of plate titanium with heat absorbing material in between.
o No, they aren't. Only in 80 per cent of accidents.

3 Students find people who read the other stories. Together they answer all the questions.

What do you think?

Answer these questions as a class. Students might be interested in talking about the articles, or they might not.

● VOCABULARY (SB p64)

Synonyms

NB *This is the first of several exercises that works on textual cohesion.*

Read the introduction as a class.

SUGGESTION

Write the word *bad* on the board. Ask students for other words meaning *bad*. Write them up.

Sample answers

awful terrible lousy dreadful horrible nasty

1 Students find words in the text 'King of the Eccentrics' with the same or similar meanings.

Answers

a author
b curious
c a goal
d remarkable
e obstinate
f belief
g admit
h insane

2 Students match a word in A with a synonym in B.

Answers

boring – dull
terrified – scared stiff
nasty – unpleasant
handy – useful
annoying – irritating
'd prefer – 'd rather
noise – sound
miserable – unhappy
clever – talented
argue – row
hate – can't stand
dangerous – risky
mend – fix
sure – convinced

3 Read the introduction and the example as a class. Students work in pairs to complete the sentences.

Answers

a boring
b annoys
c scared stiff
d remarkably/surprisingly
e handy
f believe
g nasty
h risks
i sounds
j arguments

4 **T 6.4** Students listen and reply using a synonym. This is perhaps best done as a class activity.

Sample answers

a I'd rather have red, if that's all right.
b Oh, yes. I'm absolutely convinced.
c I'll fix it today.
d Yes, I can't stand it, either.
e Yes, she's pretty miserable at the moment.
f She's very talented, it's true.
g My goal is to be a millionaire before I'm 30.
h We were having an argument about money.
i I admitted that I hadn't told the whole truth.
j I think she's totally insane.

● LISTENING AND SPEAKING (SB p64)

Advertisements

Pre-listening task

NB *You need to ask students in advance of this lesson to think about an advertisement that appeals to them. They also need to find an advertisement from a newspaper or magazine and bring it into class. Stress that this is very important, and remind them a few times. If they don't bring an advert into class, the Pre-listening task won't work.*

There are some classic pronunciation problems with the words 'advertisement' /əd'vɜ:tɪsmənt/ *and 'advertise'* /'ædvətaɪz/. *For the noun, we also talk about 'ads' and 'adverts'* /'ædvɜ:ts/.

1 Have a class discussion on advertisements using the questions in the Student's Book.

2 In small groups, students show each other the adverts they have brought to class. This can lead to an interesting discussion. Whether we like advertising or not, we are all surrounded and influenced by it.

Listening

T 6.5 Read the introduction as a class, and check students understand the two bits of information. Tell them that people in Britain have to pay a fine if they are caught watching television without a licence, and that detector vans go round the country looking for people who haven't bought a licence.
Students listen to the seven radio adverts and answer the questions by writing a letter a–g.

POSSIBLE VOCABULARY PROBLEMS

Here is a list of words for your information that might cause problems, and which students might ask you about. We are not suggesting that you should pre-teach them all.

a
scanner = a piece of computer equipment that copies an image from paper onto the screen
PC = personal computer

b
goblet = an old-fashioned cup made of glass or metal
fair maid = (here) beautiful lady
yet simmered = cooked for a long time on low heat. (old-fashioned word order)

c
on the premises = in this building
comply = do what you're asked to do
track = find
picking on me = choosing me for blame or punishment. Bullies pick on people smaller than themselves.
evaders = people who avoid doing something

d
fluffy = made of something soft and light, e.g. wool
ground-in dirt = dirt that is in the middle of the garment, not just on the surface

e
disposable users = short for users of disposable razors
Minister for Frozen Fish = a joke, of course!
micro-fins = sth on the razor with fins like a fish
in the fullness of time = a cliché which means when the right time comes, eventually
expand = say any more/give more information

f
Smartypants = someone who thinks they always have the right answer
to have the last word = to speak last in an argument, thus proving some kind of rightness

g
daunting = frightening and discouraging
back-up = support

Answers

d is selling soap powder
g is trying to recruit personnel
f is for a new car
a is selling computer hardware
b is giving a recipe
c is threatening punishment
e is about shaving

Comprehension check

1 Students complete the chart. Let them have a go at doing this for a minute or two, then play the adverts again. This way they will know what they have to listen out for.

Answers

	What's the advert for?	Name of product	Characters in the advert	Setting/ place
a	A machine that will print, fax, copy, and scan	Zubichi Multipass	John and a friend	In a pub
b	Chicken soup	Soup-in-a-box Cream of Chicken Soup	Romeo and Juliet	On a balcony?
c	TV licence		Robot/ terminator, householder, and narrator	A film? Sometime in the future?
d	Washing powder	New System Sudso Automatic	Sarah and her mother	At home and in the garden
e	A non-disposable razor	Sure Grip Supreme	Interviewer and government minister	In front of the Houses of Parliament
f	A car	Ford Escort	Father and daughter	At home
g	Joining the army		A man who sounds tough	

2 Selling point means 'the main reason you should buy this product'.

Answers

a This machine will perform four functions, and it's compact enough to fit into your office.
b The packets of soup have free recipes on them.
c If you don't have a licence, you'll be in big trouble.
d It's all you could want from a powder.
e Try the razor once, and you'll never use a disposable again.
f You get one year's free insurance with a new Ford Escort.
g Join the army if you want to be a peacemaker not a trouble-maker.

3 **Answers**

a A printer, a fax, a copier, and a scanner.
Freephone 0800 541001.
b It sounds like Shakespeare.
Chicken, onion, mushrooms, wine, and soup.
c She says her husband bought the television, not her. He said he'd buy a licence, so it's not her fault. She accuses the robot of picking on her.
d It's pink, with fluffy yellow ducks.
Something dirty and unpleasant. A worm, for example.
e He doesn't want to talk about what he chooses to do in his own home.
f Because she can get free insurance.
Because, like her mother, she always has to have the last word in an argument.
g Make the peace and keep the peace.
Visit your local army careers office, or call 0345 421633.

Group work

Students work in groups of four to devise a radio or television advert. This could be done quite simply in ten minutes or so, ending with some acting out in front of the class.
Alternatively, it could be expanded to last for up to an hour, if you and your class were so inspired. You could ask them to produce the advert, with actors, voice overs, presenters, and you could video it.

● WRITING (SB p66)

My favourite part of town

1 Before you ask students to open their books, discuss the questions in Exercise 1.

2 Students open their books. Ask them to tell you what they can see in the pictures.

Answers

1 People eating at an outdoor restaurant with tables on the pavement.
2 Colourful signs with Chinese characters outside shops and restaurants in Chinatown.
3 Pagoda-style entrance to Chinatown.
4 Theatre land – the area around Shaftesbury Avenue. Brightly lit neon signs advertising plays and shows. A red double-decker bus.
5 The 'sleazy' side of Soho – sometimes called the red light district. Shows, cinemas, and shops of an 'adult' nature, in this sense meaning 'erotic', or 'sexually explicit'.
6 Berwick Street market – lots of stalls with displays of fruit and vegetables. People buying and selling produce.

Students read the description of Soho and match the pictures to the description.

BACKGROUND INFORMATION

French Huguenots /'hju:gənəʊz/ were French Protestants who were persecuted in Catholic France in the sixteenth century. Over 250,000 emigrated.

Dim sum Chinese dumplings

Mozart (1756–1791), a child prodigy, came to London at 10 years old. He wrote his first three symphonies there.

Karl Marx (1818–1883) was a German philosopher, economist, and revolutionary. He founded Marxism, the theory of scientific socialism.

T S Eliot (1888–1965) was one of the most important British poets of the 20th century.

Answers

Picture 1	*Soho is packed with ... restaurants/There are endless ... cafés*
Picture 2	*... restaurants, 'dim sum' houses, Chinese supermarkets ...*
Picture 3	*Gerrard Street, which is pedestrianized, is the centre of London's Chinatown.*
Picture 4	*Shaftesbury Avenue is the heart of London's theatre land ...*
Picture 5	*... and there are endless clubs ...*
Picture 6	*There are also streetmarkets ...*

3 Students divide the text into paragraphs.

Sample answers

Para 1	to ... *with surprises around every corner.*
Para 2	to ... *continental food shops and restaurants.*
Para 3	to ... *New Year celebrations.*
Para 4	to ... *exciting place to live and work.*

Para 5 to the end

Paragraphs 2 and 3 could combine.

Purposes of each paragraph

1 Introduction. Where Soho is, and why the writer likes it. A description of the people, their business, and the buildings. The place is a bit of a mess, but it's interesting.
2 Origin of the name. Why Soho is so cosmopolitan. Where all the immigrants have come from.
3 The arrival of the Chinese from Hong Kong. Chinatown.
4 Famous people who have lived in Soho. Reputation for creative people. Places to go.
5 Conclusion. Why young people are drawn to the statue of Eros. You'll meet everyone you've ever known at Piccadilly Circus.

4 Students find examples of fact and opinion. Don't let this go on too long.

Answers

Fact
right in the centre
name is derived from a hunting call
has been cosmopolitan since the first immigrants arrived

Opinion
lively and colourful
a mess
buildings aren't the most beautiful
streets are interesting

5 Students underline examples of relative clauses and participles.

Answers

which is right in the centre
reasons I like it
people dashing around going about their business
which is mainly honest
who were French Huguenots
escaping the revolution
followed by Germans
packed with continental food shops
which is pedestrianized
including Mozart
which makes it an exciting place
celebrating the freedom

6 Students write a description of their favourite part of town for homework. Encourage students to attach some pictures or postcards to their essay. They might look good on the wall of your classroom.

PostScript (SB p67)

English signs

The aim of this activity is for students to recognize some very common signs that they will encounter if they ever come to Britain. There is no productive element to this exercise, obviously.
Students work in pairs or small groups to identify the signs they know. Some are international, some are particularly English. Then do the exercise as a class.

Answers

1 On a bottle of some kind of food or drink with a screw top, perhaps a can of drink or a bottle of ketchup
2 In a cafeteria
3 In a hotel or guest house
4 A pub or restaurant. The suggestion is that things are better than they were.
5 In a supermarket at the check-out
6 In the street. Conveniences is another word for toilets.
7 Pick Your Own – this is a farm in the country where members of the public can go into the fields and pick their own fruit or vegetables, which are then weighed and paid for.
8 On medicines. It means Do not take any more than it says you should take.
9 At a check-out in a shop
10 Public sign wherever crowds gather
11 In the country, near a farm
12 In a shop that is about to close
13 In a hairdresser's
14 In a pub or restaurant
15 On a bus, or in the Underground
16 In a bank, post office, or airport check-in desk
17 In the street. It's to do with parking restrictions.
18 On private property, in town but especially in the country. It means people who go into this private property will be taken to court.
19 On the road. It means there are road works, and you have to go round to get where you want to go.
20 On a small shop or office door

Don't forget!

Workbook Unit 6
Exercise 10 Nouns in groups
Exercise 11 Vocabulary – people, places, and things
Exercise 12 Vocabulary – similar words, different meaning
Exercise 13 Prepositions – adjectives + prepositions
Exercise 14 Pronunciation – silent consonants

Doing without

Verb patterns
Soundbites

Introduction to the unit

Doing without begins the second half of the book. The theme covers everything from wartime shortages, to the glut of gadgets we have in modern day life. The linguistic theme of verb patterns provides a generative and versatile base for all kinds of language practice, as well as being a necessary area for extended language study at upper-intermediate level.

Notes on the unit

LANGUAGE AIMS – VERB PATTERNS

NB See the Grammar Reference section – SB p153.

Students at this level will of course have covered basic verb patterns in English. Now is the time to bring them all together and develop their ability to produce them correctly. Infinitives and *-ing* forms occur frequently in English. They cause few problems of meaning, except when both are possible after the verb, and there is a change in meaning. This is the case with a number of verbs including *stop*, *try*, and *remember*.

Test your grammar (SB p68)

This *Test your grammar* has a dual purpose. It is designed to help inform you how proficient your students are in using all the main forms of verb patterns, and it also is a personalized activity. Your students are informing each other about themselves.

1 Ask your students to write truthful sentences about themselves.

Some sample answers from our students

a I'm (quite) good at skiing.
b I find it difficult to concentrate in lessons.
c I enjoy listening to soul music.
d I'm interested in applying for a job in the USA.
e I can't stand going to football matches with my boyfriend.
f I like being in London.
g I'd like to have a coffee break now.
h I can't afford to buy the beautiful boots I saw in Oxford Street.
i I'm thinking of going shopping after this lesson.
j I'm looking forward to seeing my family again.
k I always forget to bring my dictionary.
l Our teacher always makes us work hard.

2 Ask for some examples of each sentence from the class. Focus on interesting ones.

NB The aim is to follow the expression with a verb form in either the '-ing' form or the infinitive. However, don't worry if you get back some sentences with nouns only, for example 'I can't stand bananas'. Signify that these are fine but focus on ones with '-ing' forms and infinitives for special attention.

3 Ask students to repeat examples to illustrate *-ing* forms and infinitives.

SUGGESTION

Here you could focus the attention on yourself. Encourage students to make statements that they think are true about you. Then you comment on what they say. This can be quite a fun activity.

Example
S *You're good at listening to students' problems.*
T *Thank you. I hope I am!*

LANGUAGE IN CONTEXT (SB p68)

Verb patterns

1 **T 7.1** Ask students to comment on the photograph. *How old are the children?* Either you or a student read the introduction about Sean. Play the

tape and ask students to read and listen at the same time. (You could of course ask students to read only, but it can be quite interesting for students to hear a child speaking English.)

BACKGROUND INFORMATION

- Sean (/ʃɔːn/) and Liam are Irish names.
- *The olden days* is an expression that children often use to talk about times long ago, from prehistoric cavemen to when their parents were young!
- The war Sean is asking about is the Second World War, 1939–1945.
- The XXX at the end of the letter signify kisses.

Ask a few check questions about the letter. *Why is Sean writing to his grandma? Which war is Sean asking about? Who is Liam? What does Sean think of him?*

2 Students could work in pairs to do this exercise. Make clear that usually two are correct, but occasionally only one is correct. Go through the exercise as a class.

Answers

a 1 help him 2 agree to
b 1 has told 3 expects
c 2 advised 3 encouraged
d 2 to tell him
e 2 in remembering 3 remembering
f 1 to hear 3 her to tell him
g 2 listening to 3 hearing
h 2 is told to 3 is made to
i 1 can't stand 3 dislikes
j 1 is trying 2 isn't able
k 1 to seeing
l 2 reminds 3 asks

3 Do this quickly with the whole class. Ask for suggestions.

Answers

verb + *-ing*	She's **finished doing** her homework.
verb + infinitive (with *to*)	She **wants to go** to the cinema.
verb + sb + infinitive (with *to*)	She **wants you to take** her.
verb + sb + infinitive (without *to*)	I won't **let her go** out.
adjective + infinitive	It's **impossible to stop** her.
preposition + *-ing*	I'm interested **in coming**.

● Grammar questions

These questions link directly to the previous two exercises. Ask students to work in pairs to find examples of the verb patterns.

Answers

– verb + *-ing* g 2, 3 i 1, 3
verb + infinitive (with *to*) a 2 f 1 h 2, 3 j 1, 2
verb + sb + infinitive (with *to*) b 1, 3 c 2, 3 d 2 f 3 l 2, 3
verb + sb + infinitive (without *to*) a 1
adjective + infinitive none
preposition + *-ing* e 2 k 1

– **Sean's letter:**
verb + *-ing* *remember being love hearing hate playing*
verb + infinitive (with *to*) *'d love to hear learnt to walk want to see forget to send*
verb + sb + infinitive (with *to*) *told us to find out ask somebody old to tell us*
verb + sb + infinitive (without *to*) *help me do makes me play*
adjective + infinitive *difficult to remember*
preposition + *-ing* *no good at playing*

PRACTICE BANK (SB p70)

1 Grandma's reply

SUGGESTION

Ask some general questions to stimulate interest in the topic: *What do you know about World War II? When was it? Which countries suffered a lot? What happened to ordinary people during the war? What was their daily life like?*

1 Now ask them to read through the letter quickly and ask some check questions:
Where does Sean's grandma live? How old was she when the war started? Why were some children sent to the countryside? Where was Sean's grandma sent? What was rationed? Was she miserable because sweets were rationed? What does she say about a banana?

BACKGROUND INFORMATION

Grandma's letter talks about her life as a child during World War II.

- Newcastle is a big city in the north of England. It was badly bombed in the war because of the ship-building industry there.
- *Air raid shelters* – these were shelters to protect people from the bombs. Often built in people's gardens.
- Many city children were *evacuated* to the safety of the countryside in wartime.
- *Rationed* – there were many shortages of food and other goods during the war, therefore what there was had to shared out or rationed.

Ask students to read the text more carefully and fill the gaps with the correct verb form.

Answers

a to get	h to get	p have
b helping	i sleeping	q to eat
c to remember	j living	r getting
d watching	k to send	s to buy
e going	l to go away	t to get
f trembling/ to tremble	m to stay	u to do
g to leave	n crying	v to see
	o worrying	

2 **T 7.2** Play the tape and ask students to listen carefully and check. They are listening for detailed information. This is as much a part of the development of the listening skill as listening for gist.

2 Discussing grammar

NB *This exercise is designed to practise various problem areas in relation to verb patterns. One such area is when the verb can be followed by either the '-ing' form or the infinitive with a change in meaning. See the Grammar Reference section (SB p154).*

Ask students to do this in pairs or small groups.

Answers

a They stopped **playing football** because it got dark. (the activity ended)
They stopped **to play football** because they were tired of working. (one action stopped, *working*, in order for another to begin, *playing football*)

b I simply don't **remember giving** you any money yesterday. (looking back to the past)
Please **remember to give** my best wishes to your parents. (looking to the future)

c **Try counting** sheep if you can't get to sleep. (a method you can try)
Try to count from 1 to 10 in Arabic. (a difficult goal to aim for)

d We **prefer staying** at the Ritz whenever we're in London. (every time we come)
We'd **prefer to stay** at the Ritz next time we're in London. (one specific occasion)

e He **seems to drink** too much. He's rarely sober. (a regular habit)
He **seems to be drinking** too much. He's swaying. (this is happening now)
He **seems to have drunk** too much. He's fallen asleep. (the past)

f I **like going** to the cinema. (*like = enjoy*; a very general habit)
I **like to go** to the dentist twice a year. (*like = I think it's a good idea*; a more specific habit)
I'd like to go home now, please. (one specific occasion)

Discuss the reasons for your students' choices when you go through the exercise with the whole class.

3 *We'd love to!*

NB *This exercise has a dual purpose. It not only practises giving short answers but also the production of good stress and intonation.*

1 Model the example with some members of the class. Ask students to work in pairs to complete each dialogue and practise them together as they go.

Answers

a No, we don't have time to/haven't got time to.
b No, you're not allowed to.
c Oh, but you promised to.
d Because you told us to.
e I'm really sorry, I meant to, but I forgot.
f Sorry, I haven't had a chance to.

2 **T 7.3** Students listen particularly to the stress and intonation, and then practise the dialogues again in pairs. Round off the lesson by asking one or two students to do some of the dialogues in open pairs across the class. Student A can choose any one and then Student B must answer appropriately.

ADDITIONAL MATERIAL

Workbook Unit 7
Exercises 1–4 Basic and more complex verb patterns
Exercise 5 Verb patterns after adjectives, prepositions, and nouns
Exercises 6 and 7 Forms and uses of the infinitive
Exercise 8 *The house that Jack built* – revision of *-ing* forms and infinitives
Exercise 9 Extra input – verbs of perception: *see someone do/doing*

All of the above could be used in class but are probably best set as homework.

LANGUAGE REVIEW **(SB p71)**

Verb patterns

Read this together as a class and/or ask students to read it at home. If you have a monolingual class you could ask your students to translate some of the sentences, warning them against concentrating on form and directing them to consider overall meaning.

Ask students to read the Grammar Reference on p153 at home. Suggest that they consult this when they are doing exercises from the Workbook, and to revise.

● READING AND SPEAKING (SB p72)

The family who turned back the clock

NB As a homework task prior to starting this activity it would be a good idea to ask your students to talk to a member of their family or a friend who was alive fifty years ago. They need to ask them to compare life now with what it was like then. They need to consider areas such as: the home, work, and means of entertainment.

Pre-reading task

This is a vocabulary and discussion activity, which will hopefully motivate your students to read the text.

1 Ask students to work in pairs to consider the items in the list. They obviously won't know definitely which items were in use fifty years ago, but there can be some interesting debate.

Answers

The following were in use fifty years ago. Some of the dates may surprise you and your students.

fridge (refrigerators were first commercially produced in the USA, in 1856.)
electric razor (USA early 1900s)
radio (first radio signals transmitted in Italy by Marconi in 1895. First radio station USA 1920.)
washing machine (first motor driven machines, 1911, USA)
tin opener (tin cans were invented in England 1810 – presumably can/tin openers were invented at the same time!)
iron (electric hand irons for pressing about 1905)
vacuum cleaner (invented in 1901 by Hubert Booth, in England. First manufactured in 1908, by Hoover, USA.)
television (invented in 1926 by John Logie Baird, in London, England)

Encourage some discussion with the whole class about which items they have and don't have in their homes. Tell them what you have in yours.

2 This is where it will be useful if students have already done some preparatory work on life in their family fifty years ago. Get their feedback. You could also talk a bit about your family. Prompt them about daily life then. *What do you think was a typical day for the man of the house? The woman? The children?*

3 Ask everybody to write a personal list of what they would and wouldn't miss if the clocks turned back fifty years. Give them a couple of minutes to do this, then ask them to compare their lists with a partner and then the group as a whole. You could make your own personal list and see how it compares with those of your students.

Reading

Set a time limit for the first reading of the text. Encourage your students to read quite quickly and not, at this stage, to look up any words they do not understand. Discuss the first two questions with the whole class. They could do Exercise 3 in pairs, but before doing this throw the question open to the whole class just to see what they can remember and then ask them to scan the text again.

Answers

1 The top picture is a typical British family fifty years ago. The photograph at the bottom of the page is of some members of the Jones family: Carol the mother; Tamsin and Tom, the youngest of the four children, playing cards; Richard, the 14-year-old son, reading in the background. The father, Malcolm, and eldest daughter, Emma, are not in the picture.
2 They agreed to turn the clock back fifty years and live as people did then, doing without all the labour-saving gadgets and entertainment that we have today. Ask: *How long was the experiment?* Answer: *Three days.*
3 Items from the box mentioned are: *television, personal computer, CD player, washing machine, tumble drier, dishwasher, deep freeze, microwave oven, video recorder, jacuzzi, music system, electric razor, mobile phone.*

Comprehension check

Ask students to read the article again and then answer questions 1–4 in small groups. Students can take it in turns to read out the questions.

NB There are many opportunities in the answering of these questions for the natural use of verb patterns. Don't force these, but keep an ear open to see how well your students do, and correct them gently if they make mistakes.

Answers

1 They usually turn on their music systems. This could be radios or CD players.
2 This is a subjective answer, because what is average for one person may be a lot for another. However, the following items do seem excessive: nine TV sets, six computers, three cars, personal CD players, an electric trouser press, two power showers, Olympic-sized spa bath and jacuzzi, a music system that plays throughout the house.
3 **The three younger children** were not allowed to use their computers, watch TV, or open the freezer (deep freeze) to get out fish fingers and oven chips. **Malcolm** was allowed to use his car for work but he was not allowed to use his electric razor or his mobile phone.

Carol was not allowed to use the car, or use the telephone too often.

4 **Emma** refused to join in the experiment because she couldn't stand being without her telephone and her car, which she had only just learnt to drive.
Malcolm enjoyed it most because he liked the peace. He enjoyed hearing the birds and chatting to his wife without the noise of music and TV.
The children enjoyed it least because they missed everything. The music, the computer games, the TV. They didn't like reading books. They hated doing the washing-up.
Carol had mixed feelings. She liked the more relaxed way of life, but everything took a lot longer to do. She enjoyed doing more things together as a family, but she didn't like being without all her labour-saving gadgets, particularly the dishwasher. She liked the effect on the children, they played games together and read more, but she felt isolated without a phone and a car.

Get feedback on the above questions before continuing. For question 5, organize the groups so that members choose different parts. They will probably know enough about the members of the Jones family by now to be able to roleplay them without much preparation.

Go round and check what is happening in the groups. Ask one or two students to play their role to the whole class for them to guess which member of the family they are.

SUGGESTION

Question 5 could also be done as a piece of written work for homework. Students could then read their 'typical days' to the rest of class for them to guess who they are.

5 **A sample answer – Malcolm**

A typical day: Well, the first thing I usually do when I wake up is to turn on the TV from my bed, because I like to watch the business news. Then I press the music button – I enjoy listening to music while I have a shower. I get dressed to music too, then I race downstairs, grab some breakfast, and jump in the car and drive to work. Of course I listen to the car radio as I drive. I need to hear the traffic news to know how to avoid the traffic jams. When I'm stuck in a jam I usually make a few business calls on my mobile phone. Finally I get to work, usually late for my first meeting. I get back home late in the evening, exhausted. The children are always in their bedrooms listening to music or playing computer games. I usually have something to eat in front of the TV, and then just watch it until it's time for bed.

A typical day during the experiment: During the experiment, when I woke up I wasn't allowed to turn on the TV, so I just lay in bed and listened to the birds for a while. Carol and I sometimes chatted about this and that. I asked her about her plans for the day and she asked me about mine. We often carried on chatting while I was having a shower and she was getting dressed. The house was really peaceful without the TV and all the music. I even had a morning conversation with one or two of my children and asked them about school. The traffic jams were just the same. In the evening the kids were all in the kitchen. We all ate together there, and then argued about who was doing the washing-up. One evening I played cards with Tamsin and Tom, and another evening I helped Richard mend his bike. I felt sorry for Carol, she looked tired. But actually I'd like to throw away all nine of our TVs now, but the kids wouldn't let me do that!

6 **T 7.4** This could be done with the whole class. Ask your students to close their books and play the tape, pausing after each line. Ask one student to repeat the sentence and the others to discuss who they think said it and why. Encourage students to sound like the speaker on the tape: indignant, annoyed, fed up, tired, etc. This is to practise good stress and intonation.

Answers

a **Emma.** She refused to join the experiment because she'd just learnt to drive.
b **Malcolm** talking to Carol. He started noticing things other than the TV and the business news, during the experiment.
c **Carol** to Malcolm or Richard. She found that all household chores took longer during the experiment.
d **Tom** speaking to Tamsin. Tamsin and Tom started to play games together but they missed the TV and Tamsin just stared at the screen.
e **Richard** to the rest of the family because he didn't want to do the washing-up.
f **Carol.** Not using a car meant that it took much longer to go down to the shops.
g **Malcolm.** At the end of the experiment he wanted to get rid of all the TV sets.
h **Carol**, probably, because she found it much more difficult to run a house without modern appliances. However, they all could have said this.
i **The children** – all of them. They disliked the experiment most of all. However, Carol could have also said it, because the household chores took so much longer.

Language work

These two exercises could be set for homework.

1 Discuss the phrases as a class. Focus on the best suggestions as you go, asking those students that offer them to repeat them clearly for the rest of the class. Don't worry about small language mistakes as they try to explain what the phrases mean.

Possible answers

a Usually you can't hear the birdsong because of the loud music coming from all the music systems in the house.
b This family has every modern appliance that you can think of.
c They have all the modern appliances that most people have (and a lot more besides).
d Those things which support modern daily life.
e Household appliances that save time and means of entertainment that work with the push of a button. You can turn them on and off while lying in bed or sitting in a chair.
f She refused absolutely, not very politely.
g They were not looking forward to the three-day experiment.
h Not having a TV changed the way the children behaved in a big way.
i The children absolutely refused to admit that the experiment had any advantages at all. For them it was all bad.
j The Jones children are without doubt very pleased that it is actually impossible to turn the clock back.

2 Check the text yourself first for examples of verb patterns. Ask the class for some examples.

● VOCABULARY AND LISTENING

(SB p74)

Hot Verbs (3): *get*

Before your students open their books, write *GET* in the middle of the board. Then ask everybody to write down a sentence with *get* in it and read them out round the class. There should be a variety of examples. Tell your students that *get* is one of the most commonly used words in the English language.

1 Now ask them to open their books and read through examples from the text about the Jones family. Ask them to work in pairs to do the exercise and then go through it as a class.

Answers

a You **have/own** a dishwasher.
b I **returned** from walking the children to school.
c She found it difficult to **become accustomed** to the length of time things took.
d You **have to** keep doing the washing-up.
e All sorts of things **were done**.
f They **had a much better relationship**.

2 This is a personalized activity to practise *get*. Students answer the questions on their own and then compare their answers with a partner. Finally, they work with their partner to rewrite the questions without using *get*.

Answers

a **Do you have/own** a pet/CD player?
b What **do you have** to do when you arrive home tonight?
c How do you **come** to school?
d What time do you usually **arrive at** school? (*Note*: arrive at)
e How many TV channels can you **receive**?
f When did you last **become** angry? Why?
g **Do you have a good relationship** with your parents?
h How often do you **have** your hair cut?
i In what ways is your English **improving**?

Before the lesson consider the questions in relation to yourself. Now you can conclude this exercise with your students asking *you* the questions that they have re-written.

Phrasal verbs with *get*

1 Ask students to work in pairs to do this exercise. Make sure that your students understand that one word from the box fits all three sentences in each group.

Answers

a out	c over	e through
b at	d up	f off

Go through this exercise before doing the next.

2 Ask the class which words are not used.

Answer

away into on round

Ask students to work in pairs and find the *get* entry in a dictionary. Make sure that different pairs choose different phrasal verbs so that all four are covered. You do not want each pair choosing to look up the same phrasal verb. Ask students to make sentences to illustrate the different meanings.

Sample answers

get away = to escape
The thieves got away | *from the police.* / *with £200,000.*
= to have a holiday
We're hoping to get away for a few days.

get into = to put on
I can't get into my jeans. I'm too fat.
= to enter *The thieves got into the house through the window.*
= to become involved/interested in
How did he get into crime?

get on = to make progress
My son's getting on well at school.
= to manage/survive
I can't get on without you.
get round = to persuade *Our youngest daughter can always get round her father.*
= to overcome
How did you get round the problem?

Listening

Fast Car – a song by Tracy Chapman

SUGGESTION

It would be possible to up-end this lesson and begin all the work on *get* with this song. *Or* you could simply play it at the beginning of the lesson without studying it, and then come back to it at the end.

1 **T 7.5** Your students may know this song. Play it once through with the books closed. Ask for any examples of *get* that they heard. Open books and play it again for them to complete the gaps.

Answers

You**'ve got** a fast car
Maybe together we can **get somewhere**
But me myself **I've got nothing to prove.**
I've got a plan to **get us out of here**
You and I can both **get jobs**
You see my old man**'s got a problem**
I said somebody**'s got to take care of him**
We**'ve got make** a decision
I know things will **get better**
You'll find work and I'll **get promoted**
And I**'ve got a job** that pays all our bills
I've got no plans and I ain't going nowhere. (*I ain't = I'm not*)

2 Ask students to turn to the tapescript (SB p137) and read and check. In our experience the more the students hear the song the more they like it.

ADDITIONAL MATERIAL

Workbook Unit 7
Exercise 11 Phrasal verbs – type 4 (*get away with*)

The exercise is very suitable for use in class. However, given limitations of time, it can also successfully be set as homework.

● WRITING AND DISCUSSION (SB p75)

Contrasting ideas

1 Begin with a general class discussion. Ask some questions: *What kind of programmes do you like watching on TV? What don't you like watching? Why?*

Divide the class into two groups and ask one group to write down all the good points they can think of about TV. Ask the other group to write down only *bad* points. Give them about five minutes to do this, then ask for their ideas. When one group makes a point, for example: *We think that TV is good because it can be educational*, go to the other group to see if they have a contrasting point, for example: *Well, we think there are too many mindless programmes like game shows.*

SUGGESTION

Divide the board into two columns, GOOD POINTS and BAD POINTS. Ask representatives from each group to come up and fill out their column with their ideas. Use the points on the board as a basis for your discussion. Leave them on the board.

2 Students could work in pairs to do this. Go through the answers with the whole class.

Answers

a I always watch the news on TV, even though it's usually depressing.
I always watch the news on TV, whereas John always watches sport.
b He writes all personal letters by hand although he has a computer.
He writes all personal letters by hand despite having a computer.
c It took only an hour to get to the airport. However, they still missed the plane.
It took only an hour to get to the airport, in spite of the traffic.
d Some couples argue all the time. Nevertheless, their marriages still work.
Some couples argue all the time, whereas others never do.
e Kathy rarely uses her mobile phone. However, Kevin uses his all the time.
Kathy rarely uses her mobile phone, even though she has one.

Now ask students to look again at the lists of good and bad points about TV. This is where it would be useful to have the points on the board, so that you can focus the whole class's attention. As a class, join some of the ideas with some of the words in B.

3 Ask students to do this in pairs.

Sample answers

a His idea is brilliant in theory. However, it won't/wouldn't work in practice.
b My brothers love playing computer games, whereas I don't./can't stand playing them.
c On the one hand, cars are really convenient to get you from A to B, but on the other hand they cause traffic jams and pollution.
d I'm going to drive into London, even though the roads will be very busy at this time of day.
e Foreign travel is very exciting, but at the same time it is very tiring.
f The critics slammed Ed Newhart's latest film. Nevertheless, lots of people went to see it.
g Their daughter is often sullen and moody, despite always getting everything that she wants.

4 Ask your class how many of them would hate to be without TV. Ask them to work with a partner and discuss which modern inventions they would find it most difficult to live without. After a few minutes encourage some general discussion.
Then ask each of them to choose *one* invention which they feel is very necessary to their life and answer the questions about it.
They could make notes in class and then expand the notes into an essay for homework.

PostScript (SB p76)

Soundbites

NB *Remember – this can be done at any stage in the series of lessons that make up this unit.*

SUGGESTION

Tell the class what a *soundbite* is. It is a relatively new word, so it might not be in their dictionary. It refers to a very short part of a speech, especially made by a politician, which is used on radio or TV to sum up the main message of his/her speech or interview. Tell your students that in this activity *soundbites* are examples of spoken English from a variety of situations.

1 Ask students to discuss the soundbites in pairs. Ask: *How many can you recognize?* Tell them not to worry about those they can't recognize, because soon they will hear them and that will give them further clues. Get some feedback after a few minutes on which they think they know.

2 **T 7.6** Now play the tape, stopping after each one. Ask: *Where would you hear this? Who is speaking? What helps you identify the situation?*

Answers

1 A presenter, such as a disc jockey, announcing an interval for advertisements on a radio or TV show. This is called a 'commercial break'.
2 A child or teenager trying to persuade a parent to let him/her do something. Very typical parent reply.
3 Doctor and patient. The patient can't speak properly because the mouth is wide open.
4 Typical dialogue in a McDonald's restaurant between customer and person behind the counter. *Fries* are short for *French fries*, or *chips* in British English.
5 Very small child to parent, probably in a place where there is no toilet for miles! *I want a wee-wee* is used by very young children when they want to urinate.
6 Customer to salesperson in a music shop, asking if a certain a record/CD/cassette is available yet. An *album* is a group of songs on one record, a *single* is one only.
7 An elderly person, probably to someone at home in the family. A *nap* is a short sleep.
8 Said by a guard (or it could be a recorded message) on a crowded Underground train. Asking the public to allow people to get off the train before they get on, and to move down the carriage (= *car*) so more people can get on.
9 Said by a guest as he/she leaves someone's house. Often said by children, having been to a party, or having stayed the night with a friend.
10 Said by someone who is apologizing for using their fingers to pass you some food. *Here's one of my sandwiches. 'Scuse fingers.*
11 MPs in the Houses of Parliament, where they use very archaic and polite phrases to tell each other that they are telling lies. They are not allowed to accuse each other openly of lying, it is not protocol. *Hear, hear!* means that they agree.
12 Two old people talking about how awful the world has become.
13 Flight attendant to passengers in the departure lounge of an airport.
14 Child to parent again, probably seconds before having to leave for school. *Gym kit* = the special clothes, probably shorts, T-shirt, and trainers, for sports lessons at school.
15 A radio presenter reporting traffic news. A *hold-up* means the traffic has been stopped, probably by an accident. A by-pass is a road which goes round a town, not through it.
16 In a photographic shop. The customer wants a film developed. *Six by four* refers to the size of the prints, six inches by four inches (15 cm x 10 cm).

Don't forget!

Workbook Unit 7
Exercise 10 Vocabulary – compound nouns
Exercise 12 Pronunciation – Weak and strong forms

8 Famous for fifteen minutes

Modal auxiliary verbs
Exaggeration and understatement

Introduction to the unit

Famous for fifteen minutes comes from a quote from the late American pop-artist Andy Warhol (1928–1987, see TB p79). He once joked that eventually every human being would have their fifteen minutes of fame. He believed that the existence of television and the mass media would inevitably lead to this. The topics of the unit are mainly news items and stories from the world of entertainment.

Notes on the unit

LANGUAGE AIMS

NB See the Grammar Reference section – SB p155.

Modal auxiliaries

Modal verbs express five broad areas of meaning: probability, obligation, ability, permission, and volition. Students at this level will be familiar with these concepts. They will probably have covered them as disparate items in their English studies. This unit brings them all together. They may not know that *all* the modals can be used to express degrees of probability. They will probably know that *must/can't*, *may*, *might*, and *could* express this, but not *will*, *should*, and *would*. Don't worry too much about the differences in use between *must*, *should*, and *will*. They are very subtle. There is some explanation in the Grammar Reference.

Test your grammar (SB p77)

This *Test your grammar* begins to pull together all the uses of modal verbs, but at this stage students are only asked to *recognize* the uses. It also aims to draw attention to the fact that all modal verbs can be used to express varying degrees of probability.

1 Write the example sentences on the board *before* you ask your students to open their books. You could write them with *must* gapped to allow students to brainstorm what could go in. (This makes more of an impact than just reading the introduction aloud from the book.) Ask: *What does 'must' mean in each sentence? Which sentence means 'it is very probable'? Which is obligation?* Ask students to open their books and do the exercise in pairs.

Answers

a (✔)
b (✘) – obligation
c (✔)
d (✘) – ability
e (✔)
f (✔)
g (✘) – permission
h (✘) – willingness/volition
i (✔)
j (✘) – advice/obligation
k (✔)
l (✔)
m (✘) – obligation

2 The answers are given above.

NB When accepting descriptions of concept from your students do not necessarily expect them to be expressed as in the answers above. It is sufficient for them to use whatever means they can to get the meanings across, including L1.
Point out that sentences 'l' and 'm' are in the past.

LANGUAGE IN CONTEXT (SB p77)

Modal verbs of probability

The first part of this section only deals with verbs of probability, both in the present and in the past. It assumes students will be familiar with the forms.

1 Ask students to comment on the two newspaper headlines and read through the ideas below the first one with them. Ask them to work in pairs and go through the ideas in A again and putting a tick (✔) against their choices. (This is a recognition exercise.)

Ask them to do the same for B. Ask for some feedback on their ideas on both articles.

2 Now they are asked to do a production exercise. They have to rewrite the sentences using the modal verbs in brackets. Ask them to do it in pairs and then go over it as a full class activity. Make sure that students that you nominate to give answers produce full correct, sentences. Pay careful attention to pronunciation, especially the past modals. Write up more complex ones if needed.

Answers

- She can't have flu.
- She must have a more serious illness.
- She might be very lazy.
- The doctor couldn't (possibly) have told her to stay in bed for so long.
- Someone must have been looking after her.
- She may find it very difficult to walk again.

3 Ask students to turn the page to read the actual stories. Give them a few minutes to do this. Get some feedback on whose predictions were most/least correct. Then ask the questions to the whole class to check their understanding of the articles. Encourage full replies, not just the minimum.

Answers

a **Jason** jumped because he wanted to commit suicide. He was an unsuccessful artist, broke and lonely in a big city at Christmas time, so he felt depressed and suicidal.
Mrs Teppit stayed in bed because the doctor she first saw told her to stay there until he returned. He never returned so she didn't get out of bed.

b **Bob Stichman** was working in his office on the 85th floor of the Empire State Building when he heard Jason at the window ledge outside, so he let him in.
Hundreds of people have offered to have him for Christmas.
Dr Mark Pemberton visited Mrs Teppit in her home and was amazed to hear her story.
Norma Teppit is Mrs Teppit's daughter. She is 54, not married, and has been looking after her mother for forty years, ever since the first doctor told her to stay in bed.

Other uses of modal verbs

The second part of this section deals with the other uses of modal verbs, both in the present and in the past. It assumes students will already have some familiarity with them.

1 Ask students to work in pairs and decide who they think is saying each utterance.
Make it clear it could be any of the people in either text and they must decide who is speaking to who.

NB This is a good opportunity to encourage some real practice of modals of deduction and probability. In deciding who is speaking, encourage students to use 'must be' and 'can't be'.

Answers

'Excuse me. *May* I come in?' Jason Hosen to Bob Stichman (permission)
'You *must* stay in bed until I return.' the village doctor to Mrs Teppit forty years ago (strong advice/obligation)
'I*'ve had to* look after her since I was 14.' Norma Teppit to Dr Mark Pemberton (obligation)
'I *couldn't* believe my eyes.' Bob Stichman, probably speaking to a friend (ability)
'You *should have been* examined years ago.' Dr Pemberton to Mrs Teppit (obligation)
'She *won't* get up.' Norma to the doctor about her mother (refusal)
'I *can't* find anything wrong with you at all.' Doctor to Mrs Teppit (ability)
'I *ought to* call the police.' Bob Stichman to Jason Hosen (obligation)
'*Can* I get up soon?' (Mrs Teppit to the doctor) (request, permission)
'You *should* try to lose weight.' Dr Pemberton to Mrs Teppit (advice/obligation)
'She told me that I *couldn't* get married and that I *had to* look after her.' Norma to the doctor about her mother (permission, obligation)
'*Will* you spend Christmas with us?' A kind member of the public to Jason Hosen (willingness/offer)
'You*'ll have to* have physiotherapy.' Doctor to Mrs Teppit (obligation)
'You *mustn't* do anything like this again.' Bob Stichman to Jason (strong advice/ obligation)
'You *don't have to* do everything for her.' Doctor to Norma (obligation)

2 Get feedback with the whole class on Exercise 1. Then, again as a whole class activity, ask students to look through the remarks again and describe the concepts to you.
(Answers – see above.)

● Grammar questions

– Do these together as a class. The statements go from most certain down to least certain.

Answer

That **'ll/won't** be the postman.	**most certain**
That **must/can't** be the postman.	
That **should** be the postman.	
That **could/couldn't** be the postman.	
That **may** be the postman.	
That **might** be the postman.	**least certain**

The next two exercises are basically transformation exercises from present to past. They aim to illustrate the difference between the way the past is formed for probability modals and other modals. You could ask students to do the exercises in pairs. However, for speed and clarity of purpose it can be worthwhile doing it as a whole class activity.

Answers (In modals of probability the past is formed with the perfect infinitive)

That **'ll/won't have been** the postman.
That **must/can't have been** the postman.
That **should have been** the postman.
That **could/couldn't have been** the postman.
That **may have been** the postman.
That **might have been** the postman.

Point out the perfect infinitive form = *have* + past participle.

– Go through these and highlight the differences with the previous exercise.

Answers

He **could see** someone at the window.
She **had to call** the doctor.
He **had to tell** the police.
She **wouldn't get** out of bed.
You **should have called** the police.
We **didn't need to hurry**. (we didn't hurry because it wasn't necessary) *or*
We **needn't have hurried**. (we did hurry but it wasn't necessary)

PRACTICE BANK (SB p79)

Some of these activities and exercises could be set for homework. We'll suggest which are most suitable for this.

1 Discussing grammar

NB *These two exercises could be set for homework and then discussed in pairs or small groups in the next lesson. Students could consult the Grammar Reference section on p155, whilst doing the exercises.*

1 Ask students to do this exercise in pairs or small groups first, then go over it together.
It is important to spend time going through the exercise with the whole class because the discussion generated by the different possibilities can be very interesting.

Answers

a can, may, could (*might* sounds excessively polite and old-fashioned.)
b can, could, will
c have to
d may, might, should, 'll
e could
f may, might
g must, should, 'll
h must, may, might, could, should, will
i should, 'll
j has to
k must, may, might, could, should, 'll

2 Adopt a similar approach for this exercise.

Answers

a had to go	f could
b don't have to	g wouldn't
c mustn't	h couldn't
d may not	i shouldn't
e were you able to	j didn't need to pay

2 Listening and speaking

NB *This is not suitable for homework. It not only practises modal auxiliaries, but it also provides a solid base for discussion as students try to work out what exactly Rod and Miranda are talking about.*

1 **T 8.1** Tell the class that they are going to hear *one side only* of a telephone conversation. You could ask them to keep their books closed at this stage, and play the tape for listening purposes only. However, if you feel they would benefit from the support of the written word, ask them to read and listen at the same time. After listening ask them to work in pairs to discuss the questions below. The following are some of things you might expect them to deduce. Go round and listen in to their discussion pushing them at times to the use of modals. Don't overdo this at this stage or you will spoil their enjoyment of the activity.

Sample answers

- they must be friends. They may be studying together. They could be brother and sister.
- she might have won a competition. She must have entered a competition in the *Daily Express*.
- she must have been doing the competition in the coffee bar.
- she must be going to New York. She must have won a holiday in New York.
- she must be/it sounds like she's going to travel on Concorde.
- he must have always wanted to travel on Concorde.
- he can't be her husband. He could/may/might be her boyfriend or ex-boyfriend.
- they may/might become boyfriend and girlfriend.

Bring the class together to go through their deductions. This is the stage to push them to use the modals. Also sometimes ask them to give reasons for their deductions. At this point ask them to discuss and write down in their pairs what they think were Miranda's exact words.

2 **T 8.2** Play the complete telephone conversation. Ask students to check their answers.

3 This could be done for homework. There are a mixture of all types of modal auxiliaries in the conversation.

3 Stress and intonation

This is quite a controlled pronunciation activity designed to widen the voice range and give practice of sentence stress and intonation.

1 Use the example to model the activity for the class. You be Student A and choose another student to be Student B. Then nominate an A and a B to repeat the dialogue in open pairs across the class. Encourage good stress and intonation at all stages. You could continue through the exercise in this way in open pairs, doing each dialogue a few times with different pairs, so as to standardize the answers and really work at the pronunciation. Or you could ask the students to complete the other dialogues in closed pairs with the student next to them, finally asking a few of them to act out their dialogues in front of the others.

2 **T 8.3** Play the sample answers for your students to compare. They could then do a few of the dialogues again having heard the stress and intonation on the tape as a model.

ADDITIONAL MATERIAL

Workbook Unit 8

Exercises 1–4 Present and past modals of probability

Exercises 5–9 All modals

Exercise 7 *The 1901 Teaching Contract* – a text which practises modals of obligation and permission

Exercise 10 Extra input – *need*, both as a full verb and as a modal verb

All of the above could be used in class but are probably best set as homework.

LANGUAGE REVIEW (SB p81)

Modal auxiliary verbs

Read this together as a class and/or ask students to read it at home. If you have a monolingual class you could ask your students to translate some of the sentences, warning them against concentrating on form and directing them to consider overall meaning.

Ask students to read the Grammar Reference section at the back of the Student's Book at home. This gives a much fuller description of the uses and forms of modals other than modals of probability. Suggest that they use this to revise from and when they are doing exercises from the Workbook.

● READING AND SPEAKING (SB p81)

Get me Jane Austen's fax number!

NB *Jane Austen's books are still so popular today that TV and movie producers find it very lucrative to make them into films. The title is a joke at the expense of a film producer, who doesn't realize that Jane Austen is dead, hence it won't be possible to reach her by fax.*

Pre-reading task

1 Ask students to comment on the meaning of the title. *What is strange about it? Who might have said this?* Discuss Jane Austen briefly. (See below for your information.) It doesn't matter if your students don't know the answers. Tell them that they will find out later when they read the text.

Ask students to discuss the other names in pairs and answer as many of the questions as they can. The answers are given in the profiles below.

BACKGROUND INFORMATION

Jane Austen (1775–1817)
A world famous writer, born in the county of Hampshire in England. She wrote six very witty and romantic novels, which are a satire on the lives of people at that time. The most well-known of these are *Pride and Prejudice*, *Sense and Sensibility*, and *Emma*. She and her family were never well off. During her lifetime her books were published anonymously and she made very little money from her writing.

Marilyn Monroe (1926–1962)
Born Norma Jean Baker. US film actress and sex symbol. Most famous films *Gentlemen Prefer Blondes* and *Some Like it Hot*. She is said to have had an affair with President Kennedy. She died from a drug overdose.

Anne Frank (1929–1945)
German Jewish girl, who wrote a diary while hiding from the Nazis in Amsterdam, from 1942–1943. After her death her diary became a symbol of Jewish resistance. She died in a concentration camp in 1945.

Mozart (1756–1791)
Austrian, born in Salzburg. He showed extraordinary musical talent from the age of four. He composed many great works, including such masterpieces as *The Marriage of Figaro* (1786), *Don Giovanni* (1787), *The Magic Flute* (1791). He did not achieve much fame in his life, poverty and overwork contributed to his early death.

William Shakespeare (1564–1616)
Born in Stratford-upon-Avon, England. He worked

at the Globe theatre in London, acting and writing plays. His most famous include: *Hamlet*, *Macbeth*, *Romeo and Juliet*, and *A Midsummer's Night's Dream*. He also wrote poetry, 154 sonnets. He was quite successful in his life, but his fame has spread throughout the world since his death.

Andy Warhol (1928–1987)
American artist and filmmaker. Famous as a member of the Pop art movement of the 1960s. He was particularly well-known for his paintings of everyday consumer goods, such as Coca-Cola bottles and cans of soup, and his photographic prints of Hollywood celebrities such as Marilyn Monroe.

Eva Perón (1919–1952)
Second wife of the Argentinian president Juan Domingo Perón, responsible for many reforms in Argentina, including votes for women. She also did a lot of work for poor people and was idolized by them, both during her life and after her death.

Vincent Van Gogh (1853–1890)
A Dutch painter whose genius was ignored and misunderstood in his own lifetime. He sold only one painting. He was an energetic painter but suffered from deep depression and periods of insanity. (Once he cut off one of his ears.) Finally he committed suicide.

2 Ask your students to comment on the pictures. *Who are they?* Your students can probably work out that the connection is to do with making a film of a book.

Answers

The pictures are of Jane Austen and the British actress Emma Thompson.

The connection is that Emma Thompson directed and starred in a film of one of Jane Austen's books, *Sense and Sensibility*, for which she won an Oscar.

Reading

NB In order to discourage your students from looking up too many items of vocabulary as they read, you could give them the following list of words to look up as part of their homework prior to the lesson, and/or pre-teach some in class.

POSSIBLE VOCABULARY PROBLEMS

adaptation	*governess*
anonymously	*haunted*
enduring	*matrimony*

on the shelf = considered too old to be likely to marry (old-fashioned expression, also sexist because it usually applies only to women.)

Oscar = an annual American award for good work in the cinema. It is in the form of a small statue.

propensity	*to satirize*
rambling (adj)	*spinster*
to rival	*to screen*

Ask students to comment on the photographs. *What's happening in them?* Ask a student to read aloud the title of the text *Jane Austen – the hottest writer in Hollywood*, and ask what they think this means. Read out the introduction and the question at the end. The answer is, of course, that when people see the films, which are so colourful and historical, they then want to read the books.

1 Ask individual students to read through the sentences. After each one ask what they learn about Jane.

NB Here, if you are lucky, your students may use some modals of probability. However, don't force this – just be pleased if you hear something other than 'perhaps' and 'maybe'!

Sample answers

a The family can't have been very rich/have had many friends.
b She can't have been famous in her lifetime.
c She must have had some unhappy times in her life.
d She wrote romantic novels.
e In the days of Jane Austen girls must have married early. (Ask for the meaning of 'on the shelf' – see above.)
f This may be referring to films made about Jane's books.
g This may have been the year she started writing.

2 Ask students to read the text quite quickly. (They should be able to do this if they have researched the vocabulary for homework.) Then discuss in pairs where they think the sentences should go. Conduct a full class feedback.

Answers

1 b 2 d 3 a 4 e 5 c 6 g 7 f

Comprehension check

1 Divide the class into small groups to discuss the first two sets of questions. Then ask for feedback from the whole class. You may want to do Exercise 3 as a whole class activity to vary the pace and to help students with the explanations.

Answers

Chawton – The house in Hampshire where Jane used to live. It is visited by 200 people a day.

The BBC – It screened an adaptation of *Pride and Prejudice*, which was watched by 18 million people.
The Internet – There is a special Jane Austen discussion group on the Internet.
Iceland – Her books are sold in 18 countries including Iceland.
Bath – Her family moved to Bath in 1801.
Devon – She fell in love with a man called Samuel Blackall when she was on holiday in Devon.
Uruguay – She is popular all over the world, even in Uruguay.
Winchester Cathedral – Her grave is here.
Edward – He was her brother, richer than the rest of his family.
Cassandra – She was her unmarried sister, poor like Jane.
Nigel Nicolson – He wrote a book about Jane called *The World of Jane Austen.*
P D James – An author (a woman) who describes Jane as a genius.
John le Carré – Sales of Jane's books rival those of the modern best-selling author, John le Carré.
Tom Lefroy – A handsome law student who Jane met in 1795.
Winifred Wilson – a member of the Jane Austen Society, who thinks the screen adaptations are too romantic.
Emma Thompson – an actress who adapted *Sense and Sensibility* for the cinema.
'Emma' – one of Jane's novels.
Oscar – Emma Thompson won a Hollywood Oscar for her film.

2 Call out the numbers in feedback and nominate individuals to supply the answers.

Answers

41 – Jane's age when she died.
18 – 18 million viewers; 18 countries round the world; July 18th – the day Jane died.
four – only four of her six novels published; three or four families in a country village; for four years they moved from house to house.
£648.65 – the total she earned from her books.
200 – it's nearly 200 years since Jane's death; her house is visited by 200 people a day.
eight – she was seventh of eight children.
12 – she was writing stories by the time she was 12.
1802 – in 1802 she agreed to marry Harris Bigg-Wither.
1805 – her father died.
1811 – her first novel *Sense and Sensibility* was published.

3 Ask students to find the lines and ask one of them to read them aloud to the class.

Sample answers

lines 29–31 She writes about a very small section of English society, so perhaps it is surprising that her books are successful all over the world. (Ask your students how they think this can be.)

lines 39–42 She describes how young people behave in romantic situations in a way that was not only true then, but is still true today.

lines 74–6 She changed her mind about marrying him (the aptly named Harris Bigg-Wither!) because the only thing that was good about him was his height.

lines 118–121 Jane Austen, who had a quiet and unexciting life, has become world famous because of her books being made into films.

lines 127–8 This is a criticism of the way the films concentrate on the romance in Jane's stories rather than the wit and fun.

What do you think?

Use these questions to try to stimulate some discussion on wider issues. You could ask students to consider them in pairs or groups before getting the opinions of the whole class. Don't worry if not a lot of discussion is forthcoming, but they should be able to comment on the differences in the lives of women then and now.

● VOCABULARY AND PRONUNCIATION

(SB p84)

Making sentences stronger

1 Adverbs and adjectives that go together

SUGGESTION

Begin the lesson by writing the following words haphazardly on the board: *nice*, *wonderful*, *small*, *tiny*, *big*, *enormous*, *ugly*, *hideous*, *sad*, *miserable*. Ask your students to pair them and to say what is different about the meaning of each pair. This will prepare them for the activity to come.

1 Ask students to work in pairs, look at the adjectives and make a list of those which have similar meanings. Next ask them to say which go with *very* and which with *absolutely*. Ask *What is the rule?*

Answers

very **+ base adjectives**	good	***absolutely*** **+ extreme adjectives**	fabulous, fantastic
	bad		awful, disgusting
	big		huge
	hungry		starving
	valuable		priceless
	silly		ridiculous

funny	hilarious
interesting	fascinating
pleased	delighted
tired	exhausted
frightened	terrified
clever	brilliant
dirty	filthy
beautiful	gorgeous
cold	freezing
surprising	incredible
	right

2 Do this with the whole class immediately following the feedback to the previous exercise. Read out the sample sentences. Be sure that your stress and intonation reflect the meaning: forceful stress and falling intonation on *quite* and *right* in the first one; rising intonation on *quite* and *good* in the second one and greater stress on *quite*.

You're quite right.   The film was quite good.

Ask them to give some more examples with the adjectives above.

NB When asking for more examples you must ensure that your students use the correct stress and intonation to convey the meaning.

Then ask: *What is the rule?*

Answer

The rule is that *quite* means *absolutely* when used with an extreme adjective but it means *not very/fairly* when used with a base adjective.

3 **T 8.4** First ask your students to look at the short dialogues and ask for ideas for words that could fill the gaps. Play the tape and ask them to compare their ideas and complete the gaps with the words they hear.

Answers

A That film was **very good**, wasn't it?
B Good! It was **absolutely fantastic**!

A You must have been **quite pleased** when you passed your exam.
B Pleased! I was **absolutely delighted**!

Now ask them to practise the dialogues in pairs, either with the examples from the tape or their own examples. After this encourage them to make similar short dialogues using the adjectives and paying particular attention to practising the stress and intonation.

Go through the possible topics. They should prompt some ideas even from the least imaginative students. However, if necessary you could prompt yourself with some possible first lines: *Was that book interesting? Our holiday wasn't very good last year. Maria's quite clever, isn't she?*, etc.

2 Adverbs and verbs that go together

SUGGESTION

Again you could begin this section by some work on the board which will prepare them for the activity to come. Write haphazardly: *shout*, *loudly*, *write*, *illegibly*, *speak*, *fluently*, *work*, *hard*. Ask which are verbs and which are adverbs and which go together and point out that there is often a logical link and that *hard* is irregular.

1 Ask your students to work in pairs or small groups to do this exercise and the next one. It is important to make clear that although there is sometimes a logical link, there are no actual rules of use. Say that sometimes more than one adverb is possible with the verb.

Answers

agree – totally, fully	forget – totally
advise – strongly	lie – convincingly
behave – badly	recommend – fully, strongly
believe – sincerely, strongly, totally	remember – distinctly
consider – seriously	die – tragically
	understand – fully

2 This exercise should be done very speedily. You need to point out the position of the adverbs – they can sometimes go either before or after the main verb.

Answers

a totally	e tragically
b convincingly, totally	f fully
c strongly	g absolutely
d distinctly	h seriously

Discuss the answers to both exercises with the whole group.

3 The Oscar ceremony

This is obviously a 'take-off' of the gushing type of language used by film stars at Oscar ceremonies. Check that all your class are familiar with what an Oscar ceremony is.

1 Explain that the short text is the speech of a film star accepting an Oscar. Ask them to look quickly through it and tell what is strange about it. (It is not in the normal extreme and exaggerated language used by film stars.) Ask them to work in pairs or small groups to make it sound like a real film star by replacing the words underlined.

2 **T 8.5** Ask them to listen to the sample answer and compare their choice of adjectives and adverbs.

Possible answers

quite pleased – absolutely delighted/thrilled
very grateful – sincerely/extremely/deeply grateful
nice – wonderful
interesting – fascinating/thrilling
clever – brilliant
very good – absolutely fantastic/marvellous/wonderful
really – possibly
big – huge/enormous/gigantic/mega
silly – ridiculous/stupid
very wrong – quite/totally wrong
good – marvellous/excellent/wonderful
beautiful – gorgeous/fabulous
funny – hilarious
exciting – thrilling/nail-biting
really – absolutely

ADDITIONAL MATERIAL

Workbook Unit 8
Exercise 11 Words that go together

● LISTENING AND WRITING (SB p85)

The greatest superstar of all!

NB *You might think that a musical about Jesus Christ is a delicate subject for a listening text because it may involve controversial discussion about religion. This could be the case in some teaching situations; only you can be the judge of this. However, one of our main reasons for using it is precisely because it does provide an opportunity to talk about religion, but in a way which we hope is not likely to cause offence.*

Pre-listening task

1 Ask your students to look at the posters and ask if they have heard of any of them and if they know who wrote them. If they don't recognize them, ask them just to comment on what they can see in the posters and learn about the musical shows.

2 **T 8.6** Play the brief musical extracts. Ask your students if they recognize the songs and if they know which musicals they come from.

Answers

'Jesus Christ' from *Jesus Christ Superstar*,
'Don't cry for me, Argentina' from *Evita*.

3 These words from the interviews may be unknown to your students. Ask them to work out the meaning from the context, a dictionary should not be necessary. They could do this in pairs.

Answers

a **a smash hit** = an extremely successful and popular film, play, or song.
b **intrigued** = very interested indeed.
c **hammered** = to criticize something very strongly indeed.
d **taboo subject** = not allowed to be discussed by general agreement of society. (You could use this opportunity to point out that 'religion' in some cultures or in some families can be a taboo subject.)
You could use these sentences to help your students to predict some of the content of the interviews.

Listening

Part one – The writer

Tell your class that they are going to listen to an interview with Tim Rice, a famous British writer and lyricist.

Introduce the interview with some information from Tim Rice's biographical information below. (You could give them a photocopy of it.)

BIOGRAPHICAL INFORMATION

Tim Rice (b. 1944)
Tim Rice is a very successful English writer of musical drama. While still a student he began working with **Andrew Lloyd Webber** on musical productions, writing the lyrics to Lloyd Webber's music. Their first successful musical was *Joseph and the Amazing Technicolour Dreamcoat* in 1968. This was followed by the 'rock opera' *Jesus Christ Superstar* in 1971. This was an extremely popular though controversial work which blended classical and rock music to tell the story of Jesus' life. The show ran longer than any other musical in the history of the British theatre. It was revived in London in the 1990s. The last collaboration between Tim Rice and Andrew Lloyd Webber was *Evita* in 1978. This was a musical about the life of Eva Perón, the wife of the Argentine president Juan Perón. In 1996 it was made into a film starring Madonna, the American singer and film star.

1 Ask your students to work in pairs or small groups to discuss these questions before playing the tape.

NB *These questions are all answered by Tim Rice in the tape. Your students can compare their answers to those of Tim Rice himself.*

Possible student answers

a All manner of events and characters could be mentioned. You do not want lengthy discussion, just a few facts. (Make sure that the crucifixion and Judas Iscariot are mentioned because they are relevant to the tape.)

- b Perhaps your students will suggest that Tim and Andrew are religious and therefore chose to write about Jesus, or perhaps they wanted to create controversy.
- c The choice of superstar will to some extent depend on the nationality of the students and also on topicality – today's superstar may be tomorrow's unknown. More internationally they may suggest such names as Elvis Presley, Marilyn Monroe, or even Princess Diana, especially since her death. They perhaps called Jesus Christ a superstar because he is so internationally famous.
- d Probably because they were Christians and felt that it was insulting and offensive to make the story of Christ into a rock musical.

2 **T 8.7** Play the interview with Tim Rice. Your students should be able to follow it, but if you feel they may have problems you could put the following words on the board and check them together before they listen.

POSSIBLE VOCABULARY PROBLEMS

a straight play = a play without music
to place emphasis on = to give importance to
chapel = a small church
to betray
to draft out a story = to write the outline, perhaps just the plot and main characters.
blasphemous
congregation
to christen

Tim Rice's answers

- a He says that Judas Iscariot is central to the whole story of Jesus Christ. He says Judas betrayed Jesus.
- b He says it is an obvious subject because so many people have written stories about Jesus. He also says that he learned a lot about religion at school, and he was intrigued/fascinated by the character of Judas. He had wanted to write about him but then he realized that Jesus was the most important character.
- c They called Jesus Christ a 'superstar' because he was *the* most important character and the syllables of the word fitted the music – *Jesus Christ*: dum dum dum, and *Superstar* also: dum dum dum.
- d He doesn't answer this question directly. The interviewer suggests that some people found it blasphemous. Tim says that he and Andrew didn't consider the reaction to it when they wrote it because they didn't think it would be such a worldwide success. The churchmen that surprised him most were those who didn't protest but used it to help their congregations.

3 Ask students to do these in pairs.

Answers

- a *False.* There have been lots of versions: serious music, plays, movies, and pop or rock music.
- b *True.*
- c *False.* They thought other people had hits, not them.
- d *True.* It was an overnight success.
- e *False.* He didn't see a baby being christened **with** the name of Jesus Christ Superstar. He saw a baby being christened **in** the name of Jesus Christ Superstar.
  (*I baptize you in the name of the Father, and of the Son, and of the Holy Spirit.*)

Part two – The actor

NB *Paul Nicholas is a well-known actor of stage, screen, and television in the UK.*

1 Tell the class that they will now hear the actor who first played the part of Jesus Christ Superstar. Ask: *What problems do you think he had with the role? Do you think it was an easy role? Why not?* You just need to have a few minutes of class discussion on this.

Sample ideas

Not easy to play the part of the Son of God.
People might not think he looked like their idea of Jesus.
They might think he was insulting God.
Perhaps he didn't feel 'good' enough for such a part.
Being on the cross.

2 **T 8.8** Play the tape and ask the students to discuss their answers to the questions in pairs. Your students should be able to follow the interview, but if you feel they may have problems you could put the following words on the board and check them together before they listen.

POSSIBLE VOCABULARY PROBLEMS

risky = dangerous
to do it (the part) justice = to be good enough for such a special part.
moving = causing feelings of deep emotion and sadness
crucifixion
to be overcome = to be strongly affected
vulnerability = feeling of being weak
to crack a joke = to tell a joke
slim = quite thin

Answers

a He thinks it was successful because it was a taboo subject. This made it more interesting for many people. It appealed to the young because of this.
b He found it strange because Jesus is such a recognizable figure, who is important to so many. Everybody knows about Jesus.
c He cried the first time he was on the cross because the music was so moving.
d His attitude changed after a few weeks, because with eight performances a week it became like a job. It was impossible to feel so moved each time.
e They laugh when Paul Nicholas tells the story of the man sneezing in the front row and he says 'God bless you my son.' (This is a typical saying of vicars; and we also say 'bless you' when somebody sneezes.)
They also laugh at the end of the interview when Paul Nicholas says that if he played the part today he wouldn't look so slim on the cross. (We understand that he has put on weight.)
f The interviewer asks 'If you played the part now, how would you be different from twenty-five years ago?' Paul answers that he would do it the same but probably better because he understands it better now, and he would sing better, too. But he would look fatter on the cross.

Go through the answers with the class.

Writing

A letter from a fan

NB Zubin Varla is an actor and a singer who took the part of Judas Iscariot when 'Jesus Christ Superstar' was revived on the London stage in 1997. Although this letter is written to him about that show, this writing activity is self-standing. Stress to your students that the famous people they choose do not have to come from the world of entertainment. They can be sports people, writers, politicians, etc.

1 It can be a good idea to answer the questions about yourself as part of your lesson preparation, then get your students to ask you the questions as an introduction to the activity. Ask your students to work in small groups and discuss the questions. Get feedback from the whole class.

2 Tell the class about Zubin Varla (see above). Ask one or two members of the class to read aloud different parts of the letter. Then ask them to discuss in their groups what the aim of each paragraph is.

Answers

1 The writer of the letter introduces herself and gives the reason for writing.
2 She tells Zubin what she likes about him and the show generally.
3 She requests information (about a fan club) in a very polite way and gives a little information about herself.
4 She concludes the letter, thanking him again for his wonderful performance. She wishes him luck.

Ask the students for their feedback. Write the paragraph numbers on the board and ask for suggestions from the class to fill out the aims of each one. Tell the class to write it down because it will form the basis for a letter they will write.

Now ask students in their groups to discuss possible endings for the paragraphs. Write their suggestions on the board and compare them.

Sample answers

1 ... how wonderful you were as Judas Iscariot.
2 ... were also very good.
3 ... I have quite a good voice.
4 ... you could write back to me, but I understand if you are too busy.
5 ... we could come back stage to meet you.

You should also discuss ways of beginning and ending the letter.
Beginning with a first name is only suitable in this case because it is a young girl writing to an actor and pop star. Writing to people in other fields may well require a more formal approach: 'Dear Mr/Ms X'.
Ending with 'love' is only suitable because the writer is a sixteen-year-old girl. The ending will depend on the sex of the writer and who is being written to. It could be as formal as 'Yours sincerely' if the person being written to is addressed as Mr, Miss, Mrs, or Ms. It could be 'Yours' or 'Best wishes' if the writer is male or needs to be less familiar.

3 This could be set for homework. Then students could read and check each other's work in class in a later lesson. Be sure to allocate sufficient classroom time for going over homework and help your students towards the final production of a correct letter.

SUGGESTION

Students could leave the name blank, the student reading it could try to guess who the famous person is.

ADDITIONAL MATERIAL

Workbook Unit 8

Exercise 12 A word puzzle

This is a crossword puzzle which practises words connected with the 'rich and famous' in the world of entertainment.
The exercise is very suitable for in class. However, it can also successfully be set as homework.

PostScript (SB p87)

Exaggeration and understatement

1 This activity begins with a short discussion on the stereotypical behaviour of different nationalities. This is to establish the theme. Students are asked to discuss whose behaviour is more reserved and understated and whose is more passionate and exaggerated.

Typically they will suggest that nationalities such as the English, Japanese, and Germans are more reserved and those from Latin countries are more passionate and exaggerated. Ask your students particularly to describe their own nationality in this respect.

2 Make clear to your students that these quotations are old-fashioned, and would not be said today. Do the activity with the whole class.

Answers

Exaggerated
I worship the ground you walk on.
My heart aches to be near you.
My whole being yearns and burns for you. (yearns = *longs for*)

Understated
I quite like you, you know. D'you think you might get to like me?
You're a dear old thing, and I'm really rather fond of you. (*dear old thing* = familiar person who I like. *Old* does not necessarily mean old in years.)

3 NB *In this exercise there are all kinds of colloquial expressions, said by all kinds of people in different situations. Usually one of the speakers exaggerates the situation and the other is more understated. We will indicate which applies after the answer with an E or a U.*

Ask students to do this in pairs. Tell them that although they will have to consult a dictionary (preferably a monolingual one) because there are many idioms and colloquial expressions, they should often be able to work out the meaning from the context. This list is for your information. You could round off the lesson by putting it on the board for your class to copy.

IDIOMATIC AND COLLOQUIAL EXPRESSIONS

peckish = a bit hungry
to eat a horse = to eat a huge amount
dying for a drink = very thirsty indeed
loaded = very rich
to hit the roof = to get very angry
tipsy = a little drunk
as thick as two short planks = very unintelligent indeed
vile = absolutely awful
knackered = very tired/exhausted
huge great = absolutely huge
wouldn't hurt a fly = harmless

Answers

a (E) 13 (U)
b (E) 3 (U)
c (U) 11 (E)
d (E) 9 (U)
e (U) 4 (E)
f (E) 12 (U)
g (U) 2 (E)
h (E) 6 (U)
i (E) 1 (U)
j (E) 8 (U)
k (U) 7 (E)
l (E) 10 (U)
m (E) 5 (E) Careful – this answer is exaggerated but in opposition.

4 **T 8.9** Ask students to listen and check. Ask them to give you examples of both understated and exaggerated sentences. Ask them to practise the dialogues in pairs.

NB *Some of the more colloquial expressions sound rather strange coming out of the mouths of foreign speakers unless they are truly fluent and have excellent pronunciation. Warn your students of this. However, when practising the dialogues, not only can they have fun, but their stress and intonation can benefit from trying to exaggerate their speech.*

Don't forget!

Workbook Unit 8

Exercise 13 Prepositions – verbs + preposition

Exercise 14 Pronunciation – Consonant clusters and connected speech

Nothing but the truth

Questions and negatives
Being polite

Introduction to the unit

The title of this unit refers to the oath taken by witnesses in a court of law. They promise to tell '... the truth, the whole truth, and nothing but the truth.'

The grammatical focus of the unit is on the broad areas of question formation and making sentences negative. In the Practice section there is a short general knowledge quiz. The reading text is about *Mysteries of the universe*, from a popular science magazine. The listening is a radio programme about people who changed their minds about getting married at the last minute. The PostScript deals with being polite and telling 'white lies'.

In the Workbook there is a text about Buzz Aldrin, the second man on the moon. The extra input is on the hot verbs *keep* and *lose*, and an exercise on phrasal verbs with common noun collocations.

Notes on the unit

LANGUAGE AIMS – QUESTIONS AND NEGATIVES

NB See the Grammar Reference section – SB p157.

Questions

Question formation is always a problem for learners of English. There are several reasons for this.

- Students must remember to invert the subject and the verb, and use the correct auxiliary verb.
- The subject of the sentence must always follow the auxiliary verb, no matter how long it is.
  How many times has the European section of your company won an award?
  Students often want to say *~~How many times has won an award the European section~~ ...?
- Students don't differentiate between the two questions *What ... like?* and *How ...?* and overuse the question with *How ...?*
  *~~How's your flat?~~ *~~How's your city?~~
- Having learned that questions always require an auxiliary verb, students encounter subject questions.
  *Who **wants** an ice-cream?*
  *What **happened** at the party?*
- Students are reluctant to end a question with a preposition.
  *Who are you waiting **for**?*
  *Who did you give the letter **to**?*
- It is unlikely that your students are using negative questions appropriately and accurately. They are quite difficult to form and to pronounce.
  They have two quite distinct uses. The main use expresses the speaker's surprise about a negative situation.
  *'**Haven't** you **got** a computer?' '**No**, I haven't.'*
  ***Can't** you **swim**? I thought everyone could swim!*
  The other use means *Confirm what I think is true.* In this use, it refers to a positive situation.
  *'**Weren't** we at school together?' 'Yes, we were.'*
  In some languages, especially Far Eastern languages, the answer to negative questions is the opposite to English.
  A Can't you swim?
  B *~~Yes.~~ (You're right.) I can't swim.
  They answer the truth value of the question and not the reality of the situation.

Negatives

Making sentences negative doesn't usually present such a problem for upper-intermediate students. This unit concentrates on how other parts of the sentence can be made negative, not just the main verb.
*I told you **not to do** it.* = negative infinitive
*There are **no** onions left.*
*'Who likes grammar?' '**Not** me.'*
There is also practice of transferred negation. In English we usually say *I don't think* + affirmative verb rather than *I think* + negative verb. Other verbs like this are *believe*, *suppose*, and *expect*.
***I don't think** you're right.*
***I don't suppose** you know the answer.*

Test your grammar (SB p88)

NB Remember to keep this brief. Avoid teaching everything through the Test your grammar section.

1 Students work in pairs to make the sentences negative. The aim is to show students that negatives work in a variety of ways.

- We can use a prefix as in *disagree*.
- When there are two verbs as in *I think you're right*, we make the first one negative.
- Infinitives can be negative, as in *I told her not to go home*.
- A sentence with *had* is included to remind students that in the past the negative (and the question) is formed with *did*.
- *Must* has **three** negative forms. (These should be revision for students.)
  1 *Mustn't* = a negative obligation. It is important not to do something.
  You mustn't smoke in here.
  2 *Don't have to* = an absence of obligation. It isn't necessary to do something.
  You don't have to wear a tie.
  3 *Can't* = the negative of *must* probability.
  She must be his sister, she can't be his wife.

Answers

a I disagree/don't agree with you.
b I don't think you're right. I think you're wrong.
c I didn't tell her to go home. I told her not to go home. (*NB: two different meanings*)
d We didn't have lunch at 12.00.
e I haven't done my homework yet.
f You mustn't get a visa. You don't have to get a visa.
g The postman never has anything for me.
h (Who wants an ice-cream?) Not me.

2 Students complete the questions. You could do this as a class to save time and get on with the next section.

Sample answers

There might be some variations.
a What sort/kind of music do you like? (*what* + noun)
b How often do you go to the cinema? (*how* + adverb)
c What's she like? (*What does she look like?* is not possible, because of the character description in *She's very nice.*)
d Who discovered America? (Subject question)
e What did you talk about? (Question with preposition at the end)

LANGUAGE IN CONTEXT (SB p88)

Questions and negatives

1 Discuss this question as a class, to launch the topic of lies.

Sample answers

A young boy might tell his mother that it wasn't him who stole the cake, it was his baby sister.
A salesman might say that a car has only done 20,000 miles, but in fact it has done 100,000 miles.
A politician might say that he would never accept a bribe, never do anything illegal or immoral.
A student might tell the teacher that he did his homework, but his dog ate it.
An estate agent might say that a house is in good condition, whereas in fact it is falling down.

2 In pairs, students look at the cartoons and discuss what the people are lying about.
Have some feedback as a class.

T 9.1 Students listen to the truth and compare it with their own ideas.

3 Students match a question to a cartoon, and put a number 1–7 in the right box.

Answers

a 7 b 6 c 1 d 4 e 2 f 3 g 5

Grammar questions

Answer the Grammar questions as a class.

Answers

Questions without auxiliary verbs
– *Who wants to speak to me?*
– *What happened last night?*

An indirect question
– *I wonder why she doesn't like him.*

Questions with a preposition at the end
– *Who's she going out with?*
– *What did she buy it for?*
– *What's his room-mate like?*

A question that asks for a general description of someone
– *What's his room-mate like?*

A question that asks about someone's health
– *How is he really?*

Another way of asking *Why?*
– *What … for?*

You might want students to read the Language Review on p91 before starting the Practice exercises.

PRACTICE BANK (SB p89)

1 General knowledge quiz

NB You need to photocopy the quiz (TB p142). There is one copy of the quiz for Student A and one for Student B.

1 Students work in pairs to do the quiz. Read the instructions and the example as a class.
Give out the quizzes. Tell them they have ten questions to ask and ten to answer.
Go round the pairs checking that the questions are well-formed.

POSSIBLE PROBLEMS

- Bram Stoker wrote the fictional horror stories of *Dracula* in 1897. Count Dracula is a vampire who lives in a castle in Transylvania.
- William Tell is a legendary hero of the Swiss struggle for independence from the Austrian Hapsburgs.
- *Spark off* means *to be the cause of trouble or violence.*

Answers

1 a Who wrote the stories of *Dracula*? Bram Stoker.
  b Which country are they set in? Transylvania.
2 a Which ceiling was painted by Michelangelo? The ceiling of the Sistine Chapel in Rome.
  b What do the frescoes depict? *The Last Judgment.*
3 a Whose son had an apple shot off his head by his father? William Tell.
  b What did he shoot it off with? A crossbow and arrow.
4 a Why was the Eiffel Tower built? To celebrate the Centennial Exposition.
  b How high is it? 300 metres.
5 a What did Einstein write to President Roosevelt for? To warn him that an atomic bomb could soon be built.
  b What did Einstein campaign for? Nuclear disarmament.
6 a How long was Nelson Mandela sent to prison for? 28 years.
  b Who released him? President de Klerk.
7 a Which countries developed Concorde? France and Britain.
  b How fast does it travel? 2,179 km an hour. Twice the speed of sound.
8 a Which war was sparked off by an incident in Sarajevo? World War I.
  b What happened to Archduke Ferdinand? He was assassinated.
9 a Whose statue stands on a mountain overlooking Rio de Janeiro? The statue of Christ the Redeemer.
  b Which mountain is it situated on? Mount Corcovado.
10 a Which plants produce opium? Poppies.
  b What has it been used for for centuries? For the relief of pain.

When students have finished, it might be worth checking the questions quickly as a class.

2 Students make some comments about the answers in the quiz. If students don't produce much, move on!

2 Short questions

1 Read the explanation and example as a class. This area seems quite easy, but it can take students a while to work out which preposition to use.
Do the first few questions as a class, then ask students to do the rest in pairs.

Answers

a Who to?
b What about?
c Who with?
d What for?
e What about?
f Who from?
g Who for?
h What about?
i Where to?
j What with?

2 Again, this exercise presents students with more problems than you might anticipate. This is probably because there seem to be prepositions everywhere!
Do the first few as a class, than ask students to do the rest in pairs.

Answers

a Who did she give all her money away to?
b What do you want to have a word with me about?
c Who did you dance with?
d What do you need £5,000 for?
e What's he writing a book about?
f Who did you get a present from?
g Who did you buy a birthday card for?
h What are you thinking about?
i Where do you want me to give you a lift to?
j What do you want me to clean the sink with?

T 9.2 Students listen and check their answers. You could use the taped sentences as models for some pronunciation practice.

3 *Vegetarians don't eat meat*

1 **T 9.3** Read the instructions as a class.

POSSIBLE VOCABULARY PROBLEMS

Check students understand the following words.
insomniac
dyslexic = describes someone who has difficulty reading and writing because they confuse letters.

atheist *teetotal* *anti-social*
basement flat *caffeine*
drive = the area between a house and the road, sometimes with a space to park a car.
barking *hangover*
overslept *crosswords*
mate = familiar word for a friend

Students read and listen at the same time. The story is the basis of a joke, which students in all likelihood won't understand. This is probably because they won't be expecting a joke of this nature. You'll have to explain it, and nothing kills a joke more!
Ask: *Why did he say KO? What did he mean?* (OK.)
Ask students to look at the last four lines again. *What can't an insomniac do? What does a dyslexic person do? What doesn't an atheist believe in? So why does he lie awake wondering about the existence of dog?* (God)
Maybe students will see the joke and laugh, and maybe they won't. If they don't get it, move on!

Read the first paragraph again as a class, then the beginning of the second paragraph, when the contradictions start to emerge. Pause after *I walked up the drive*. Hopefully someone will say *He hasn't got a drive. He lives in a basement flat.*
Read the next bit: *his dog started barking*. Someone should say *But he hasn't got a dog. He lives alone.*
Similarly read the next bit: *His wife answered the door* and get from students *But he isn't married. He's single*.

By now students should have the idea. They can work in pairs to finish finding all the contradictions.

Sample answers

He hasn't got a drive. He lives in a basement flat.
He hasn't got a dog. He lives alone.
He isn't married. He's single.
You don't go upstairs to a living room. The living room is usually downstairs. He lives in a flat, not a house.
He's an atheist, so he doesn't believe in God. Why did he go to church?
If he's teetotal he doesn't drink alcohol, so how has he got a hangover?
He doesn't touch caffeine, so why is he having a coffee?
If he's anti-social, it means he doesn't like being with other people, but he'd had a party the night before.
He's a vegetarian, so he doesn't eat meat. Why was he eating a hot dog?
He's dyslexic, so he gets letters confused. How can he do crosswords?
He's unemployed, so he can't have a lunch break at work.

2 You could do this activity as a class, so that it doesn't take up too much time.

Answers

Agnostics aren't sure whether God exists or not.
Vegans don't eat any animal products.
Claustrophobics don't like being in enclosed spaces.
Agoraphobics don't like being in open spaces.
Workaholics can't stop working.
Animal rights campaigners don't want animals to be exploited in any way.
Traditionalists don't like change.

4 ***Who is it?***

This activity is best as a short warmer. Make it fun, not heavy! You could set it up by describing yourself using negative sentences only. This way, you could get across the idea that the activity should be fun.

5 Negative questions

NB *See the section LANGUAGE AIMS at the beginning of this unit of the Teacher's Book for some of the problems students have with negative questions.*

1 **T 9.4** Students read and listen to the questions a–f, answer the three questions in pairs first, then as a class.

Answers

Questions b, d, and f express the attitude of the speaker. The others are normal, 'unspecial' questions. (The grammatical word for this is *unmarked*.)
The speaker is expressing surprise.
In questions d and f, *Yes* means *You are wrong. I* ***have*** *done it/I* ***can*** *swim.*

2 **T 9.5** Students listen to the questions. Stop the tape after each one and drill the sentences around the class, correcting intonation and pronunciation mistakes carefully.

3 In pairs, students ask and answer negative questions, using the prompts. Do a few as a class first, so students see what they have to do. Make sure their intonation is wide, so that they sound surprised!

Answers

Haven't you got a dictionary/a boyfriend/a girlfriend/a computer at home?
Don't you like pizza/learning English/parties?
Haven't you ever been to a disco/abroad?
Didn't you come to school yesterday/have anything to eat yesterday?
Can't you cook/dance/play the piano?

ADDITIONAL MATERIAL

Workbook Unit 9
Exercises 1–3 Negatives
Exercise 4 *I don't think you're right*
Exercises 5 and 6 Questions
Exercise 7 Questions and prepositions
Exercise 8 *How … ?* and *What … like?*
Exercise 9 Negative questions

LANGUAGE REVIEW (SB p91)

Questions and negatives

Read the Language Review as a class, and/or ask students to read it at home. Students read the Grammar Reference at home. Encourage them to study this carefully whilst doing the exercises in the Workbook.

● READING (SB p91)

Mysteries of the universe

Pre-reading task

SUGGESTION

Write on the board the question *Why are we here?* Ask students for their comments. Their answers might be humorous, religious, or non-existent!

Do the Pre-reading task as a group activity. There isn't supposed to be any prescribed reaction from students, other than maybe a smile, or a cry of 'Yes! I've always wondered that!' Maybe students will want to propose answers to some of these questions.

Students look at the ten paragraph headings in the text on p92–3 and say which of the topics they think will be discussed.

Sample answers

Why are we here? probably won't be answered.
Why are people different? might be answered in paragraph 5.
When I lose things, where do they go? might be answered in paragraph 10.
Is the person sitting next to me a time traveller? might be discussed in paragraph 8.
Why did the dinosaurs disappear? probably won't be answered.
Is there life on another planet? is discussed in paragraph 1.
How did the world begin, and how will it end? is discussed in paragraph 9, and possibly in paragraph 4 as well.
What do animals think about? probably won't be answered.
Will we ever find a cure for all disease? might be mentioned in paragraph 3.

Reading

POSSIBLE VOCABULARY PROBLEMS

This list is for your information only. You might decide to focus on these words at some stage of the lesson, and/or students might ask about them. See the extra vocabulary photocopiable activity on p143.

plagued = caused problems and worries
alien life forms *light-years*
sustaining *minute* /maɪ'nju:t/
long shot (last sentence from paragraph 1, in Exercise 2) = an attempt that is not very likely to succeed, but it is still worth trying

condensed	*fundamental*
comets	*genetics*
chunks	*blueprints*
to rid	*inherited*
combat	*recuperation*
viruses	*deprivation*
guaranteed	*hallucinations*
expanding	*infectious*
matter	*tough (problem)* = difficult
fatigue	*barrier*
trigger off	*critical density*
heart rate	*gravity*
alert	*alternatively*
zooming off	*consensus*
paradoxes	*odd (socks)* = socks that don't match
range	
black holes	*lurks*

1 Students read the texts and answer the questions. Allow adequate time for this. When there is silence in the classroom, language teachers can become unnerved. We are trained to engender noise. Monitor students carefully to see who's finished reading, who's answering the questions, and who's got their nose in a dictionary.

When students have finished reading and have had a few minutes to think about the questions, ask them to work in pairs and compare answers. Then have some class feedback.

Answers

a Because the universe is so big.
Definitely not.
b Frozen vapour, dust, and water.
c Because there are so many cold viruses, and they keep changing.

d Matter, space, and time.
No one knows. Maybe there was nothing.

e Because being left-handed runs in families.
Identical twins aren't necessarily both left-handed or right-handed.

f They recover from the stresses of the day.

g When we're tired, bored, or anxious.
Our mouth opens wide, and we take in a long, deep breath. This raises the heart rate, and forces more blood to the brain.

h There is nothing to stop us.
They worry about paradoxes such as going back in time and stopping something happening.

i It will contract and implode billions of years from now. Alternatively, it might expand forever.

j They disappear down black holes; they are eaten by washing machines; there is a place in every house where all the missing things live.

2 Read the instructions as a class, and do the first one together, as it is quite easy. Then ask students to do the rest in pairs. Encourage students to say *why* they think the sentence goes with a particular paragraph.

Answers

a 3 b 7 c 8 d 5 e 6 f 1 g 4

3 You might decide to discuss these questions as a class.

Answers

There is a planet capable of sustaining life just **50** light-years away.
The chance that alien life will resemble us is **zero**.
There are **1.4 billion billion** tonnes of water in the sea.
In **1929** astronomers discovered that the universe was expanding.
At the time, it was thought that the universe was **a few billion** years old.
Now, we think the universe is between **9 and 12 billion** years old.
10 per cent of the population is left-handed.
We spend **a third** of our lives sleeping.
Billions of years from now the universe might start to implode.
After **decades** of research, astronomers still don't know how much matter there is in the universe.

What do you think?

Maybe your students want to talk sincerely about other aspects of life that they find mysterious. Or maybe after quite a serious text, they just want a bit of fun.

SUGGESTION

There is a vocabulary exercise you could do after the *What do you think?* on p143 of the Teacher's Book.

● VOCABULARY (SB p94)

Making connections in texts

NB This is one of several exercises that works on textual cohesion. Other units are 6 and 12.

SUGGESTION

Before you start, ask students if they know other words for the following adjectives.

big small rich beautiful

Answers

huge, enormous, vast tiny, minute
wealthy, well off gorgeous, lovely

Do they know the opposite of these words?

useful crowded popular success

Answers

useless deserted unpopular failure

1 Read the introduction as a class. Students identify the antonyms and synonyms in the sentences.

Answers

beginning and **end** – antonyms
expansion and **contraction** – antonyms
precisely and **accurately** – synonyms

2 Do the first few words together as a class, then ask students to do the rest in pairs.

Answers

huge	tiny, minute
happiness	unhappiness, misery
guilty	innocent
criticize	praise
reward	punish
cruelty	kindness
dangerous	safe
succeed	fail
genuine	false, fake
improve	deteriorate, get worse
admit	deny
permanent	temporary
profit	loss
brave	cowardly
attack	defend
crazy	sane

3 Do the first of these together, so students get the idea that the same adjective can have more than one opposite.

Answers

a tough question	an easy question
tough meat	tender meat
fair hair	dark hair
a fair decision	an unfair decision
rich food	plain food
a rich person	a poor person
a sweet apple	a bitter/sour apple
sweet wine	dry wine
a strong man	a weak man
a strong taste	a mild taste
a hard exam	an easy exam
a hard mattress	a soft mattress
clear instructions	unclear/vague/ambiguous instructions
a clear sky	a cloudy/overcast sky
a free man	an imprisoned man/a prisoner
a free seat	an occupied seat

4 Read the introduction as a class. This fact is probably true of all languages. You could translate the two sentences if you have a monolingual class.

5 Do the first few sentences together, so students see what they have to do. Then ask students to finish the exercise in pairs. This is quite a difficult exercise, so be prepared to help and nudge.

Answers

a successful	failed
b good fun	a disaster
c improvements	has got worse
d casualties	survived
e mystery	solved
f dangerous	safe
g critical	encouragement

6 Read the dialogues and answer the question as a class.

Answer

It sounds more tactful and less brutally honest to say *not very* + positive adjective.

In pairs, students write similar dialogues.

SUGGESTION

On a piece of paper, write A's lines only from the following sample answers and ask students to complete B's responses. This might trigger their imagination.

Sample answers

A What a terrible dinner party! Who were those dreadfully boring people?
B *Paul and Marilyn. They weren't very interesting, were they?*
A And the food was disgusting.
B *True. It wasn't exactly tasty, was it?*
A I thought it was never going to end.
B *Yes. It did drag slightly.*

A Thank goodness we're home at last. What a disastrous holiday!
B *It wasn't the most relaxing holiday we've ever had.*
A True, and the sun never shone.
B *No, it wasn't very warm.*
A And the locals were all thieves.
B *Mmm. It was difficult to trust them, I agree.*

A That meeting was a complete waste of time.
B *We didn't achieve very much, did we?*
A It started late.
B *Mm. The director wasn't quite on time, it's true.*
A And Charles made a mess of his presentation.
B *Yes, he wasn't terribly organized. Never mind.*

A That was the worst hotel I've ever stayed in.
B *It wasn't very comfortable, was it?*
A The waiters were rude.
B *Yes, they weren't always very kind or helpful.*
A And the manager's an idiot. The bill was all wrong.
B *No, he wasn't very good at maths, it's true.*

A Our team were absolute rubbish today.
B *No, we didn't play well at all, did we?*
A The goalkeeper was asleep.
B *He didn't have a good match today, did he?*
A And the ref was blind.
B *There were one or two things he missed, it's true.*

A That was impossible. I couldn't do any of it.
B *Yes, it was a bit tricky, wasn't it?*
A Did you understand question 2?
B *It wasn't very clear, I agree.*
A My hand is killing me after all that writing.
B *Yes, mine's a little painful as well.*

ADDITIONAL MATERIAL

Workbook Unit 9
Exercise 10 Antonyms and synonyms

● LISTENING AND SPEAKING (SB p95)

Saying 'I won't'

1 Students work in pairs or small groups to discuss question 1.

2 Students write a list, first alone, then with a partner.

Sample answer

First, find someone who wants to marry you!
Tell your parents, meet your future in-laws.
Choose bridesmaids and best man.
Book a church and somewhere for the reception.
Invite family and friends.
Get a dress/a suit.

Order flowers for bouquet and church.
Book a photographer.
Decide on a menu.
Book a honeymoon.
Decide where you're going to live.

On the actual day, the bride and groom have to get dressed carefully, so that they look their best. The bride needs to have flowers. Everyone needs to get to the church on time, and be sitting in the right place for when the bride arrives with her father.

3 Answer this question as a class. Encourage students to say what they can see in the cartoons. What do they think has happened at the weddings?
Obviously, students are guessing about what might have happened at the weddings, as they have no way of knowing for sure.

Listening

POSSIBLE PROBLEMS

This list is for your information. Students might ask if there is something they're not sure of.

There is a song *Waiting at the church* played at intervals during the radio programme. It is a well-known music hall song from the beginning of the century. It is repeated in tapescript 9.7, if you want to play it to your students.

There are some words in the song your class might not know.
left me in the lurch = abandoned me at a time when I needed help
Lor = short for Lord

Possible problems from the interviews:
iced = cakes are covered in a mixture made from sugar and water, called icing.
it's all off = the wedding is cancelled
wedding gear = wedding clothes
stationery = invitations
pluck up courage = force yourself to be brave
distraught = very, very upset
fancy dress party = a party where everyone dresses up in unusual or amusing clothes
the brides of Frankenstein = 'Frankenstein' is a horror story written in 1818 by Mary Shelley. Frankenstein creates a monster with supernatural strength, but it is terribly ugly, so it wants Frankenstein to make a bride for it.
the best man = the bridegroom's helper at a wedding
smashing = very good, brilliant, very enjoyable
Nicole is American. Manhattan is in New York.
aisle = long passage, down the middle of a church
I will survive = a pop song in which a woman who is let down by a man vows to carry on, despite being badly treated

1 **T 9.6** Students read and listen to the introduction to the radio programme.

2 Students look at the cartoons. These illustrate what actually brought the wedding to a stop. Encourage students to give their opinions.

3 Play the rest of the programme. Answer the questions as a class.

Answers

Elizabeth and her sister are at a fancy dress party, wearing their wedding clothes.
George and Vicky are having a picnic on the day they were going to get married.
Nicole is having a non-wedding reception. She's drunk, and singing *I will survive*.

1 This is Michael's note to Nicole, which she received in the church.
2 Elizabeth is panicking as the pressure builds up. She can't cope, and everything costs so much.
3 Vicky is having a panic attack as she and George are at the church having a rehearsal.

Comprehension check

Students work in pairs to answer the questions.

Answers

1 Elizabeth was going to get married to Paul.
George was going to get married to Vicky.
Nicole was going to get married to Michael.
2 Elizabeth didn't get married because she suddenly realized that she didn't love Paul any more. He was more like a brother.
George didn't get married because Vicky panicked while they were having a rehearsal and realized she couldn't face the idea of the wedding.
Nicole didn't get married because Michael changed his mind at the last minute and didn't turn up at the church.
3 Elizabeth did.
Vicky did. (But it was George who told the minister to postpone the wedding.)
Michael did.
4 **Elizabeth**
Everyone had bought their wedding clothes.
Everyone said how good her wedding dress looked.
She felt all the pressure on her to keep everyone happy.
She tried to explain the situation to her mother.
Her mother said that she'd also felt nervous before marrying her father.
Her sister was the most distraught, because she'd

been looking forward to being a bridesmaid.
Her family were very understanding.

George
The best man and the bridesmaids were at the rehearsal.
The minister was in the church with them.

Nicole
A man ran out of the church and gave Nicole a message from Michael.
All the people in the church had a party even though the wedding didn't take place.
Both their parents are Greek.

5 a Elizabeth. She realized she didn't love Paul as a lover, but a brother.
b Nicole. This is how she learned that Michael was not coming.
c George. He's referring to the picnic he had with Vicky on the day they were going to get married.
d Elizabeth's mother. She was trying to reassure Elizabeth.
e George. This was when Vicky realized she couldn't go through with the wedding.
f Elizabeth. This is how she felt after she told Paul that she couldn't go through with the wedding.
g Nicole. She danced non-stop at her non-wedding reception.
h Vicky. She couldn't go ahead with the wedding.
i Nicole. They were both Greek.

6 In groups of three, students retell the stories from different people's points of view.

The song

T 9.7 This is an optional extra. Do it to round off the lesson if you have time.

● WRITING (SB p96)

Joining sentences

NB This exercise deals with conjunctions and comment adverbs. These adverbs are also dealt with in the PostScript of Unit 12.
You will need to photocopy the exercise on conjunctions (TB p143).

SUGGESTION

Write these sentences on the board.
As I was having a bath, I listened to the radio.
As I didn't have to go to work, I stayed in bed till 10.

Since I arrived this morning, I haven't stopped working.
Since I haven't got her address, I can't write to her.

Ask students if *as* mean the same in both sentences. Does *since* mean the same in both sentences?

Students will probably be familiar with *as* and *since* as conjunctions to refer to time, but not to reason.

Answers

In the first sentence in each pair, the conjunction refers to time.
In the second, it refers to reason.

POSSIBLE PROBLEMS

- *As* and *since* are used when the reason is already known, or when it is not the most important part of the sentence.
  ***As** you know, it's my birthday next week.*
  ***Since** it's nearly 10.00, I think we should begin the meeting.*

  As and *since* often come at the beginning of a sentence.
- *Because* makes the reason more important, and often comes at the end of a sentence. The reason is the strong part of the sentence.
  *We can't play tennis **because it's raining**.*
- It can be difficult sometimes to differentiate between *so* to express a reason and *so that* to express purpose. This is made more difficult by the fact that we can drop the word *that* in the purpose clause.
  *I was tired, **so** I went to bed.* (= so that is why)
  *I'm learning Japanese **so (that)** I can talk to our Japanese customers.* (= in order to be able to)
- *In case* means *as a way of being safe from something that might happen.*

1 Read the introduction as a class. Look at the list of conjunctions. Be prepared to write some illustrative sentences on the board for the conjunctions your students might not be familiar with. Give out the photocopies. Students work in pairs or small groups.

Answers

TIME
a I didn't know what love was until I met you.
b Whenever I hear this song, I think of my first boyfriend.
c When she saw what the hairdresser had done to her hair, she burst out crying.
d Joe, come home as soon as you can. We've been burgled!
e While I was having breakfast, the phone rang.
f I've made a lot of friends since I started at this school.
g After we'd eaten, we did the washing-up.
h I didn't like George at first, but as time passed I grew to love him more and more.

REASON
i I didn't have any money, so I went to the bank.
j I'm tired because I didn't sleep well last night.
k As you all know, I'm retiring next year.
l I looked round for a chair, but since there wasn't one, I sat on the floor.

RESULT
m I was so tired that I fell asleep in front of the television.
n We had such a big meal at lunchtime that I didn't want anything in the evening.

PURPOSE
o I'll give you my key, so that you can let yourself in whenever you want.
p Take your umbrella in case it rains.

CONDITION
q If I'm going to be late, I'll give you a ring.
r As long as I know where my children are, I don't worry about them.
s You'll fail your exam unless you do some work.

CONTRAST
t I tried to carry the bag, but I wasn't strong enough.
u The two boys like each other, even though they're always fighting and hitting each other.
v Although I can understand French, I can't speak it.

2 Read the information about adverbs that express the speaker's attitude. These are known as comment adverbs.

3 This exercise is best set for homework. In class, ask students to work in pairs or groups of three to check. This is quite a tricky exercise, so be prepared for students to have problems that need sorting out.

NB *This exercise tests one or two other items besides conjunctions and comment adverbs.*

- *Except* is usually a preposition followed by a noun; *when it's raining* is a noun phrase.
- *As if* is found after verbs such as *look*, *sound*, *feel*. It means the same as *as though*.
  You look ***as if*** *you've had some bad news.*
  It sounds ***as if*** *the party was a success.*
- Purpose can also be expressed by the infinitive.
  I'm learning English to get a better job.
- *Still* and *always* are adverbs that students sometimes confuse.
- *By the time* is another conjunction of time.

Answers

It happened at about 6.00 yesterday evening, (a) while I was coming home from work.
(b) Whenever I can, I walk to work (c) except when it's raining, (d) because I like the exercise. (e) Anyway, I was coming down Station Road, and (f) just as I was walking past number 38, I heard a noise. It was (g) such a loud noise that I stopped. It sounded (h) as if a chest of drawers had been knocked over. I know that a lot of old people live alone on this street, so (i) naturally I was a little concerned. (j) At first I didn't know what to do. I went up to the front door and listened (k) to see if I could hear anything. (l) In fact the front door was ajar, (m) so I pushed the door and went in. It was (n) so dark that I couldn't see anything, (o) but my eyes soon got used to it.
I went into the dining room, and there on the floor was the body of an old man. He had been attacked. (p) As soon as I saw him, I was scared (q) in case the burglar was (r) still in the house. I knelt down to feel his pulse. (s) Although he had been badly beaten up, he was still alive, (t) fortunately. I went to look for a damp cloth (u) so that I could bathe his wounds, then found his phone and dialled 999. I stayed with him (v) until the ambulance arrived, and (w) by the time the police came, he had woken up and was talking about the attack. (x) Apparently, he had been working in his garden when a man had jumped on him. He didn't see him, and he didn't hear him, (y) either.
The old man is now in hospital, and (z) as long as he takes things easy, he should make a complete recovery.

4 Students write a description of a crime or accident for homework. If you think that this would tax their imagination too much, you might want to prepare them for this in class. You could find or draw some pictures that tell the story, or you could do a mime story as a picture composition. This will act as the outline of the story for students to add detail to.

PostScript (SB p97)

Being polite

SUGGESTION

Ask the class this question: *A friend of yours has bought a very expensive coat, which you think looks awful. He or she says to you* 'What do you think of it? Don't you think it's beautiful?' *What would you say?* Teach the expression *white lies*. Have a short discussion on the acceptability of white lies.

1 Do question 1 as a class. Students might have a lot to say, or not much.

Possible answers

- That's very kind, but I'm full. It really was delicious, but I couldn't possibly eat any more. Thank you.
- Yes, he's beautiful! What big eyes! And such lovely hair! You must be so excited!

2 **T 9.8** Students listen to the pairs of dialogues and say which one is more polite. This is usually pretty

obvious. Polite forms tend to be longer, and pronounced with a wide voice range. A narrow voice range sounds ruder and less considerate of other people's feelings.

Answers

The following sound more polite.

a 1 b 2 c 1 d 2 e 1 f 2 g 2 h 1 i 1

Students look at the tapescripts as you play the dialogues again. Ask if students' L1 has similar fixed expressions which show politeness. What is considered to be polite or impolite in their country?

3 Again, do this exercise quite quickly, encouraging students to produce good pronunciation. It is probably best done as a class, so you can push the pace and correct mistakes.

4 **T 9.9** Students listen and respond.

T 9.10 Students listen and compare their answers. Point out the pronunciation, and especially the wide voice range.

Answers

a A Hi! Listen, can you come round for a meal tomorrow evening? I'm cooking Chinese.
  B Oh, I'd love to, but I'm afraid I'm already going out. Oh, what a shame!

b A Can you help me with my maths homework? We're doing algebra.
  B Believe me, I would if I could, but I don't know the first things about algebra. Sorry.

c A Would you like me to babysit this evening so you can go out for a meal?
  B That's very kind of you, but we've arranged for my sister to come over. Thanks for the offer, though.

d A Can you tell me where the nearest post office is, please?
  B I'm afraid I don't know. Sorry.

e A Hi, it's Susan here. Could I ask you a big favour? Could you look after my dog next week? I have to go away.
  B I'm terribly sorry, Susan, but I can't. I'd love to have Molly, you know I adore dogs, but I'm going away myself for a few days.

5 **T 9.11** Read the instructions as a class. This exercise is perhaps best done in two stages, first as a class to establish a variety of answers, and then in pairs to practise. Remember that this is a semi-controlled speaking practice, so you need a fair degree of accuracy from students. Correct mistakes carefully.

Sample answers

1 Hello. Thank you very much. What a lovely house! I've brought you some flowers. I hope you like them.
2 Hello, Henry. And you/Nice to meet you, too.
3 I'm from (Germany) actually. From Bonn.
4 I'm doing a language course at International House, in Piccadilly. It's very interesting.
5 Well, it's certainly very different from where I come from. But I like London very much. What I like especially are the shops.
6 What I'd really like is a Coke, if that's all right.
7 No, thanks.
8 All right. Thank you.
9 Cheers! It's very nice to meet you all.
10 Sorry, I don't understand. What are they?
11 Just a little, yes, please.
12 Thank you, but I couldn't eat another thing. It was delicious.
13 Yes, please. That's enough, thank you.
14 It was delicious, really wonderful. I've never eaten anything quite like it.
15 Yes, I know. But I've had a lovely time. Thank you so much. I really enjoyed meeting your friends, and the food was excellent. Thank you.

Don't forget!

Workbook Unit 9

Exercise 11 Hot Verbs – *keep* and *lose*

Exercise 12 Phrasal verbs and nouns that go together

Exercise 13 Pronunciation – Question tags

Things ain't what they used to be!

Expressing habit
Time expressions

Introduction to the unit

The title of the unit comes from a popular song called 'Things ain't what they used to be'. 'Ain't' means either *isn't* or *aren't*. The song is humorously nostalgic about the way life used to be in 'the good old days'.

This unit brings together most of the ways that habit can be expressed in English, and it compares and contrasts subtleties of use. It covers a range of topics which describe habits both past and present. Also some of the differences between a London accent and standard English are focused on in the Listening section about homelessness.

It is worth pointing out here that in preparation for the writing activity towards the end of the unit, students are required to do some of research into a period of history in their own country. This should concern social history, the way the people lived, not wars and politics.

Notes on the unit

LANGUAGE AIMS

NB See the Grammar Reference section – SB p157.

Expressing habit
Many of the expressions of habit will already be familiar to students at this level, but not all. They should be familiar with all the forms involved, but some of the uses will be new. Also, they will probably not have had all the different ways of expressing habit brought together before.

Present habit
The principle form used to express present habit is, of course, the Present Simple. Students also meet the Present Continuous which can express an annoying habit or characteristic behaviour; *will* in its unstressed, contracted form to express typical behaviour, and in its full, stressed form to express irritation in the speaker.

Examples
She's always asking me for money. (annoying habit)
He'll spend hours just doing nothing. (typical behaviour)
He ***will*** *keep asking me for money.* (irritation)

NB It is important not to confuse this stressed use of 'will' with the stressed use which expresses insistence or strong volition, e.g. 'I will pass my driving test this time. I'll make sure I do!' (Do not teach this use to your students at this stage.)

Past habit
The Past Simple can, of course, be used to express past habit. However, English often prefers to use *used to* + infinitive to illustrate the idea of habit. Students are often introduced to *used to* at quite an early stage in their learning, but fail to use it on the occasions when it would sound better. *Would* can also be used for past habits, but not past states. (Like *will*, *would* in its stressed form can express irritation.)

Examples
1 *When we were young, we went to the seaside for our holidays.*
When we were young, we used to go to the seaside for our holidays.
When we were young, we'd go to the seaside for our holidays.
When we were young, my little brother would always spoil my games.

The first sentence needs the addition of *every year* or *always* (etc.) to convey the idea of habit. The second sentence does not need an adverbial to do this. The third does not need one, and conveys the idea of 'typical behaviour for my family.' The fourth expresses irritation.

2 *I loved hamburgers when I was young.*
I used to love hamburgers when I was young.
*I~~'d love~~ hamburgers when I was young.

love is a state verb, not an action verb, and cannot be used with *would.*

Common mistakes
1 Students can find it puzzling that *used to* can only exist in the past, and try to use it in the present.

* He ~~uses to~~ get up early.
Here we need the Present Simple + time expression.
He usually/always gets up early.

2 Students often omit the final *'d'* when writing *used to* because it isn't pronounced.
*I ~~use~~ ~~to~~ smoke but now I don't. /juːstə/

3 Forming the question and negative can be difficult, because the *'d'* is dropped but the pronunciation is the same.
Did you use to wear a uniform at school? /juːstə/
I didn't use to wear a uniform. /juːstə/

4 *used to* is sometimes confused with *be/get used to* + noun or gerund because the forms are similar and both are to do with habit.
I used to get up early when I worked in London.
used = a verb and the idea of a discontinued past habit.

I'm used to getting up early to go to work.
used = an adjective and the idea of a present habit that was difficult at first.

5 Students can find it surprising that in the expressions *be/get used to*, the *to* is followed by the *-ing* form. It can be pointed out that here *used* is an adjective followed by the preposition *to*, and *-ing* forms follow all prepositions (see Unit 7).

Test your grammar (SB p98)

This *Test your grammar* checks both time adverbials and verb forms that convey the idea of habit.

SUGGESTION

Before your students open their books, write the first sentence on the board. Ask the class: *Which word in this sentence expresses frequency?* (*Rarely.* It's an adverb of frequency.) Now ask: *Which tense is used? Why?* (The Present Simple because it is a present habit.) This will illustrate that you want them to look for both verbs and adverbs.

1 Ask students to open their books and work in pairs. Ask them to read the sentences and underline those words which express habit and frequency. If you haven't done the first sentence on the board with them before, do it now to illustrate how to do the exercise.

Answers

a I very rarely go to church.
b My Aunt Dora used to go to church regularly.
c I usually watch my son's football matches.
d My father used to watch me playing football.
e I have to take this medicine regularly.
f We occasionally visit my uncle in Scotland.
g We used to stay with my grandparents in the country.
h We'd go skating on the village pond.
i She hardly ever writes home but she often phones.
j She'll frequently e-mail us.
k My computer's always breaking down.

Sentences a, c, e, f, i, j, and k express present habit.
Sentences b, d, g, and h express past habit.

Go through the exercise with the class quite quickly. Do *not* be tempted to discuss any subtleties of use at this stage, especially the uses of *will* and *would.* Just point out that they can be used to express habit and more work on them will follow.

2 Obviously answers to this section will be to some extent subjective, because the frequency that the time adverbial represents depends on the nature of the activity, viz. *I brush my teeth regularly* = twice a day; *I go to the dentist regularly* = twice a year. Do it with the whole class and not too seriously. Use the examples to illustrate the activity before you begin.

Sample answers

a twice a year
b every Sunday
c every week
d every weekend
e three times a day
f once a year
g three times a year
h every Christmas
i once a month, every Sunday
j twice a week
k once a week

LANGUAGE IN CONTEXT (SB p98)

Past and present habit

1 Ask students to comment on the photograph of Rosemary Sage. *How old do you think she is? What kind of a lady is she? Rich? Poor? What's in the photo?*

BACKGROUND INFORMATION

2s 9d is 'old' English money: pounds, shillings, and pence or £ s d (d = old pennies). There were twelve pence in a shilling, and twenty shillings in a pound. Britain did not use decimalized coinage until 1971.

Write these questions on the board. They will check your students' general understanding.

Check questions

a Why is the title *Living History*? What does it mean?
b How old is Rosemary?
c Where does she live?
d Has she travelled much in her life?

e What is so different about her life and most other people's?
f Is she happy?

Answers

a This lady is 100 years old, and her way of life hasn't changed. She shows us how people used to live.
b 100 years old.
c In the village of Hambledon.
d No.
e She doesn't have any modern appliances. She doesn't move out of her own village.
f Yes.

Ask them to read the text about Rosemary quite quickly and answer the questions. Tell them not to worry about the gaps at this stage. Now ask students to work in pairs and suggest how the gaps could be filled. Make it clear that often a few words will be needed to fill each gap. Give them five to ten minutes to do this, then go through the text getting their ideas. There are quite a few possibilities for each gap.

NB *All the gaps require verb forms which express habit. At this stage you want the students' own suggestions for filling each gap. The aim is to make the point that their ideas may well be correct, but in the next part of the question they are likely to meet more varied and subtle ways of expressing habit.*

2 Read the introduction to this part aloud to the class. Ask them to work in pairs again to select the correct words. Tell them to check any new words in their dictionary or with you, but most of the words should be familiar. Expect to be questioned about the use of *will* in c, d, e, f; and *would* in j, k, l.

T 10.1 Listen and check your answers. You could have class discussion about Rosemary's life here.

Answers

a commute	h used to own
b gathers and chops	i rented
c 'll boil	j would freeze over
d 'll carry	k 'd go skating
e 'll get washed	l 'd spend
f 'll make herself	m get used to
g 's always telling	n 'm used to

3 This is an important section because it should begin to broaden the linguistic horizons of your students. Do it with the whole class. Your students will probably have used the Present Simple, Past Simple, and *used to* quite frequently (and correctly) when filling in the gaps themselves. They may also have chosen different items of vocabulary. Finally, they may have found difficulty with m and n, although they will probably have met *be/get used to* before.

Grammar questions

Move immediately to this section as it will help to pull together points you have been making. Give them a few minutes to think about both sets of questions before you do them together as a class.

– Read aloud the questions and nominate students to give answers.

Answers

We **used to live** in London when I was a child.
Used to is possible but *would* isn't correct because *live* is a state verb.

We **used to/'d go** to the park every Sunday.
Both *used to* and *would* are possible. A habit is being expressed and *go* is not a state verb.

We went to the zoo last Sunday.
Neither *used to* nor *would* are possible because this is not a habit, it is one particular time.

– Repeat the procedure.

Answers

a does not express the speaker's attitude, b expresses irritation, or the fact that this habit is typical.

The past

a Our cat played with a ball of string for hours.
Our cat would/'d play with a ball of string for hours.
b Our cat was *always* playing on the kitchen table.
Our cat *would* play on the kitchen table.

SUGGESTION

You could ask your students to read the Language Review on p101 at this point, or read it for homework. It should consolidate all the work you have been doing.

PRACTICE BANK (SB p99)

Some of this bank of activities and exercises could be set for homework. We will suggest which are most suitable for this.

1 Discussing grammar

NB *This exercise could be set for homework and then discussed in pairs in the next lesson. Ask your students to consult the Language Review p101 and the Grammar Reference section p157, whilst doing the exercise.*

Ask students to do this exercise in pairs, then discuss it as a class. It is important to do this because the discussion generated can be very worthwhile.

Answers

a My grandfather smokes a pipe. It's a habit he's had for over fifty years.
He'll sit and smoke it every evening after dinner. He always enjoys doing this.
He *will* smoke it at the dinner table. My mother gets really annoyed at this.

b We once went skiing in Colorado. We flew to Denver and then we drove up into the Rockies.
We used to go to skiing in Colorado. We'd fly to Denver and then we'd drive up into the Rockies.

c John usually does the cooking, but he isn't tonight.
John used to do the cooking, but he doesn't any more.
John's used to doing the cooking, because he's been doing it for so many years.
John's getting used to doing the cooking, but it's taking a long time.

d It rained on my wedding day. Everybody got very wet.
It *would* rain on my wedding day. This is so typical of the kind of thing that happens to me.

e He always brings Mel to our parties, which is just fine by us.
He's *always* bringing Mel to our parties, and nobody can stand her! It drives us crazy!

2 Listening and speaking

SUGGESTIONS

Set a short pre-lesson task. Ask students to think about their first best friend and make some notes. This will be useful on two counts.

- You can begin the lesson (before opening the coursebook) by asking them to tell you a little bit about their friend. You could also get them to ask you about your first friend.
- At the end of the activity they are asked to give a short talk about their first friend or teacher, so this would be good preparation and save classroom time.

1 Read aloud the introduction and ask students to read through the sentences about Gillian. To save time you could answer any queries about vocabulary yourself.

POSSIBLE VOCABULARY PROBLEMS

spoilt rotten = *very badly spoilt* (colloquial)
ice lolly = frozen, fruit flavoured ice on a stick.
bursting into tears = suddenly starting to cry.

Ask if they think Gillian and Kathy are still friends. (The truth is – they are not!)

NB The aims of the next two sections are to focus on different ways of expressing past habit and to give practice in listening for details.

2 **T 10.2**

POSSIBLE VOCABULARY PROBLEMS

You may need to pre-teach:
brewery = a place where beer is made.
nauseating = sickening and ridiculous.
ice-cream van = a van which travels the streets of towns selling ice-cream.

Tell students that they will now *hear* Kathy talking about Gillian, and that although what she says is similar to what they have read, the verb forms she uses are not exactly the same, so they have to listen very carefully to find the differences. Point out that they must find the sentence not on the tape.

Play the tape and ask students to work in pairs. In feedback you can either go through the answers orally with the whole class or ask individual students to write the sentences on the board, one by one, for the others to comment on and discuss. Begin by asking which sentence was *not* on the tape (k).

Answers

(Comments on the uses are to aid discussion.)

a She **lived** up the road in a big white house.
(*live* = state verb, so *used to* can be used.)

b We **went** to the same school but we **didn't use to see** much of each other at school. (*never used to* is often used instead of the negative.)

c Her dad **had** a really good job.
(*have* = state verb, so *used to* can be used.)

d We **used to fight** a lot.

e We both **loved** going to the cinema.

f We**'d learn** all the words of the songs.
(*would* used for typical past behaviour.)

g We **were always having** these huge rows.
(*would* and Past Continuous to convey attitude.)

h I **used to think** that she was spoilt rotten.
(*think* = state verb.)

i She **would get** four flavours and an ice lolly.

j She **wouldn't share** a thing and she**'d just burst** into tears. (typical behaviour.)

k (Not on the tape.)

l I **once went** on holiday to Blackpool with her and her Auntie Ethel. (not a habit. This is a specific event.)

3 Probably some of the extra information will have emerged when you were going through the previous exercise. Go through the sentences encouraging contributions from the class.

Answers – extra information

a Gillian's house was bigger than Kathy's.
b They were in different classes. Gillian was older.
c Her father worked in the local brewery.
d Gillian and Kathy had a lot in common but ...
e They liked seeing musicals.
f They learned the songs by heart and acted out the musicals.
g They had rows about nothing.
h Gillian got everything she wanted.
i When the ice-cream van came round ...
j She was mean and she ran home to mummy.
k (Not on the tape)
l Kathy once went on holiday with her, but it was a disaster.

If you feel it is unnecessary to play the tape again, you could ask students to read the tapescript on p141.

4 Ask students to form small groups and tell each other about their first friend (or teacher). Then ask one or two individuals to tell the whole class, encouraging questions from the others at the end of each one.

3 Short answers and pronunciation

This exercise gives controlled practice of the target language and combines it with stress and intonation practice. The topic is all to do with learning English and thus can be personalized quite easily.

SUGGESTION

If you feel that your students may be unsure about the use and meaning of *be/get used to* you could write the following on the board and ask them to match the two sentences above with their correct explanation below.

1 I'm used to starting work early.
2 I'm getting used to starting work early.

a I usually start work early.
b I'm gradually finding it easier to start work early.
c I now find it easy to start work early.
d I used to start work early, but I don't now.

Answer: 1 c 2 b

1 Read the introduction to the class. Ask students in open pairs across the class to read aloud the two examples. Correct their pronunciation carefully. Ask them to work in closed pairs to do the exercise.

Answers

a Well, we usually get it twice a week.
b Well, yes, I do now, but I didn't use to.
c I didn't at first, but I soon got used to it.
d Well, I don't now, but I used to when I was a beginner.
e Well, I suppose I'm used to it.
f Oh, yes we did. We used to do it every lesson.
g It's not easy, but I think that gradually I'm getting used to it.

2 **T 10.3** Play the tape for your students to check their answers. Tell them to pay attention to the stress and intonation. Ask them to practise them with their partner. Finally, personalize the activity. This can either be done in pairs or with the whole class, with you asking the questions. At this point they can answer any way they want, not necessarily with an expression of habit.

ADDITIONAL MATERIAL

Workbook Unit 10
Exercises 1–4 Past and present habit
Exercise 5 Text about a secret millionaire
Exercise 6 *Get*, *become*, and *be* in changes of state

LANGUAGE REVIEW (SB p101)

Verb forms expressing habit

You may well have already been through this with your class. If not, read this together now and/or ask students to read it at home.

Ask students to read the Grammar Reference section at the back of the Student's Book at home. Suggest that they use this to revise from and when they are doing exercises from the Workbook.

● VOCABULARY (SB p101)

Money, money, money!

NB *This activity checks some of the vocabulary needed for the reading and speaking activity on p102.*

1 Quickly illustrate the idea by asking the class what the opposite of *poor* is. They will certainly offer *rich*, but encourage them further and you may get *wealthy*. You could also ask them for the opposite of *cheap*. Now ask them to open their books and run their eyes down column A and then B, to see if any opposites immediately strike them. They could work on their own to complete the activity and then check their answers in pairs or small groups, before you conduct a class feedback session. Some words are quite difficult, so make sure that there are sufficient dictionaries in class for them to consult.

Answers

generous – stingy
spendthrift – penny-pincher
in the black – overdrawn
debt – loan

luxury – necessity	tight-fisted – extravagant
brand new – second-hand	income – expenditure
hard up – well off	worthless – priceless
deposit – withdraw	beggar – millionaire
save – waste	profit – loss

2 Ask them to work in pairs to do a–i. Then get some of their ideas in feedback and do j with the whole class. Ask the class if anyone has heard of Mr Micawber and if they know anything about him.

BACKGROUND INFORMATION

Mr Micawber is a character from Charles Dickens' novel *David Copperfield* who always has money problems. This is one of his many famous quotes.

3 (p102) These are all expressions to do with money. Ask your students to consider them in pairs or small groups, then ask for feedback from the whole class. Ask them to illustrate their answers either by using the expression or explaining it.

Answers + examples of use

- miserable. *He **fell on hard times** when his business went bankrupt and his wife left him.*
- miserable. *We were so poor when we were first married. We had to **live on a shoestring**, we had only £10 a week for food.*
- happy. *They won the lottery and now they **live in the lap of luxury**.*
- miserable. *His father threw him out of the house and since then he's been **living rough** on the streets of London.*
- miserable. *We never have enough to pay the bills at the end of the month. We simply **can't make ends meet**.*
- happy. *Donald Trump is **rolling in money**. I think he's a billionaire.*
- miserable. *When I was a student I had to be very careful with my money. I **had to penny-pinch** to save enough money to buy books.*
- happy. *They buy everything they want. They must be **made of money**.*
- miserable. *He has no money and no home. He's been **down and out** on the streets of the city for over two years.*
- miserable. *We can't spend as much as we could when we were both working. We've had to **tighten our belts** a lot.*
- happy. *My uncle is a very successful man. **His business is doing a roaring trade**.*
- happy. *You look very happy! You look like you **lost a quid and found a fiver**.*
  ('a quid' and 'a fiver' are colloquial words for £1 and £5 respectively.)

ADDITIONAL MATERIAL

Workbook Unit 10

Exercise 7 This introduces further expressions to do with money. It includes a text called *A lesson in thrift at the supermarket*.

● READING AND SPEAKING (SB p102)

Money makes the world go round

NB *This is a jigsaw reading activity. There are four quite short texts and students are required to study two in detail and then swap information with those who have read the other texts.*

Begin the lesson by writing the title *Money makes the world go round* on the board and asking the class what they think it means and if they agree with it.

Pre-reading task

This should take a maximum of ten minutes. Read out the introduction.

1 Check that your students know the meaning of *miser*. Go through the questions and encourage contributions from the class. (If you're lucky they will use some of the vocabulary and expressions from the previous exercise!)

- Here are some typical comments from our students.

The aristocrat:
Rich, rolling in money. Perhaps doesn't think about money much. Has a big country house. Shops in Harrods. Goes to parties. Goes hunting and fishing.
The divorced mum:
Poor. Hard up. Has to tighten her belt, penny-pinch, lives on a shoestring, can't make ends meet. Lives in a block of flats. Doesn't go out much. Watches TV. Buys second-hand clothes. Doesn't have holidays.
The taxman:
Not poor or rich. Lives in quite a nice house. Doesn't like his job. Spends his money carefully. Has a holiday in Spain every year.
The miser:
Probably rolling in money but pretends he's poor. Only buys necessities, no luxuries. Never buys presents. Hates birthdays and Christmas. Rarely goes out. Never has a holiday. A stingy penny-pincher with few friends.

(As you might expect, the real answers to these questions in the texts provide a few surprises!)

2 Ask students to work in pairs or small groups to do this. Some of the statements are easy to place, but again your students will find some surprises when they read the texts.

NB This activity has two aims. It prepares the way for the topic content of the texts and also pre-teaches some necessary vocabulary, viz: 'split up', 'social leper', 'collection', 'baulk', 'splash out', 'cheer up', 'leaks', 'stash away'.

Obvious answers	**Actual answers**
a divorced mum	a divorced mum
b taxman	b taxman
c divorced mum, taxman, miser	c aristocrat
d miser, taxman	d miser
e miser, divorced mum	e taxman
f divorced mum	f divorced mum
g divorced mum, miser	g aristocrat
h miser, aristocrat	h miser

Reading

1 Give your students a strict time limit for this, about three minutes. Stress that they have to *scan* read (look through the texts very quickly, looking only for the sentences and *not* reading every word). Go through the answers, asking which they found surprising.

Answers

- probably c, e, g are the most surprising.
- the aristocrat is obviously worth the most money because her husband is a financier and they own a large house and land. However, they have huge expenses because of the house. Therefore it could be argued that the miser is the richest because of his salary and his miserly ways.
- The divorced mum is obviously the poorest.

2 Now ask each student to choose two texts only and read them more carefully. Give them ten to fifteen minutes to do this.

NB You will need to allocate texts to some extent to make sure that they are all covered, otherwise the information swap will not work.
The list of vocabulary problems below does not include those words taught in the vocabulary section on SB p101.

SUGGESTION

Do not pre-teach this list. You can either photocopy it and give it out for your students to use as they read, or just use it for your own information in case students want to check some of the words with you.

POSSIBLE VOCABULARY PROBLEMS

The aristocrat
upholstery = material covering furniture.
funeral parlour = a place where dead people are prepared for the funeral.

The divorced mum
state benefit = money from the state for poor people.
barmaid = a lady who works in a bar, selling drinks.
treats (n) = something that gives great pleasure.
beans on toast = a cheap meal of baked beans on a piece of toast.
packed lunch = food, such as sandwiches, biscuits, and fruit, taken to school or work for lunch.
school dinner = dinner provided by the school, which is subsidized and therefore cheap.

The taxman
to baulk /bɔːk/ at = to refuse to
to buy in bulk = to buy a large quantity of something. It's often cheaper that way.
to indulge yourself = to allow yourself to have or do exactly what you want.
to boast = to talk proudly about oneself.
to dodge paying tax = to avoid paying tax. *Tax dodger* = noun.

The miser
a tag = a label attached to something to identify it, for example, *a gift-tag*
to mislay = to lose
wishing well = a well where you throw money to have a wish come true!
to recycle = use again and again.
charity shop = a shop which sells second-hand things, and gives the money to charity.
a garment = a piece of clothing.
to stash away = to hide *(informal)*

Answers

The aristocrat

a She runs Knebworth House as a business, but doesn't have a regular salary. Her husband is a financier.
b Yes, in general they get on well. The only thing they row about is money.
c She says she doesn't have much money, but she spends £2,000 a year on clothes. She feeds lots of guests.
d She doesn't like spending money but her husband likes having parties and going to restaurants.
e She doesn't mention giving money to any good causes.
f She decorates the house and makes her own curtains and upholstery. They do their own repairs.
g Not really, but perhaps having so many guests for weekends in summer is extravagant. Also the parties and visits to restaurants.
h Her husband, David, is a financier. She has four grown-up children. She wants the next generation to inherit the house. They have lots of friends to stay. Her family were not well off when she was a child – she'd sell flowers from the garden to the funeral parlour.

The divorced mum

a She works part-time as a barmaid. She earns £21 a week for this, and £585 a month state benefit.
b We don't know, but presumably not. She split up from him four years ago.
c She takes the kids to McDonald's once a month. She buys second-hand school uniforms. She spends £350 a month on food, they have lots of beans on toast at the end of the month. Usually she makes a packed lunch for the kids, but sometimes there isn't enough food, so they have school dinner and pretend they have forgotten the money to pay for it. She once spent £30 on clothes and regretted it. She wants new shoes for the children.
d A packet of ten cigarettes. Lottery tickets.
e No, impossible.
f She buys second-hand clothes. She's careful with money, but she doesn't get enough to save.
g A packet of ten cigarettes. Sometimes she buys something to cheer herself up.
h She has four children, aged 5 to 10. No husband. Her family gave her lots of treats as a child.

The taxman

a He's a tax inspector. He earns £23,558 a year.
b Yes. They never row about money.
c He buys and cooks food in bulk and puts it in the freezer. He'll buy a round of drinks but not a packet of crisps. He won't eat in motorway service stations. He doesn't spend much on clothes, £95 (a year) because a taxman doesn't need to look smart.
d He buys good malt whisky. His wife spends £40 at the hairdresser's.
e Yes, he does. He'll give £1 to down-and-outs and helps his mum. His wife gives £20 a month to animal charities, but not to beggars.
f He buys in bulk. He won't buy unnecessary food like crisps and snacks. He doesn't use one of his credit cards. He saves on clothes.
g Whisky. Credit card debts.
h His wife, Denise, is 20. She's a part-time secretary. They have no children. His mother is a widowed pensioner, who lives alone. He buys his friends a round of drinks.

The miser

a He's a BBC journalist and author. He earns £50,000 a year.
b They don't row but she is embarrassed by his meanness.
c They grow their own vegetables. They only buy second-hand clothes, paying £2 a garment. He never invites people to dinner.
d Nothing!
e No. (He gets his clothes from a charity shop and he organizes collections for good causes but doesn't give anything.)
f He never buys luxuries or a round of drinks. He never has dinner parties. He once gave just the wrapping paper and tag as a wedding present! He has a wishing well in the garden and collects the money that passers-by throw in. He recycles everything and buys from charity shops. He used to give his mother flowers from her own garden.
g No.
h His wife, Jo, is 32. They have two young children. He's never bought flowers for his mum. No friends come to dinner but he accepts their invitations.

Get some feedback on the questions. You could give copies of the answers to different students for them to check themselves.

Speaking

1 Ask students to form pairs or groups with those who have read different texts to them, and go through the answers together. The idea is that by doing this they will be telling each other about the people in their texts and comparing information.

2 Ask students to consider these words in relation to the people.

Answers

thrifty
Lady Cobbold because she does her own repairs and decorating. **Angie Cross** because she doesn't get treats for herself and the kids and buys second-hand clothes. **Bob Wilden** because he buys in bulk and doesn't spend much on clothes. **Malcolm Stacey** because he recycles and buys second-hand clothes. However, most of what he does is stingy rather than just thrifty.

skinflint
Malcolm Stacey is a skinflint. He is very mean indeed despite his good salary. He especially does not like spending money on other people.

well off
Malcolm Stacey earns the most. His lifestyle does not indicate that he is well off, but he is. **Lady Cobbold** doesn't think she's well off, but her home and her lifestyle show that there is still wealth in the family. Compared with most people she is well off.

hard up
Lady Cobbold feels hard up because she cannot have the grand lifestyle that befits her home and background. **Angie Cross** is poor rather than just hard up. **Bob and Malcolm** are 'careful' with their money, but not really hard up.

privileged
Lady Cobbold because of her background and home. She has inherited a stately home.

underprivileged
Angie Cross because she lives on state benefit money.

3 Ask students to do this in small groups and then have a feedback session. They could discuss themselves in relation to the words in Exercise 2.

Language work
Hot Verbs (4): *come* and *go*

SUGGESTION

Write the words *come* and *go* on either side of the board. Ask students to come up to the board and write any words or expressions that go with each.

Read through the introduction with them. Ask them to find the examples in the texts. Ask them to go quickly through the exercise on their own, and then check their answers with a partner. Get feedback with the whole class.

Answers

a came	e come	i go	m went
b gone	f comes	j came	n goes
c go	g goes	k going	o come
d go	h comes	l come	

Ask the class which other *hot verbs* they have studied. Encourage examples and expressions to remind them. We have now done *take*, *put*, *get*, *have*, and *be*.

● LISTENING (SB p105)
Homelessness

NB *This is quite a serious topic but we felt it to be a common problem in the world today. However, only you can be the judge of whether your students would be interested to discuss the subject or would find it too depressing.*
You will need to photocopy the transcript (TB p144) for part 2 of the listening activity.

Pre-listening task

Ask questions about the photographs and lead this to a general class discussion of the three questions. Relate the questions to your students' own experiences. Where and when have they met homeless people? Is it a problem in their countries? (Don't spend too long on this at this point because after the listening there is an opportunity for fuller discussion.)

Possible answers

1 They live on the streets, often sleeping in shop doorways, in cardboard boxes, and under newspapers. They sometimes beg for money and look for food and clothing in rubbish bins. There are usually charity groups who help them with handouts of food and clothing. There are also some hostels for homeless people.
2 All kinds of people: young people who have fallen out with their parents; alcoholics and drug addicts who have lost their jobs or who can't find work; businessmen whose businesses have gone bankrupt; divorced people who have lost their homes to their ex-wives/husbands, etc.
3 They have to appear interested so as to seem caring about society. However, homeless people can't vote, so they are not very useful to politicians. They cost money and don't contribute any taxes. There are complaints that they can affect the tourist trade.

Part 1 Listening

T 10.4 Read aloud the introduction to the radio interview with Oliver McGechy. Check that your students understand Oliver's job: running a special home for the homeless and alcoholics. Also, go through the questions with the class *before* playing the tape, pausing to sort out any vocabulary problems.

NB *Warn your students that Oliver has a Scottish accent. They may find him quite difficult to follow, but should get used to his voice as they listen.*

Play the tape once and see how much information your students can get from one playing, by going through the questions to see which they can answer. They could go through it in pairs to get ideas from each other. Reassure them that they will hear it again, if necessary. Play it again, building up their level of understanding. If there are still difficulties your students could read and listen at the same time, following the tapescript on p141.

POSSIBLE VOCABULARY PROBLEMS

a long-term commitment = a promise over a long period of time.
lifespan = length of time someone is likely to live.
GP = General Practitioner, who is a family doctor.
clergy = priests
ex-service men = people who used to work for the army, airforce, or navy.

Answers

a Because he used to be homeless and an alcoholic himself.
b Homeless people have short lives, 42 years in Europe on average. This is similar to how long people lived in Victorian times.
c The people you actually see sleeping on the streets are just 'the tip of the iceberg'. Many more people are actually homeless.
d '... lost all of the network' – means that they have probably lost not only their home but all their family and all those things that supported them in society such as doctors, dentists, and jobs.

'... downward spiral ...' The more they move down in society, the more difficult it is to climb back. Unemployment can start this process.
'... little political gain ...' The homeless can't vote so they are not very important to politicians.

e All kinds of people. Oliver mentions: doctors, members of the clergy (priests), factory workers, postmen, ex-service men (soldiers, sailors, airmen). Oliver emphasizes the spread of people.
f Oliver asks the interviewer what he would do if he had lost everything. He suggests that he might easily turn to alcohol and drugs to escape and forget the horror of life.

Part 2 Listening and reading

NB The reason for including the transcript of the first part of Chris Caine's interview is to focus students on the differences between standard English and what is quite a strong regional accent. This will also help students when they listen to what he says.

1 Read through the introduction about Chris. Ask your students to work in pairs or small groups to study and discuss the transcript. Tell them to 'translate' what he says into standard English and note the differences.

Differences from standard English

- 'h' is often dropped. Chris says *'ad* (*had*); *'er* (*her*).
- 'th' becomes 'f' or 'v'. He says *wiv* (*with*); *fings* (*things*).
- *took on* means *took responsibility for*.
- *patch fings up* means *to mend the relationship*.
- 'ing' is pronounced 'in'. Chris says *workin'*.
- *'n' all* means literally *and everything*. But it is more of a conversation 'filler', it doesn't mean much.
- *All of a sudden, like ...* 'like' is another filler. It means *you see/you understand*.
- *dunno* = don't know
- *yer* = you
- *yeah* = yes

Go through them with the whole class.

2 Give out the complete photocopied transcript (TB p144) of Chris's interview. Play part 2 of the tape and ask them to read and listen at the same time. Focus their attention on the glossary of difficult words and expressions in the transcript.

NB We suggest reading and listening at the same time here in order to help students understand Chris's accent. It can be quite a shock hearing dialects in a foreign language. We hope this will raise awareness of different types of spoken English.

Ask students to discuss answers in pairs or small groups.

Answers

a His relationship with a woman and her children ended after two years. So he left home.
b He's surprised because Chris lives in the woods. Perhaps he thinks that most people live rough on the streets, not in the woods.
c He feels freer and safer in the woods. He thinks the towns are full of risk and 'hassle' (trouble) and stress.
d He had a breakdown and the doctor suggested that he came to the home. He used to light fires, cook his food, sleep in his sleeping bag. Also he used to work in the woods as a survival instructor.
e He's worked for the post office and he's been a survival instructor for the army.
f He misses family life, particularly the company of a woman and someone to talk to. He gets very lonely.
g When he sees people with families in the street, holding hands. He knows he had that once and he lost it.
h In doorways, in parks, on benches.
i It takes him much longer to get used to living in society. It takes him only about a week to get used to being on the road.

Part 3 Listening

This is just a short conclusion to the programme. By now students should be quite used to Chris's voice. Play part 3 and discuss the questions with the whole class, leading this to the final discussion.

POSSIBLE VOCABULARY PROBLEMS

sleeping rough = sleeping outdoors
grim = unpleasant and depressing
rock-bottom = the lowest point you can reach

Answers

Chris is basically saying that drink (and drugs) cannot be the answer to problems, because the escape is only temporary. The next day your problems are still there. Chris does sound determined despite all his difficulties, so maybe he will find a job and build a home again. At least he knows it won't be easy.

Discussion

Put students into small groups to discuss these questions. Go round and listen and comment on their ideas.

● WRITING AND RESEARCH (SB p106)

Writing about a period in history

NB This activity is not meant to entail detailed research. We want students to draw primarily on knowledge they already have about their country's social history.

SUGGESTION

Set homework before this lesson requiring your students to do a little research into a period of history in their own country. This can be any period, ancient or more recent, but it should be a time that particularly interests them and should concern social history, the way the people lived, not wars and politics.

Ask students to look at the pictures on the page. Ask some questions about them.
What period of history is it? What kind of lives did people have then? What are they doing in the pictures? Do you know anything about life in your country in this period?

POSSIBLE VOCABULARY PROBLEMS

Teach some of the vocabulary for the text from the pictures: *mansion, chimneys, sewers, typhus, plague, feast, hunting, wild boar, jousting.*

Other words:
monarchs = kings and queens
cobbled streets = streets made from small round stones
thrive = grow and develop well
venison = meat from deer
lark = a small bird
turnip = a round, white root vegetable
fencing = a sport of fighting with swords

1 and 2 Ask for some feedback about periods of history in their country which interest them. (If students have not done this, continue talking about the pictures.)

3 Ask students to read the text quite quickly, then in pairs decide which heading goes with which paragraph.

Answers
1 Health 2 Homes and food 3 Education 4 Pastimes

4 This can be done first in pairs, followed by a full class feedback. Also ask your students to underline the adverbs of frequency used in the text. Set up the writing task for homework from the discussion. Ask them to do a first draft from the notes they have (hopefully!) previously made. They can use the text as a model. In a subsequent lesson check the rough drafts, before setting them to write up a final version.

PostScript (SB p107)

Time expressions

1 The activity begins with some dictionary work. However, if you want to save time go through the sentences as a class, asking for suggestions for the meaning of the words underlined in column A.

Vocabulary answers
brush up – get back the skill you once had
come across – find by chance
a cutting – something you cut out of a newspaper
make it (to) – manage to reach
blizzard – a bad snowstorm
put up with – tolerate
poky – small, not big enough
trade figures – the amount of money involved in buying and selling products
in touch – in contact
moan – complain
rambling – walking for pleasure
muttering – speaking in a low voice so that it's difficult to understand
tights – worn over legs by women (US 'pantihose'). About 300 years ago worn by fashionable men.
gobble – eat very fast
drop in – pay a casual visit

2 Ask students to work on their own and then check their ideas with a partner before you get full class feedback. Remind them that sometimes more than one answer is possible.

Answers
a lately.
b the other day.
c in record time/just in time/on time.
d on time.
e for the time being.
f by Friday at the latest/by the end of the week/at the end of the week/some time soon.
g some time soon/at the end of the week.
h all day long/for hours upon end.
i all day long/for hours upon end/many years ago.
j all day long/for hours upon end.
k in the olden days/many years ago.
l Take your time!
m before long/some time soon.
n It's a waste of time.

3 Now see if your students can write a sentence each for the expressions in B. They could do this in pairs. Don't let this go on too long. Set a time limit of five minutes and then ask them to compare their ideas in small groups. Go round and check. If you see interesting examples ask the students to write them on the board for the whole class to comment on.

Don't forget!

Workbook Unit 10
Exercise 8 Prepositions – verb + object + preposition
Exercise 9 Pronunciation – Rhymes and limericks

11 If only things were different!

Hypothesizing
Moans and groans

Introduction to the unit

The topic of this unit is wishing things were different about the past, present, and future. A variety of people express their frustrations, from a boy with Monday morning blues to a couple with six children and no job. The reading text is a short story about two lovers who cannot find the words to tell each other how they really feel about each other. The lead-in to this reading is via a short radio play. The listening exercise is about family secrets, and the black sheep of the family.
This topic of regret obviously fits the grammatical aims of the unit, which is expressing hypothesis – *If I hadn't … If only she didn't …/I wish you'd …/I'd rather you didn't …*
The unit ends with a PostScript on moans and groans, with people complaining about their lives.

Notes on the unit

LANGUAGE AIMS

NB See the Grammar Reference section – SB p158.

Hypothesis

- Students will of course be familiar with conditional sentences. This doesn't mean that they aren't making mistakes with them! What it does mean is that in their English learning career they have had many lessons where teachers have tried to get across the difference between the basic patterns.
- There are, of course, an infinite number of permutations of verb forms following the word *if*. Nevertheless, it is still helpful to students to point out that the basic forms of first, second, and third conditionals, and the zero conditional, are the foundations on which all the others are built.
- Students need to perceive the difference between tense usage to express fact, and tense usage to express non-fact. The first, second, and zero conditional refer to fact in real time.
  The third conditional refers to non-fact, and this is expressed by shifting the verb form back in time.
  If I'd passed my exam … (I didn't pass)
  … I'd have gone to university. (I didn't go)
- It is possible to mix the time reference in conditional sentences.
  If we'd brought a map … (we didn't)
  … we wouldn't be lost. (we are)
- This shift back in time to express unreality is also seen in the way *I wish …* is used.
  I wish I knew the answer. (I don't)
  I wish he hadn't gone away. (he did)

Test your grammar (SB p108)

1 Ask students to look at the picture of Tom, and describe what they can see. You might need to explain that if you have the blues, you feel depressed. Students might have heard of the musical style called the blues. Students read the sentences in column A.

2 Students join a regret in A with a wish in B. Obviously there are large hints for students. They can match the subjects of the sentences (*flatmate – he*; *it – it*; *my alarm clock – it*, *there – there*), which should make this activity quite easy and quick to do. Avoid the temptation to teach the whole of the grammatical aims of the unit via this *Test your grammar* section. Keep it quite brief. This exercise does illustrate the tense shift backwards very clearly, however, and you might like to point this out. Note that both Present Perfect and Past Simple go back to the Past Perfect.

Answers

a It's Monday morning. I wish it wasn't.
b I've overslept. I wish I hadn't.
c My alarm clock didn't go off. I wish it had.
d I drank too much last night. I wish I hadn't.
e I feel sick. I wish I didn't.
f There isn't any coffee. I wish there was.
g My flatmate *will* play his music very loudly. I wish he wouldn't.
h I haven't ironed my shirt. I wish I had.
i I can't go back to bed. I wish I could.

3 Students complete the sentences. Note that the first sentence is a second conditional, the middle sentence is a third conditional, and the last sentence is an example of a mixed conditional. Again, don't linger over explanations.

Answers

If it was/were Sunday morning, Tom would/could stay in bed till lunchtime.
If his alarm had gone off, he wouldn't have overslept.
If he hadn't had too much to drink last night, he wouldn't feel sick now.

You could ask some of the class to repeat these three sentences, paying attention to sentence stress and weak forms. This is more difficult than it might appear to the average upper-intermediate student!

LANGUAGE IN CONTEXT (SB p108)

Past and present wishes

1 Students work in pairs to look at the pictures and guess what someone's wish is. It doesn't matter if their ideas aren't identical to those in tapescript 11.1 as long as they are relevant to the pictures.

SUGGESTION

When students are making their suggested wishes for each picture, there will inevitably be mistakes. Correct them, but decide when you want to establish the rules, to make sure they understand about tense usage to express non-fact. You either need to do it now, or wait until after Exercise 3 when they will have seen a lot of examples. Remember that recognition always exceeds production – students have *seen* examples of tense usage with *I wish* …, but that doesn't mean that they can produce them accurately.

Possible answers

1 I wish I'd found a proper parking space.
2 I wish I lived on a desert island.
3 I wish I didn't get so angry.
4 I wish I could speak another language.
5 I wish my dog could talk.
6 I wish I didn't like chocolate cake.
7 I wish my grandmother was/were still alive.
8 I wish I had more time to read.

2 **T 11.1** Students listen to the people expressing wishes and put a letter a–h next to a picture.

Answers

a 2 b 3 c 8 d 5 e 1 f 7 g 4 h 6

3 Students complete the wishes. It isn't important that they reproduce every word, but obviously the tense usage must be correct. This exercise could be done in pairs or as a class. Encourage students to write the contracted forms. When getting feedback, make sure students pronounce the contracted forms.

Answers

a I wish I lived somewhere warm.
b If only I weren't such a quick-tempered person. If I hadn't shouted at George the other day, we'd still be friends.
c I wish I could read faster. I wish I had longer holidays.
d If only animals could talk!
e If only I hadn't parked my car on the double yellow line, I wouldn't have got that ticket.
f I wish I'd listened to my grandmother more.
g I should have studied languages. But if I hadn't studied politics, I might never have met Andy.
h I shouldn't have eaten that huge slice of chocolate cake.

4 As a class, students say what the facts are. Keep it brief. Once you've established the use of tenses to express fact, there's no need to labour the point.

Answers

a He lives in a cold climate, probably in England.
b He loses his temper easily. He shouted at George, and now they aren't friends.
c He reads slowly. He doesn't have long holidays.
d Animals can't talk.
e She parked on the double yellow line. She got a parking ticket.
f She didn't listen to her grandmother.
g She didn't study languages. She met Andy.
h She ate the chocolate cake.

● Grammar questions

Answer these as a class.

Answers

– a present b past c present d past e past
– The Past Simple is used to express unreality about the present. The Past Perfect is used to express unreality about the past.
– If I had taken I would have met he had given

PRACTICE BANK (SB p109)

1 Reading and roleplay

1 **T 11.2** Students read and listen to Leanne and Holly. They underline realities and unrealities.

Answers

'Colin and I got married when we were both sixteen. Of course, now I wish we'd waited and I wish I'd had more time to enjoy myself as a teenager, 'cos by the time we were seventeen we had the twins. Now we've got six children, which wouldn't be so bad if Colin wasn't unemployed and if we lived somewhere bigger. This flat has only two tiny bedrooms and it's on the tenth floor. If only there was a park nearby, where the kids could play. I'd rather we had a house with a garden, though. I try to be optimistic but the future's pretty bleak, really.'

'Of course, I know that I'm very lucky. I have a hugely successful career and a beautiful apartment overlooking Central Park. But now I wish I hadn't had to focus so single-mindedly on my work. I know my marriage wouldn't have been such a disaster if I hadn't. I was devastated when Greg and I split up. My mom keeps saying, 'Holly, you're not getting any younger. It's time you started dating again.' I must admit, when I look out of my window at the kids playing in the park, I kinda wish that I lived out of town and had some kids of my own.'

You could ask students to say what regrets the two women have about their lives.

2 Students work in pairs to form conditional sentences. In class feedback, pay particular attention to correct auxiliaries, sentence stress, and weak forms.

Answers

- a Leanne's life would be better if Colin had a job.
- b If she hadn't got married so early, she would have had more time to enjoy her teenage years.
- c If she hadn't got married so early, she wouldn't have six children now. (mixed conditional)
- d If Holly hadn't worked so hard in the past, she wouldn't/might not have a successful career now. (mixed conditional)
- e If she had spent less time at work, her marriage wouldn't/might not have broken up.
- f If she didn't work in New York, she'd live in the country.

3 and 4 Students work in pairs to interview one of the women. Ask one or two of the pairs to re-enact their interview so the whole class can hear.

2 Wishes to facts

These two exercises could be set for homework and checked in class. Read the introduction as a class. Students work in pairs.

Sample answers

- a I wish I spoke English fluently, but I don't. I'll have to keep trying.
- b If only I didn't get so nervous before exams, but I do. I always panic.
- c You should have worked harder for your exams, but you didn't. Now you'll have to take them again.
- d I'd rather you didn't borrow my things without asking, but you do. It really annoys me.
- e I wish my brother wouldn't keep interrupting me when I'm working, but he does. I'll never finish this.
- f If you'd told me you loved me, we would never have split up, but you didn't and now it's too late.
- g If my father hadn't gone to work in Malaysia, he wouldn't have met my mother, and I'd never have been born, but he did and I was.
- h It's time those children were in bed, but they aren't. They'll be tired tomorrow.

3 Facts to wishes

1 Students read the reality and write some wishes.

Sample answers

- a I wish we'd had some pets. I would have had a cat. If only we hadn't lived in a flat!
- b I wish I had blond hair. I'd rather have anything other than mousy-brown. If only I weren't short-sighted! If I weren't short-sighted, I wouldn't have to wear glasses.
- c My parents wish I hadn't become/wasn't a teacher.
- d They wish my youngest brother wasn't so lazy. If he had a job, he'd get out of the house more.
- e I wish I didn't come from such a huge family.
- f If only I could remember my grandmother. If only she hadn't died when I was three.
- g I should have started learning a language before I was fifteen. I'd be totally fluent by now.
- h If only I spoke Spanish, I would have got the job in Barcelona.

2 Do this activity either in pairs or as a class. Students discuss their wishes and regrets.

4 *Would* or *had*?

T 11.3 Students listen to the sentences, and say if the contracted *'d* = *would* or *had*.

Answers

1 had 2 would 3 had 4 would, had 5 had, would 6 would 7 had, would 8 would, had, had

You could play the tape again and ask students to repeat the sentences.

ADDITIONAL MATERIAL

Workbook Unit 11

Exercise 1 Real or hypothetical past?

Exercises 2 and 3 Wishes and regrets

Exercises 4 and 5 Third conditional

Exercise 6 Revision of all conditionals
Exercise 7 Ways of introducing conditionals
Exercise 8 Revision of fact and non-fact

LANGUAGE REVIEW (SB p111)

Hypothesizing about the present/past

Read the Language Review as a class, and/or ask students to read it at home. Students read the Grammar Reference at home. Encourage students to study this carefully whilst doing the exercises in the Workbook.

● LISTENING AND READING (SB p111)

Things we never said

NB *This is a two-part activity. First students listen to a short radio play and from this make predictions about the story on which it is based. They then read the complete story.*

Listening

This section should take a maximum of twenty minutes.

1 Encourage a few minutes of discussion through these questions. The topic is concrete and universal enough for most students to contribute something. You could give them a personal account of someone you have lost touch with to prompt their experiences.

2 **T 11.4** Read through the introduction and then play the tape. Afterwards ask them to discuss the questions in pairs, then go through them with the whole class.

Answers

a No, they met by chance. Neither knew the other was visiting their home town.
b Peter has returned for his father's funeral. Amanda for her sister's wedding.
c They both live in London. Peter in north London and Amanda in the south.
d No, they clearly have not kept in touch, because they don't know anything recent about each other.
e Peter wanted to become a foreign correspondent but he's now a lawyer. Amanda wanted to be a world-famous artist but now only paints doors and walls, i.e. decorates her room.

3 Ask students to discuss their predictions in pairs and then bring the class together to compare all their ideas. Don't give away anything about the story. Tell your students they will find out when they read it.

Reading

POSSIBLE VOCABULARY PROBLEMS

to loathe = to hate
to beat = to hit somebody hard again and again
to spotlight = to highlight
cascading = falling (like water in a waterfall)
unruly = not easy to control
bedsit = (informal) a room for living and sleeping in
damp = a bit wet

See also the Language work section and Vocabulary section on idioms which follow.

BACKGROUND INFORMATION

'Cliveden' is a beautiful old English country house in the countryside north west of London on the bank of the River Thames. The grounds are popular for walking and picnicking.

Students read the story. Get class feedback on how their predictions compared. Discuss the other questions.

Possible answers/reactions

It's possible to feel both sorry and angry for Peter and Amanda. It is frustrating to read the thoughts which they don't express. However, both of them are probably afraid of being hurt again, especially Peter who suffered so much when Amanda left him before.

The tragedy of the situation is that two people who clearly love each other don't end up together because they don't put their real feelings into words.

Comprehension check

1 Ask students to do this in pairs, finding the correct information for the false ones. Check through the exercise with the whole class.

Answers

a True (and false!) They used to be in love when they were young and they still are in love, they just have not confessed this to each other.
b True. They parted fifteen years ago when they were both eighteen.
c False. Peter looks much the same, but his shoulders are broader and his face rounder. Also his clothes are not as casual. He looks like a lawyer, not a student. Amanda is still very beautiful but now has a few white hairs.
d False. His mother is not at all distraught. His father had obviously been a bully so his mother will be happier without him. She'd been trying to find the courage to leave him for years.
e False. She was twelve when Peter last saw her so

she must now be twenty-seven. She's getting married.

f False. She has had a series of failed relationships.

g False. Neither of them have had the career they planned. He wanted to be a foreign correspondent, she wanted to be an artist.

h True. She in south London, he in the north. He wishes he had someone to go home to.

i True. He'd written letters begging her to come back. He knew he'd never meet anyone like her again.

j True. He seems to dismiss their romance as just something young people do.
Amanda is very upset but she holds back her tears so as not to show him how much.

k False. They both love each other but they're afraid to confess to it for fear of getting hurt.

2 **T 11.4** Ask your students to close their books and play the radio play one more time. This time pause the tape after every few lines and ask what was really going on in Peter and Amanda's minds behind the actual words of their conversation.

Roleplay

1 Divide the class into two groups: 'Peters' and 'Amandas'. Ask them to go through the text again and note all the problems and regrets according to who they are. These could be such things as:
Peter: *I wish I'd told Amanda that I'd never love anyone as much as her. I'm really lonely, I wish I didn't live alone. I should have tried harder to become a foreign correspondent. I don't enjoy being a lawyer.*
Amanda: *I wish I'd never walked out. I should have answered his letters. He's the only man I've met that I really want to marry. If only I'd continued to paint and draw. I'm not happy with my life now.*
Students could consider the following areas: their relationship with each other, past and present; their families; their work; where they live.

2 Ask each 'Peter' to find an 'Amanda' and to try to have a different and more truthful conversation than in the radio play. They can begin with the words given. Go round and listen to the roleplays.

SUGGESTIONS

- Ask one or two of the pairs to act out their roleplays for the rest of the class.
- Record some of the roleplays and compare them with the original radio play.

Language work

These exercises could be set for homework if class time does not allow. Whether to do them or not may depend on how well the roleplay goes. You may like to check the pronunciation of some of the words in Exercise 2, e.g. *bald, plump, swallow, tears*. Conduct a feedback session after each section with the whole class.

Answers

1 he rested his *head* on her *stomach*, twisting grass in his *fingers*. (l. 12–13)
her *heart* quickened (when she heard his voice). (l. 9)
Peter's father died of a *heart* attack. (l. 26)
his *shoulders* were broader. (l. 24)
her *hair* cascaded over her *shoulders*. (l. 70–1)
his *face* slightly rounder. (l. 24)
burying his *hands* in the pockets of his coat. (l. 14–15)
laughing and holding *hands* under the table. (l. 52)
she pushed her *hair* behind her *ears*. (l. 35–6)
He could see a few white *hairs*. (l. 71)

2 *bald* (adj) a bald head
blink (v) to blink your eyes
waves (npl) her hair fell in waves.
swallow (v) to swallow food (the mouth)
beat (v) to beat with a stick (the hands)
tears (npl) her eyes filled with tears.
plump (adj) the baby was plump all over: from plump legs to plump cheeks.

ADDITIONAL MATERIAL

Workbook Unit 11
Exercise 9 Vocabulary – physical appearance and personality. Both sections of the exercise could be used in class or be set for homework or private study.

● VOCABULARY (SB p114)

Idioms

NB *Students at this level invariably seem to like learning idioms. However, remind them that it is much more difficult to use idioms naturally and correctly. They can sound strange when uttered by those who are not yet truly fluent. The activity is also designed to practise the dictionary skill of identifying the keyword in idioms to help look them up successfully. Two are taken from the reading text: 'time to kill' and 'a far cry from'.*

Make sure that you have sufficient good monolingual dictionaries in class for this activity.

1 Use this exercise with the whole class to illustrate how to do the activity and use the dictionary. Tell students that they need to identify the keyword in the idiom in order to find it in a dictionary. Ask: *Which is the keyword (the most important word) in the first sentence?* Tell them to try it out in their dictionaries and get feedback. (In fact *time* is the keyword, but a good dictionary like *The Oxford Advanced Learner's Dictionary* also cues the idiom if you look up *kill*.) Go through the questions with them one by one.

Answers

a I had time to kill and I was at a loose end
b The last two are not.
c I had time to kill = I was early and needed to pass the time; I was at a loose end = I was bored and had nothing else to do
d time, loose.

2 Now ask students to work in pairs and do the same for the next groups of sentences. Check through the exercise with the whole class.

Answers

A a is a far cry from and isn't a patch on
b The middle two.
c is a far cry from = is very different from
isn't a patch on = isn't nearly as nice as
d far, patch

B a A lot of water has flowed under the bridge and gone up in the world
b The middle two.
c A lot of water has flowed under the bridge = so much has happened; gone up in the world = become much more successful
d water, world

C a went down the drain and hit the jackpot
b The middle two.
c went down the drain = went bankrupt
hit the jackpot = became very successful
d drain, hit

D a on the tip of my tongue and rings a bell
b The last two.
c on the tip of my tongue = I'll remember in a minute
rings a bell = sounds familiar
d tip, ring

3 Students match the cartoons in A with the idioms.

Answers

1 = bury your head in the sand; 2 = break someone's heart; 3 = fall head over heels in love;
4 = have butterflies in your stomach; 5 = break the ice;
6 = be over the moon; 7 = go through the roof;
8 = get cold feet

4 Students discuss in pairs before a full class feedback.

5 Students can continue to work in pairs to complete the sentences, or you could set it for homework.

Answers

a ... was over the moon. b ... buries her head in the sand. c ... broke the ice. d ... fell head over heels in love. e ... had butterflies in my stomach.
f ... 'll go through the roof. g ... got cold feet.
h ... broke my heart.

● LISTENING AND WRITING (SB p115)

Family secrets

Tell your students that they are going to listen to stories from two family histories. The first is set in Japan; the second in Canada. (The second story is very short.)

Pre-listening task

1 This is a personalized start to introduce the topic of families. Have a general information exchange with the whole class using their family trees.

2 Now focus students' attention onto the family tree. Ask them to discuss the questions in a in pairs. Then go through these and b and c with the whole class.

Answers

a Deborah is Ralph's granddaughter. Christine is Ruth's sister-in-law. Christine is Yuri's half-sister. Christine and Clive are Isuzu's step-children.
b Students may be able to guess that Deborah didn't know about her grandfather's second marriage and her Japanese aunt. It is clear from the names that Isuzu and Yuri are Japanese.
c They may notice that the dates show that Yuri was born when Ralph was probably still married to Lily Margaret. This would make him 'the black sheep'.

Listening and writing

T 11.5

NB The listening activity develops into a writing activity where students are asked to finish a short dramatic scene based on the story. This is in preparation for the final writing activity after part 2 of the listening.

Part One My Japanese aunt

Play part 1 of the tape and ask students to circle people mentioned as Deborah tells the story. Check after that they know who each one is in relation to Deborah.

Answers

Deborah's family:
Jennifer and Rowena are her sisters. Alan is her husband. Christine and Eric are her mother and father. Clive and Ruth are her uncle and aunt. Lily and Ralph are her grandmother and grandfather. Yuri and Hans are her (half) aunt and uncle. Isuzu is her step-grandmother.

Comprehension check

1 Ask students to answer these questions in pairs. Then conduct a full class feedback.

Answers

a Because her grandfather married Isuzu after his wife died and always took responsibility for Yuri. Deborah calls him 'naughty'.
b Ralph: a silk dealer in Japan. Isuzu: a maid in his family. Hans, Yuri's husband: a Swiss businessman.
c The baby is Yuri, the daughter of Ralph and Isuzu.
d They learned about the family secret at the dinner table, when their Aunt Ruth (their mother's sister-in-law, married to Clive) suddenly mentioned Yuri and they asked who she was.
e Christine (Deborah's mother) is clearly ashamed of her father, Ralph. Otherwise she wouldn't have kept Yuri's existence secret.
f Christine is angry with Ruth. She wishes she hadn't spoken about Yuri and let slip the family secret.
g Because she met her half-aunt, Yuri, and she found it amazing to have a Japanese family.
h Deborah was born in 1955, so work out her age today, then take away sixteen. She will have been in her late twenties/early thirties.
i Isuzu was probably about 70. Yuri in her forties.

2 Read the introduction.

a Ask students to read through the scene quickly to themselves. Then allocate the roles to some of the students and ask them to perform it to the rest of the class. Ask them to follow the stage directions showing the feelings of the characters and doing the actions described. Encourage the student playing Christine to continue the story in her own words.

POSSIBLE VOCABULARY PROBLEMS

napkin = a square of cloth or paper used at meals to wipe lips and fingers.
splutters = makes coughing and spitting sounds.
icily = very coldly

b Encourage the other 'actors' to comment on Christine's story, asking questions and expressing their feelings. Now ask students in small groups to write down a final version, completing Christine's story and adding comments and questions from the other characters. Ask at least one member of each group to write down the scene.

c Ask the groups to act it out. A few sets of 'actors' could do it in front of the class. (It gets better with each 'performance'!)

Part Two My Canadian aunt

Read aloud the introduction, and check that students know the meaning of 'great aunt'. Play part 2 of the tape.

POSSIBLE VOCABULARY PROBLEMS

midwife = a nurse trained to help with births.
wood stove = an oven heated by burning wood.

Comprehension check

Go through the questions as a class.

Answers

- She was born in Winnipeg, Canada, in December, 1900.
- The mother, the midwife, the grandmother.
- The baby wasn't breathing when it was born, so the grandmother put it into the wood stove and it started crying.
- the baby would probably have died. (She in fact lived until she was nearly one hundred years old!)

Writing a play

Students should ideally work on this in small groups in class. However, if time is short it could be started for homework and refined in class in small groups. Tell students to use the scene in part 1 as a model, particularly as to how to insert stage directions. You can give them the following opening lines to help prompt their ideas.
Midwife: It's a beautiful baby girl! *(gasps)* Oh dear!
Mother: *(very worried)* What's the matter? …

Discussion

This is simply an opportunity for you or anyone with an interesting family story to contribute it to the class. There may be one or two examples, if you're lucky!

PostScript (SB p117)

Moans and groans

1 Read the introduction as a class. Students work in pairs to match a line in A with a response in B and an item from the box.

Answers

a 5 homework b 7 a painting c 1 a tin opener d 9 a TV programme e 2 shoes f 3 a washing machine g 6 an exam h 8 a sweater i 4 a meal

2 **T 11.7** Students listen and check their answers.

3 and 4 Discuss these questions as a class.

Don't forget!

Workbook Unit 11
Exercise 10 Phrasal verbs – nouns from phrasal verbs
Exercise 11 Pronunciation – ways of pronouncing *-ea-*

12 Icons

Noun phrases
Adding emphasis
Linking and commenting

Introduction to the unit

This is the third unit in *New Headway Upper-Intermediate* where the main grammatical focus is on noun phrases. Units 4 and 6 are the other units. There are also exercises on adding emphasis to both spoken and written texts.

The theme of the unit is icons. As you explain to students what an icon is, tell them that you want them to talk about one of the following topics over the course of the next few lessons: a person they admire, a hero or icon, a pet hate. This will allow students time to think of something, and to plan what they're going to say.
The skills work takes a reflective view of key events of the twentieth century. The reading text is taken from a magazine article about the explosion of the first atomic bomb. In the listening activity, a variety of people express their opinions on the great events of the twentieth century.

The PostScript section ends the unit with a final activity on the grammar of spoken English. It deals with expressions, mainly adverbs, which link and comment, for example *honestly*, *still*, *surely*, *as a matter of fact*.

Notes on the unit

LANGUAGE AIMS

NB See the Grammar Reference section – SB p158.

Noun phrases

- The *Test your grammar* section revises the input on noun phrases from Unit 6. This includes prepositional phrases, relative clauses, participle clauses, and compound nouns.
- Unit 6 concentrated on determiners that express quantity. This unit works on the distributives *all*, *every*, *each*, and the demonstratives *this*, *that*, *these*, *those*. These are practised in the Workbook.
- The use of articles presents students with difficulties. Some languages have no system of articles at all. These include Turkish, Russian, Thai, and Chinese. Other languages have articles, but their use is very different from English, for example Arabic and Japanese. European languages such as French, Spanish, Italian, and German have many uses of articles in common, and just as many exceptions. Fortunately, mistakes in the use of articles don't often cause communication to break down, but they certainly single out the low-level and the high-level speaker of English. You need to correct carefully. Explain the rule when possible.

Adding emphasis

- Adding emphasis is a feature of both the spoken and the written language. This unit works on word order, selecting active or passive voice, and the use of structures such as *What I like about London is …* Adding emphasis when speaking is practised with work on sentence stress and the addition of *do/does/did*. These are areas of the language that are not necessarily difficult to understand, but it is not easy for students to incorporate them immediately into their active store.
- The idea of unmarked or non-special word order might be difficult to convey. In some languages, word order is very flexible, but this is not so in English. Deviations from an unmarked word order usually express emphasis of some kind.
- Students will have had many lessons on the use of the passive, but might not have been asked to comment on the resulting shift of sentence focus.
- When we express spoken emphasis via word stress, the voice range in English is very wide. We start high and drop low.

  I did do my homework!

  Students are often reluctant to stretch their voices as much as English requires!

Test your grammar (SB p118)

Read the title of the unit as a class. Ask if they know the word *icon*. You will probably have to explain that an icon is someone famous who is admired by a lot of people and who is thought to represent an important idea or ideal. Read the instructions as a class. Students work in pairs to match the words in the box to a picture and then make a sentence about each picture.

Answers

b It's a country cottage with a thatched roof and roses growing round the front door.
c She's a traffic warden wearing a uniform and giving someone a parking ticket.
d It's a boy sitting on a wall licking an ice-cream.
e It's a pair of dirty football boots stuffed in a bag.
f It's a driving licence which expires in February 2020.

LANGUAGE IN CONTEXT (SB p118)

Noun phrases and adding emphasis

NB Photocopy the exercise on p145 of the Teacher's Book.

POSSIBLE VOCABULARY PROBLEMS

carve	*inspired*	*block of marble*	*sling* (n)
dome	*sculptor*	*trickling*	
stiff	*scaffolding*	*contemporaries*	

1 You could begin by asking students who their favourite artists are. Students read Text A. Write the following questions on the board and discuss the answers as a class.
How did Michelangelo express his creativity?
What did he like about Florence?
What do you learn about the statue of David?
Was it easy to paint the ceiling of the Sistine Chapel?
Why was his work on St Peter's Basilica important?
Why is Michelangelo compared to Beethoven and Shakespeare?

2 Students read Text B and compare the two texts. In pairs they discuss which text sounds better. This is quite difficult.

Answer

Text B sounds better. There is more variety. The important parts of a sentence are in a strong position, perhaps because of word order, or structures that 'point', for example *... it was Florence that he considered ...* or *What he loved above all was ....* In Text B the passive is used correctly, unlike in Text A, where often the passive is used when the active would be better and vice versa.

Go through the texts again as a class. Students should now be better able to comment.

Answers

Paragraph 1 In Text B, there is a build-up with the nouns *sculptor, architect, painter,* and *poet.* We are in suspense as we wait to know what they all refer to. In comparison, Text A sounds flat and uninteresting.
Paragraph 2 There are two emphatic structures in Text B – *... it was Florence that ...* and *What he loved above all was ....* These point and focus our attention on the important part of the sentence.
Paragraph 3 The first part is mainly about time, so the adverb *Initially* and the time expression *In 1501* balance each other at the beginning of the first two sentences. The passives *This was finished* and *David is shown* are better than the active because our attention is on the statue, not the artist.
Paragraph 4 The adverb *Later* also links back to the adverb *Initially* at the beginning of the previous paragraph. Our focus of attention is on the man, Michelangelo, so it is appropriate that he is the subject of the sentence, not Pope Julius II. In passive sentences, we often don't use *by* + the agent, so when we do, it is in a strong position. The information that it was no less than the Pope who asked Michelangelo to paint the ceiling comes at a strong point *after* the verb. The time expression *Every day for four years, from 1508 till 1512* comes in a strong place at the beginning.
Paragraph 5 Michelangelo is still the focus of our attention, so it is right that he is the subject of the sentence, not *Many buildings.*
There are two emphatic structures in this paragraph – *it was his work at St Peter's Basilica that ...* and *What is difficult to appreciate nowadays is ....*
Paragraph 6 In Text B, the whole paragraph builds up to the line *Michelangelo belongs to this group.*
It is a very dramatic end to the text. Text A sounds very flat and boring.

3 Give out the photocopied exercise (TB p145). This is a gapped version of Text B. The aim is to test understanding of articles, determiners, demonstratives, and possessive adjectives. Students close their books and work in pairs to fill the gaps. Get feedback before they check their answers with the completed text.

● Grammar questions

Answer these as a class. The questions aren't particularly difficult, but don't be surprised if students have problems finding the right words to express themselves.

Answers

- There is a 'normal' word order where no information is particularly stressed. If we play with that word order, we can make parts of a sentence more important.
- *It was Florence that he considered ...*
  ... it was his work at St Peter's Basilica that ...
  What he loved above all was ...
  What is difficult to appreciate nowadays is ...
  In Text A, there is nothing special about the sentences. The information isn't presented in an interesting way. The emphatic structures announce the fact that something interesting is coming.

- (*was born* is passive, but there isn't really an active form, so ignore this.) *This was finished ...* Focus on the statue. *David is shown ...* Focus on David. *... Michelangelo was asked by Pope Julius II ...* Focus on the Pope.

PRACTICE BANK (SB p119)

1 Adding emphasis

Read the introduction as a class. Practise the example sentences to establish the sentence stress.

What I like about Tony is his honesty.

Do the first few questions as a class, asking individual students to repeat the sentences to practise rhythm and sentence stress. Students finish the exercise in pairs.

Answers

These are sample answers. There are many possibilities, depending how freely students rephrase the sentences.

a What annoys me about my daughter is her untidiness.
b The thing I like about Tom is the fact he always buys you a drink.
c What I can't stand about my son is his moods.
d The thing I admire about the Italians is the way they love life.
e What makes the Germans work hard is their sense of duty.
f What makes Mercedes Benz cars so popular is their reliability.
g The thing I can never resist in a restaurant is chocolate desserts.

2 Emphasis and sentence stress

1 **T 12.1** Read the introduction and listen to the examples as a class. Practise the two-line dialogues in the examples in open pairs across the room, making sure that pronunciation is good.

T 12.2 Read the instructions. This exercise is best done as a class, so that you can monitor students' responses and insist on good sentence stress. Try to do this exercise at a brisk pace.

Sample answers

a Did Ann give James a blue shirt?
No, she gave one to David.
Did she give him a white shirt?
No, she gave him a blue one.
Did she give him a blue jumper?
No, a blue shirt.
Was it a Christmas present?
No, a birthday present.

b Did James fly to Rome?
No, he flew to Paris.
Did he go to Paris by Eurostar?
No, by plane.
Did he want to do some shopping in Paris?
No, he went to learn French.
Did he go there just for the weekend?
No, he went for a month.

c Do you go to Scotland in summer?
No, we go every autumn.
Do you go to Ireland in the autumn?
No, we go to Scotland.
Do you go there to relax?
No, we go there to go walking.

d Is your daughter at Bristol university?
No, my son.
Is it your youngest son that's studying at Bristol?
No, my eldest son.
Is he studying modern languages?
No, he's studying law.

2 Students ask and answer similar questions. Don't ask them to do all four questions. Just one or two will be enough, as long as they do them thoroughly.

Sample answers

a Did he write to you?
Did he phone last week?
Did he invite you to a party?
b Are you going alone?
Are you going to India?
Are you going for a couple of weeks?
Are you flying?
c Did John lose his wallet?
Was there twenty pounds in it?
Was he sunbathing in the park?
d Are you meeting Mary?
Are you meeting her at quarter past seven?
Are you meeting her inside the cinema?

3 Do this exercise as a class. Ask students where they think the stressed word is in the second line of the dialogues. Ask them in pairs to read out the dialogues as they think is correct.

T 12.3 Students listen and check their answers.

Answers

a A Why weren't you at school yesterday?
B I **was** at school.
b A Come on, Dave. Its time to get up.
B I **am** getting up.
c A It's a shame you don't like parties.
B But I **do** like parties!
d A I wish you'd tidy your room.
B I **have** tidied it.
e A What a shame you didn't see Tom.
B I **did** see Tom.

4 For this exercise, the best thing is for you to think up

some sentences that are factually wrong for students to correct. Here are some examples to guide you.

About you	**Students' reply**
I never arrive on time.	You **do** arrive on time.
I'm never strict.	You **are** quite strict.
About your students	
We watched a film in the last lesson.	We **didn't** watch a film. We studied grammar.
Peter hasn't got a dictionary.	He **has** got a dictionary. He uses it all the time.
About your school	
Our school is very small.	It **isn't** small at all! It's huge.
The receptionists aren't very nice.	They **are** nice! They're very friendly.
About the world	
The weather's been lovely lately.	No it **hasn't**. It's been raining for days.
What a shame X didn't win the election.	He **did** win the election!

3 Active or passive?

Read the introduction as a class. Students work in pairs to complete the sentences.

Answers

a He was sentenced ... b He sentenced him ...
c They show ... they serve ... d They are shown ... they are served ... e ... you'll be told ...
f She'll tell you ...

4 Articles and determiners

NB Students could read the Grammar Reference on p159 of the Student's Book before doing these exercises. You could set this for homework before the lesson. There are further exercises on articles, determiners, and demonstratives in the Workbook.

1 Do the first four or five questions as a class, then students work in pairs to finish off. Ask them if they know the rule.

Answers

a I had lunch ... (no article with meals)
b ... in the States (with a few countries we need the definite article)
c ... in a taxi (several languages have the same word for *a* and the number 1)
d Unemployment is a world problem ... (no article with abstract nouns)
e ... about the life of Beethoven ... (only one)
f ... broke her leg ... (we use possessive adjectives to refer to parts of the body)
g Computers have changed ... (a general statement with a countable noun)
h ... only one ambition ... (we need the number to contrast with two, three, etc.)
i ... as an interpreter ... (we need the indefinite article with professions)
j In the kitchen. (we both know which kitchen)
k I'd love one. (we are not talking about a particular drink, but an indefinite example)
l ... the truth. (only one)
m ... to a restaurant (indefinite – we don't know which) The food ... the service ... (these are things associated with being in a restaurant, so are defined by the context)

2 This exercise is intended to be short and fun, with the grammatical aim of practising the zero article when talking about things and people in general. The obvious way of setting it up is to divide the class into two groups, boys and girls! They can brainstorm the topic. Then compare notes as a class.

3 Students work in pairs. This short exercise aims to make students think about articles and determiners. The area is practised more in the Workbook.

Answers

Would you like an egg? (any egg)
Do all birds lay eggs? (in general)
Where did I put the egg? (the one I had a minute ago)
Borrow either one. (not both, just one)
I said goodbye to everyone. (the whole group)
I gave a present to each one. (each individual person)
Love is everything. (abstract noun in a general statement)
A love of animals is vital for a vet. (an example of love)
The love I have for you ... (defined)
Both my parents ... (two)
All my friends ... (the whole group)
Every student ... (seen as a whole)

5 Speaking

You could set this activity up quite early in your timetable for this unit. Ideally, you would have one or two students giving their short talk each lesson over a series of lessons. While the students are speaking, avoid correcting. Obviously, if they are having a problem you will want to help, but that is different from interrupting the flow to point out a mistake.

ADDITIONAL MATERIAL

Workbook Unit 12
Exercise 1 Adding information before and after a noun
Exercise 2 Articles
Exercises 3 and 4 Determiners and demonstratives
Exercises 5–8 Adding emphasis
Exercise 9 Nouns in groups

LANGUAGE REVIEW (SB p121)

Noun phrases/Adding emphasis

Read the Language Review as a class, and/or ask students to read it at home. Students read the Grammar Reference at home. Encourage students to study this carefully whilst doing the exercises in the Workbook.

● READING AND SPEAKING (SB p121)

It blows your mind!

NB *You will probably have to explain what this title means. It is an informal expression. If something blows your mind, it is incredible, surprising, amazing, unimaginable, e.g. 'Seeing India for the first time really blew my mind.' There is a play on words with 'blow' meaning 'explode'.*

Pre-reading task

Discuss the photograph as a class. It is the first atomic bomb. In pairs, students discuss whether the information is true or false. Don't let this go on too long. Get some feedback, but don't say yet what the answers are.

Reading

POSSIBLE VOCABULARY PROBLEMS

This list is for your information only. You might decide to pre-teach some of the words, or you might allow students to use their dictionaries.

summed up	*foothills*	*plain*
redefine	*stunned*	*eye-witness accounts*
blasted	*pounced*	*bored*
luminosity	*dingy*	*fast-food joints*
watchtower	*censored*	*barbed-wire fence*
sworn to secrecy	*protégés*	*tailed*
urging	*villain*	*surrender*
summoned	*dismisses*	*consciences*
sceptics	*imminent*	*call it quits*
devastating	*bet*	*speculated*
fateful	*cargo*	

Students read the text and find the answer to the nine questions. Allow adequate time for this. Monitor students carefully to see when the majority have finished reading. Then ask them to work in pairs to check their answers.

Answers

a False. It was first tested on July 16, 1945.
b False. They came from Italy, the Ukraine, Austria, Hungary, and Germany, as well as the United States.
c False. It took place at Los Alamos, New Mexico.
d We don't know the answer to this.
e True. This is what some scientists hoped.
f False. He wrote a letter encouraging the bomb's development, but that was his total involvement.
g True.
h False. There was disagreement.
i We don't know the answer to this.

SUGGESTION

You might want to go through the text again, with either you or students taking it in turns to read aloud. This will provide you with the opportunity of checking some vocabulary and asking some more comprehension questions.

Comprehension check

1 Do this as a class.

Answer

The scientists who had created the atom bomb now had unbelievable power – power to kill and destroy. (Note: *I am become ...* is poetic. Normally we say *I have become ...*)

2 Students work in pairs or small groups to answer the questions.

Answers

a No. They had no idea how powerful it would be. Most of them expected it to be smaller.
b They were stunned. They couldn't believe it.
c One said 'It seemed to last forever. It blasted. It seemed to go right through you.' Another said 'It was too bright to look at. We all knew we had seen one of the great events in history.'
d There are road signs that say the land on either side belongs to the government. It is forbidden to remove dirt. There is a high watchtower and a barbed-wire fence.
e Because it didn't exist.
f They thought it would be an end to all wars, a way of establishing global government.
Politicians probably saw the bomb as a way of achieving supremacy, and a means of winning a war and beating their enemy.
g Harold Argo has no regrets about using the bomb against the Japanese. He says the war might have gone on a lot longer.
Carson Mark has doubts. He says no one knew how soon the Japanese would surrender. Perhaps it was unnecessary to kill so many people?
h It carried the first atomic bomb to be used in warfare. It left from San Francisco. It sailed to the island of Tinian. After it unloaded the bomb, it was sunk by a Japanese submarine. Many of its sailors were killed either in the explosion, or by sharks.
i August 6, 1945 at Hiroshima.

3 Do the first three or four of these as a class, so students see what they have to do.

Answers

a They are the physicists who created the first atomic bomb. They were all together at Los Alamos.
b The scientists. None of them knew what would happen when they exploded their bomb.
c The scientists. They were stunned by their creation.
d The inhabitants of Los Alamos today. There are just over 18,000 people.
e People who travel on State Highway 84. They are not to go on to government property, and they are not allowed to remove any dirt.
f The technicians are the people who built the bomb. The town of Los Alamos was built to house them.
g Protégés are people who are looked after, guided, and helped by someone who has influence, power, and more experience. The US government brought together this team of scientists from a variety of countries, but it didn't trust them.
h The real villain was Klaus Fuchs, but he was never suspected of espionage until too late.
i The original target of the bomb was Germany, but it was obvious by early 1945 that the bomb was not needed to make Germany surrender.
j They are the people who wonder whether it was necessary to kill so many people to bring the Second World War to an end.
k Oppenheimer named the test Trinity, partly because of the Christian concept of God the Father, the Son, and the Holy Spirit, but mainly because of the Hindu godhead of Vishnu, Brahma, and Siva.
l VIP stands for Very Important Person. Their observation point was 20 miles from the explosion.
m *Little Boy* was the nickname of the bomb dropped on Hiroshima.
n *Enola Gay* was the name the pilot gave his plane. It was his mother's name. This was the plane that dropped the bomb.

Language work

This is probably best done as a class, so you can direct and monitor.

Answers

1a ... the greatest collection of scientific brains ...
b ... their knowledge ...
The normal, unmarked word order has been reversed in both sentences to give emphasis.
2a The passive is used because the actual agents (probably the FBI) aren't important.
The focus is on the mail and the people who were sworn to secrecy.
b Oppenheimer is the focus of attention. Usually in passive sentences we do not have *by* + the agent, so when we do it is significant. The end of a sentence is a strong position. The inclusion of *by FBI men* stresses that Oppenheimer was followed by no less than the FBI – not just any ordinary detective.
c Klaus Fuchs is the focus. Who actually revealed him is irrelevant here.
d The focus is the ship *Indianapolis*. However, as in b above, the information *by a Japanese submarine* is in a strong position at the end of the sentence. It is very ironic that the boat that delivered the atomic bomb was itself destroyed by the Japanese.
e The focus is on the sailors. As in b and d above, the information that they were eaten alive by sharks comes as very dramatic news.

What do you think?

Discuss these questions as a class.

Answers

There are no set answers. It depends on one's point of view. It could be argued that the existence of nuclear weapons has kept some sort of world peace, because the use of them by one side would lead to mutually assured destruction (otherwise known as MAD). Hence they have not been used in warfare since 1945. On the other hand, it could be argued that the money spent in the development of these weapons could have been spent on more worthwhile things. The weapons were at the heart of the Cold War between West (NATO alliance) and East (The Warsaw Pact countries), which was defused in the 1970s with a move towards détente, and finally ended with the collapse of the Soviet Union in 1991. Similarly, Richard Rhodes' sentiments could be seen as correct or false. The bombs have been used in tests, but never in hostility. Nevertheless, the fact that they exist at all, and in such huge numbers, is very worrying.

● VOCABULARY **(SB p124)**

Homophones

1 Read the introduction as a class. Students work in pairs to find the two spellings.

NB *This can be more difficult than you might think. Also, students might not connect the two words as having exactly the same pronunciation.*

Answers

The first words given are the ones in the text.

a new knew
b plain plane
c sure shore
d would wood
e seen scene
f through threw

2 Students work in pairs to think of two spellings.

Answers

a peace piece
d weather whether

b court	caught	e mail	male
c way	weigh	f sight	site

Homonyms

1 Read the introduction as a class. Check that students understand the various meanings of *plain*.
Students work in pairs to fill the gaps.

Answers

a lasted	last	e long	longing
b accounts	account	f sign	sign
c sum	sum	g still	still
d race	racing		

2 In pairs, students think of two meanings for each word.

Sample answers

match	football match; a match to light a fire; to match words and pictures
draw	draw a picture; the football match was a draw
cross	a sign like X; angry; cross the road
fine	fine weather; to pay a parking fine
fair	fair hair; a fair decision
fit	healthy; be the right size
suit	wear a suit; red doesn't suit me; law suit
miss	Miss Smith; miss a train; miss your family
mind	Do you mind?; a quick mind = brain
mark	mark homework = correct; a mark on my shirt
sentence	a sentence in a paragraph; a prison sentence
point	point a finger; there's no point in complaining

Children's jokes

T 12.4 Listen to the jokes. Hopefully students will laugh, which is preferable to you having to explain! However, you will no doubt have to help a bit.

Answers

1 a football fan; an electric fan
2 a horn on a cow's head; a horn on a car
3 long = a long time; long = the shape
4 branch of a tree; branch of a bank or shop
5 sale/sail; sea/see
6 sell/cell; watch = see, watch = to tell the time
7 wave with your hand; wave on the beach
8 plain crisps = potato flavour; plain/plane
9 sore/saw; whole/hole; hoarse/horse

● LISTENING (SB p124)

Great events of the twentieth century

Pre-listening task

1 Brainstorm great events in your students' country or the world in general. Look at the photos as a class. Talk about what they illustrate. Encourage discussion if you feel your class is interested.

Answers

John F Kennedy's assassination in Dallas (1963)
Collapse of the Berlin Wall (1989)
Release of Nelson Mandela (1990)
Vietnam war (1954–75) Children in a napalm attack
First crossing from France to England by air (1909)
First man on the moon (1969)
Princess Diana's funeral (1997)

2 Students work in groups to think of a great event of the twentieth century for each of the categories. Stress that they don't have to agree on one event.

3 Discuss conclusions as a class.

Listening

T 12.5 Students listen to the six people (two of them, Pam and David, speak twice). They fill in the chart, and compare answers in pairs before class feedback. After listening to the first one, fill in the chart with students as an example.

POSSIBLE VOCABULARY PROBLEMS

This list is for your information only. We are not suggesting that all these words must be pre-taught.

apartheid = former political and social system in South Africa, in which the whites held all power and political rights, and blacks were forced to go to separate schools and live in separate areas.
seminal = important, influential
perspective
covering up = hiding
advent
the Pill (with a capital P) = birth control pill
penicillin — *congestion*
flippant — *structure of society*
decay — *drifting*
ripe for change — *it's our turn*

Answers

When students are filling in the category column, there might be some disagreement. This is fine, as there is not necessarily one answer only.

Speaker	Event	Category
Pam	End of apartheid in South Africa, the day Nelson Mandela was released	P, SC
David	Collapse of the Berlin Wall	P, SC
Alexa	Internet	Tech, SC
Penny	Feminism, the Pill	M, SC
Pam	Penicillin	M
David	Motor car	Tr, SC
Hilary	First World War	W, SC
Barry	Elvis Presley	AC, SC

Comprehension check

1 Discuss this as a class. Students discuss the rest of the questions in pairs. Have some class feedback.

Answers

2

a She can see Nelson Mandela walking to freedom with his then wife by his side. The crowds were excited. She was moved.

b The fact that communism collapsed so fast as a result of the Berlin Wall coming down.
No. He says that the introduction of capitalism is both good and bad.

c The person you're talking to on the Internet might be lying about themselves.
You talk to them in a way you wouldn't normally, because you can't judge them by their physical appearance and presence. You can only go by what they say.

d She has the right to have her own life, her own job as well as being a mother. The Pill allows women to have control over their bodies, to give them a life after babies.

e If she hadn't had penicillin, she would have died in childbirth.

f The balance between using the car properly without letting it take over our lives.

g The whole structure of society changes; everybody's life changed. Life in the 1920s was so completely different from life in the 1900s that it must have seemed like a different century.

h It seems silly to suggest that the greatest event of a whole century is a pop singer. However, the arrival of Elvis Presley changed youth culture forever. Young people used to be like their parents, dress like them, and copy their way of life. After Elvis, youth had an identity. It rebelled and challenged. Society was ripe for a change because the older generation had made so many mistakes. Young people wanted a turn at organizing things.

● WRITING (SB p126)

Focusing attention

NB *This activity is to revise ways of adding emphasis via word order, use of the passive, and emphatic structures.*

Remind students of the two texts about Michelangelo on p118–9. Why did one sound better than the other?

1 Read the introduction as a class. Do the first three or four paragraphs together, so students see what they have to do. Discuss the answers carefully. Students finish the exercise in pairs. Alternatively, you could set it for homework and check answers in class.

Answers

1 a The opening paragraph will start with the focus of attention, which is Elvis Presley.

2 b We are interested in Presley, not his parents.

3 a *As a teenager* comes at a strong point at the beginning of the sentence. This emphasizes his early age when he began playing the guitar.

4 b The focus is on Presley, not Sam Phillips. The time expression *In July 1954* at the beginning of the sentence balances with *As a teenager* at the beginning of the previous sentence.

5 b The emphatic structure *What earned him ...* in (a) is inappropriate. The unmarked word order in (b) is better.

6 a Presley is the focus of attention, not his career.

7 a The emphatic structure *It was 45 records* in (b) is unnecessary.

8 b Presley is the focus of attention, not viewers.

9 a The word order in (b) is unnatural in English.

10 a *Before Presley* is in a strong position at the beginning of the first sentence. In the second, the focus is on Presley, not youth culture.

2 **T 12.6** Students listen and check their answers.

3 Students write about the career of someone that interests them. They could make notes in class and write it up for homework.

PostScript (SB p127)

Linking and commenting

NB *This is a final exercise on the grammar of the spoken language. These expressions, mainly adverbs, express the speaker's attitude to what is being said, and link what has been said before to what is about to be said. It can be quite difficult for learners to appreciate exactly what they mean and when to use them. You should expect your students to recognize them long before they start to use them correctly.*

1 Read the introduction as a class.

2 Students work in pairs to choose the correct linking or commenting expression. Have some feedback.

Answers

a apparently Actually
b Personally However Anyway
c Hopefully After all Actually Of course
d All the same Basically Honestly
e Definitely surely Obviously basically Ideally

3 **T 12.7** Students listen and check their answers. In pairs, they practise the dialogues.

Don't forget!

Workbook Unit 12

Exercise 10 Hot Verbs *set* and *break*
Exercise 11 Prepositions – noun + prepositions
Exercise 12 Pronunciation – nouns and verbs

Photocopiable materials

Unit 1 **PostScript** (SB page 15, role cards)

You're going to	Australia
Your address is	11, Carcoola Road, Barra Brui, New South Wales 2075
You're going on	21 June
You're staying with	Jonie and Bruce Wilson
Your telephone number is	00 612 94492789
You're taking	A$ 1,000

You're going to	The United States
Your address is	699 Sutter Street (Suite 590) San Francisco, CA 94102
You're going on	17 September
You're staying with	Mike Buchanan
Your telephone number is	001 415 749 5644
You're taking	US$ 2,000

You're going to	England
Your address is	98 Main Road, Wiggington, Tamworth Staffs WM2 8GR
You're going on	5 November
You're staying with	Gaye and Barry Goldsmith
Your telephone number is	01827 648920
You're taking	£500 Sterling

You're going to	South Africa
Your address is	25, Birkett Road, Rondebosch 7700 Cape Town
You're going on	28 August
You're staying with	Peter and Jean Pooler
Your telephone number is	002 721 7192356
You're taking	ZAR 3,000 Rand

You're going to	Canada
Your address is	356 Fairlawn Avenue, MSM 156 Toronto 20, Ontario
You're going on	5 January
You're staying with	Ray and Elsie Swift
Your telephone number is	00 1416 755489
You're taking	CAD$ 1,500

You're going to	Ireland
Your address is	16 Lower Main Street, Dundrum, Dublin D14
You're going on	10 December
You're staying with	Phillip and Joan O'Doherty
Your telephone number is	00353 12988601
You're taking	IEP 900 Punt

You're going to	The USA
Your address is	198 Madison Avenue, New York, NY 10016–4314
You're going on	28 March
You're staying with	Jackie Rosenthal
Your telephone number is	001 800 441 5229
You're taking	US$ 850

You're going to	Wales
Your address is	11 Cae Mawr Gardens, Porth, Rhondda, Mid Glamorgan CF36 9RO
You're going on	9 August
You're staying with	Megan and Rhys Llewellyn
Your telephone number is	01443 649826
You're taking	£650 Sterling

Unit 2 **Practice 3 Speaking and listening** (SB page 18)

Student A

Jimmy Kramer's VIRGO GROUP

Originally *Virgo* sold records. The company was founded in (**1**) ... (***When?***). The chairman and owner of *Virgo*, Jimmy Kramer, opened his first record shop in Oxford Street, London.

He built a (**3**) ... (***What?***) in the garden of his house in Cambridge, and since then more than (**5**) ... bands (***How many?***) have recorded albums there. One of the most successful is *Black Days, White Nights*, by Pete Moor. Over 15 million copies have been sold worldwide.

In 1992 Jimmy decided to (**7**) ... (***What?***). He bought a Jumbo jet and started his own airline, *Virgo Pacific*. In 1994 he had (**9**) ... planes (***How many?***), and now he has twenty-four planes. He has been flying to Japan and the Far East since (**11**) ... (***How long?***).

Jimmy has been trying to expand his business. His company now includes book publishing, film production, clubs, and hotels. The *Virgo Group* has won over (**13**) ... awards (***How many?***) for its exports. The company employs over 22,000 people.

Student B

Jimmy Kramer's VIRGO GROUP

Originally *Virgo* sold records. The company was founded in 1980. The chairman and owner of *Virgo*, Jimmy Kramer, opened his first record shop in (**2**) ... (***Where?***).

He built a recording studio in (**4**) ... (***Where?***), and since then more than one hundred bands have recorded albums there. One of the most successful is *Black Days, White Nights*, by Pete Moor. Over (**6**) ... copies (***How many copies of?***) have been sold worldwide.

In 1992 Jimmy decided to diversify. He bought a (**8**) ... (***What?***) and started his own airline, *Virgo Pacific*. In 1994 he had ten planes, and now he has (**10**) ... planes (***How many?***). He has been flying to Japan and the Far East since 1996.

Jimmy has been trying to (**12**) ... (***What?***). His company now includes book publishing, film production, clubs, and hotels. The *Virgo Group* has won over twenty awards for its exports. The company employs (**14**) ... people (***How many?***).

Unit 2 **Practice 4 Roleplay** (SB page 18)

Information for the journalists

You are going to interview the chairman of the *Virgo Group*, Jimmy Kramer. Work together to decide on some questions to ask him. Here are some suggestions.

Personal background:

When ... born?
... brothers and sisters?
Where ... school?
... favourite subjects?
... university?
... like adventure?
... ever flown a plane yourself?
... a plane of your own?
... ever climbed a mountain?
How old ... got married?
... children?
How many times ... married?
How long ... married?
Where ... live?
How long ... lived there?
... sport?
... hobbies?
... ever thought about writing a book?

Questions about the *Virgo Group*:

... always wanted your own business?
How ... start *Virgo*?
How many people ... employ?
... still expanding?

Information for Jimmy Kramer

Here is some information about you. If you are asked a question to which you don't know the answer, use your imagination!

You were born in 1960. You are the oldest of three children. You were educated at Manchester Grammar School. You weren't very academic, and you didn't do very well at exams. Your favourite subject was geography because there was never any homework.

You have always liked adventure. You learned to fly a helicopter when you were still a teenager, and since then you have gained your private pilot's licence. You have two light aircraft. You have also climbed Mount Everest and Mont Blanc.

You are married to Penny, your second wife. You got married in 1989. You have two children, Sally aged 8, and Ben aged 4. You live in London and Cambridge, and you also own an island off the Scottish coast.

You play tennis and cricket. You like chess. You go skiing three or four times a year. You also adore doing crossword puzzles. You have been writing a book about your approach to business for the past three years, but you are finding it difficult to find the time to complete it.

Virgo employs over 22,000 people. You are moving the company into financial services, business loans, and insurance. You are also opening radio stations, and you're thinking about having a television channel.

Unit 3 **Reading and listening** (SB page 30)

A synopsis of

***The Mayor of Casterbridge* – a story of characters**

by Thomas Hardy (1840–1928)

Michael Henchard, a hay-maker, his wife, Susan, and young daughter Elizabeth-Jane go to a country fair and horse auction. Michael gets very drunk, and, inspired by the auction, he ends up selling his wife and daughter for five guineas to a sailor called Newson. The next day, when Michael is sober again, he is horrified at what he has done and vows not to touch alcohol for twenty years. From then on he works hard, becomes rich and respected and finally the mayor of the town of Casterbridge. Meanwhile Newson has taken Susan and the child to Canada. They work hard but with little success and eventually return to England. Their relationship is not good and Newson sails off again to Newfoundland. A short time later Susan hears that Newson has been lost at sea.

So, after 18 years, she decides to look for her first husband. She soon finds him in Casterbridge, and she and Elizabeth-Jane are reunited with him. Susan leads Michael to believe that Elizabeth-Jane is his child, but in fact she is Newson's, (Michael's daughter, the first Elizabeth-Jane, had died just three months after her arrival in Canada.) Finally Susan Henchard falls sick and dies, leaving Michael a letter in which she tells him the truth about Elizabeth-Jane. His life then starts to go to pieces. His business is ruined; the story of how he had sold his wife and child many years before is made public, and he starts drinking again. His business rival becomes the mayor of Casterbridge and marries Elizabeth-Jane. Then Newson, not drowned, only missing, returns from sea and claims Elizabeth-Jane as his daughter. The unfortunate Michael Henchard finally dies lonely and alone in a hut in the wilds of Egdon Heath near Casterbridge. He has lost everything that he ever possessed.

Unit 4 **Language in context** (SB page 38)

I left England with £5 and now I'm a multi-millionaire!

A British woman who began a new life in Australia with just £5 in her pocket a few years ago has sold her business for a huge amount of money.

Cherry Haines, 39, who once worked as a market stallholder, made all of her fortune from marketing a new kind of make-up. She left England because there weren't many jobs, caught a flight to the other side of the world, and arrived without any qualifications. She only knew two people.

'The flight cost £1,500, which left me penniless. At first I stayed with a friend. Then I had a bit of luck.' The friend gave her the name of Peter Maddox, an Australian businessman. 'I rang him and told him I was the best salesperson in England and that he should give me a job.'

He liked her idea for a sort of make-up that stays on all day, so together they formed a company to market it. At first she was earning just A$10,000 a year, but later she was getting a great deal of money every year. 'Hard work means happiness to me,' she said.

Her brother, Roger Haines, who is spending several weeks with her in Brisbane, said 'She left school when she was 16. She had very little work experience. But she could sell a fridge to an Eskimo. Ambition has led to success.'

a How much money did she have when she left England?
b When did she leave England?
c How much has she sold her business for?
d Why did she leave England?
e Did she have any qualifications?
f Did she have many friends?
g How much did she pay for her flight?
h How much did she earn at first?
i How much did she earn later?
j How long is her brother staying with her?
k What did he say about her work experience?

44

You are ready to open the fast food restaurant, but no one knows about it. You need to generate some awareness in the town, but you only have a limited budget. You must spend the money wisely.

- The budget could be spent on traditional advertising in the local press. It has an excellent readership so everyone will see the ads. *go to* **37**
- Or you could do a public relations stunt! You could make some 'funny food' costumes and dress up as a carrot! Then you could go around town handing out leaflets to everyone. Wouldn't it be fun? *go to* **20**

22

Your friend agrees to join you and contribute half the funds. Now you have to decide what type of restaurant you want.

He/she wants to open a fast food restaurant as there aren't any in town, and it would be easy to set up.

You don't want to be serving fast food. You'd rather open an upmarket bistro. As well as being more enjoyable work the profits will be far higher.

What are you going to do?

- Open a fast food restaurant. *go to* **44**
- Open a bistro. *go to* **31**
- Conduct some market research. *go to* **2**

64

You give the police the information. Fortunately there is no trace of your 'ex-friend'.

Your good relations with the police mean that they use your fast food restaurant quite a bit. It makes a lot of money but the presence of the police does tend to keep other customers away.

- So what? The police give you easily enough business to keep going and you're not likely to get burgled with so many police around. You could tailor your restaurant to them. *go to* **55**
- You politely and very tactfully persuade the police to use a different restaurant from yours. *go to* **6**

2

You conduct some research and discover that a bistro will be opening in town before yours. However, there aren't any plans for more fast food restaurants.

- You are determined to carry on with the bistro and are not worried about competition. *go to* **31**
- Maybe a fast food restaurant would be easier to run anyway. *go to* **44**

69

Discounting prices doesn't seem to be working. People now think your food is of poor quality just because it's cheap, but they haven't even tried it yet!

You can't win! If you put prices up, people will stay away too! What can you do to make the restaurant busier and make more money?

- You put the prices back up but give the customers something extra for free. Your friend still has the soft drinks that he/she can sell you so that you can give them away. *go to* **39**
- How about staying open 24 hours a day? There are factories nearby that do night shifts. There is sure to be lots of business. *go to* **29**

8

The banks agree to lend you as much money as you need. That seems very generous, until you see the amount of interest they want to charge.

- The interest charges look huge. You decide to look for a partner to share the start-up costs. *go to* **22**
- It's a high cost but you'll be successful enough. *go to* **33**

20

Oh dear! It was a great stunt and everyone in town certainly knows about your restaurant. Unfortunately your partner has been arrested for obstruction of the pavement. The problem is the bail money would take the last of your cash and may stop you from opening on time.

- You decide to use the money to pay your partner's bail. *go to* **38**
- You decide to open the restaurant. *go to* **59**

59

You don't pay your partner's bail, but open up instead. Business is pretty slow, so you don't miss your partner.

When he/she is finally released, you need to start attracting more people into the restaurant. You have two ideas on how to do it.

- A friend of yours has offered you several cases of soft drink at an extremely good price. You could give free drinks with every meal. *go to* **39**
- Or you could discount your food as a special offer. *go to* **69**

38

You've got your partner out of jail and still managed to open on time. However, all this activity hasn't brought in many customers. You need a special opening offer. You have two ideas. You could buy some cheap soft drinks from a friend, and give them out free with every meal. Or you could discount your prices.

- You want to give soft drinks out free with every meal. *go to* **39**
- You discount your prices on food as an opening offer. *go to* **69**

39

Success! The free drinks idea has gone down very well. It's bringing the people in. However, it has also brought the police in! Apparently that consignment of drinks was stolen from a nearby factory and they want to know where you got them from.

- You tell the police the truth, that you bought the drinks in good faith from a friend of yours and give the police his/her name and address. *go to* **64**
- You lie to protect your friend and say that a travelling sales representative came to the restaurant and sold them to you. *go to* **73**

11

Word gets around town that you sacked him. Feeling is running very high, and people start to boycott the restaurant. Boy, was that guy popular! You try to track him down without success. Business gets worse and worse, you're ruined.

- You have come to the end of this activity.

  BAD LUCK!

6

The police understand your position and now are far less regular visitors. However, instead of the rest of the town now rushing to use your restaurant you only get the local kids coming in. You've got nothing against kids but they just use the place as a meeting place and buy one drink between ten of them that lasts for two hours.

- You tell them to leave or you'll report them to the police for loitering. *go to* **63**
- You leave them alone. After all, they haven't got anywhere else to go. *go to* **54**

63

Things are very quiet now! You got rid of the police and now the kids as well. Is there anyone left?

You've got one last chance to make it all work. The situation is that bad.

- You could try and get the police to come back and use the restaurant. *go to* **55**
- You could sell out to a large national chain of restaurants. They've guaranteed you a job and a good price for the restaurant. *go to* **18**

55

You are doing quite well since you specialized for the police. Unfortunately, a canteen opens at the police station itself, and overnight half of your business has gone. You need to find some more customers from somewhere.

- As the market is competitive you look for a niche to exploit. You could open a fast food vegetarian restaurant. *go to* **23**
- People are all so obsessed with their weight these days. A place that specializes in low-fat food could be successful. *go to* **47**

37

The ads appear and trade starts to pick up, but it's not great. One of your customers tells you that the restaurant in the next town is doing special offers, so most people are going there. You need some special offers of your own to bring them into the restaurant.

- A friend of yours has offered you several cases of soft drinks at an extremely good price. You could give free drinks with every meal. *go to* **39**
- You could discount your food to be more competitive with the other restaurant. *go to* **69**

73

You tried to protect your friend, but they really want to know where you got the drinks from. You have to tell them the truth to be able to get on with running your restaurant.

- You tell the police where the drinks came from. *go to* **64**

18

Well, at least you've got a job and a nice uniform to go with it!

It is certainly not what you had in mind when you set out to run a restaurant. You have very little control over what goes on. You're never going to be happy there.

- You have come to the end of this activity.
  BAD LUCK!

23

It sounded like a good idea, but the number of vegetarians is still quite low in the area, and you are fed up with telling people that no, you don't sell hamburgers.

- You decide to try the low-fat fast food restaurant idea. *go to* **47**

26

You took the food around and got the money. You nearly got away with it, until someone with an allergy to butter falls ill the next day. They find out the truth, demand the money back and the story makes the headlines in all the local press. Your restaurant is ruined.

- You have come to the end of this activity.
  BAD LUCK!

29

Now you're making more money. The night-time business is good. The problem is you're drinking most of your extra profits in the amount of coffee you need to stay awake! It's time you employed some staff. Unemployment is high so you won't need to pay them much, and you need to save some money. However, if you pay a reasonable wage you'll probably get a better standard of applicant.

- You offer a low wage for the position. *go to* **56**
- You offer a high wage for the position. *go to* **32**

57

You tell the customer you cannot make the food. They ask for whatever you can do. You prepare a range of completely oil-free foods that are a massive success with all the health freaks in the area. The restaurant becomes famous for its recipes and you become a wealthy and healthy restaurateur.

- You have come to the end of this activity.
  WELL DONE!

35

Your new 'celebrity' restaurant is proving to be very popular with families. To add atmosphere you put up some signed pictures of Hollywood actors. People start to ask you whether the actors have actually eaten in the restaurant. The fact is that they haven't, but will it upset the customers if you tell them the truth?

- You tell them that a famous actor did pop in for a snack one day to keep them impressed. *go to* **17**
- You admit that you simply put the photographs up to impress customers. No one famous has actually eaten in the place. *go to* **67**

47

It's a very original idea and the people eating fast food like the idea that yours is better for them. You do outside catering for special events and offices as well. You get a large order one day, but unfortunately you have run out of olive oil. You've only got butter. You don't want to lose the order. Will you make the food using the butter or turn down the order?

- They won't notice the difference. You can make the food and take it around. You need the money after all. *go to* **26**
- You have to turn the order and the money down. They won't be impressed, but if they found out what was in the food you could be in even more trouble. *go to* **57**

54

You let the young people stay. Word soon gets around and you end up having so many young people in that you start to make a profit.

You worry your restaurant isn't trendy enough. You could lose your business! Should you renovate the restaurant to appeal to all the young customers?

- You decide to renovate the restaurant to appeal to your young customer base. *go to* **25**
- Don't bother! Hopefully, the restaurant will be just as appealing to the new youngsters in the area. *go to* **58**

67

You told them the truth, but customers don't seem to mind. They keep coming in just in case someone really famous is there. When they never see anyone famous, you become well-known as the Restaurant of the Stars where no star has ever eaten.

> You have come to the end of this activity.
> **WELL DONE!**

32

You get a lot of good applicants and employ someone who works extremely hard. Your twenty-four hour fast food restaurant is doing really well. An opportunity arises to expand into next door. You're sure you could fill the seats.

> Expand in to next door. It's quite a lot of money, but nothing ventured, nothing gained. *go to* **34**

> Wait a while, you've only just become this busy and successful. It would be best to consolidate your position and build up some cash reserves. *go to* **51**

56

The people turning up for interviews are pretty appalling. You don't see anyone you would consider employing, and decide to increase the wages you are offering.

> You increase the wage you are offering for the position. *go to* **32**

34

The risk has paid off! Business is excellent. You and your partner are very confident in your ability to run a restaurant. You believe the concept would work in lots of other locations. You could become extremely rich. If you do this, you will need to raise some investment capital.

> You decide to take the idea further and bring in a number of investors to open up more restaurants. *go to* **71**

> Stick with what you've got. You might not become extremely wealthy, but things will be all right. *go to* **16**

71

You now have a chain of restaurants in the area. The problem is, there are now a lot of people who influence the business, not just your partner and yourself. The other investors are demanding some changes be made to increase profitability. You don't believe they will work, but the others could fire you from the company if you don't agree.

> Agree to their demands. They are all respected business people, so they should know what they are talking about, even if they don't run restaurants. *go to* **65**

> Refuse their demands and stick to your plans, even though you're risking being made redundant. *go to* **15**

17

They're extremely impressed and soon tell their friends. Business picks up as people come in just in to see a celebrity dining. As the talk continues, the famous Hollywood actor finally gets to hear about it. He/she promptly files a lawsuit against you. You lose the case and your restaurant as part payment of the fees. The restaurant is now owned by a famous person but you've lost your livelihood.

> You have come to the end of this activity.
> **BAD LUCK!**

51

You haven't expanded. There are now queues at certain times of day. This is no bad thing, as some of the most fashionable eating places always have queues outside. You have a couple of ideas that could work in this situation.

- Expand into next door. You think people might become fed up with queueing for fast food at some point. go to 34
- Take the restaurant upmarket like Planet Hollywood, which is run by celebrities. They make lots of money and always have a queue outside. go to 35

66

That is a lot of money! You're not going to have to work for a year.

After all the hard work you've put in, you feel it's been worth it and will get stuck into another project next year.

- You have come to the end of this activity.
  WELL DONE!

31

Your bistro is being decorated and will soon be open. However, another one has opened before you and is quickly building up its business. There is going to be a lot of competition in town. Will you both be successful?

- Maybe fast food wouldn't be so bad. There is still time to change your mind. go to 44
- Competition never hurt anyone and you're confident that your restaurant will be successful. go to 5

65

The changes they forced you to make are a disaster. To increase profit you buy cheaper food from a bad supplier and lower the wages. This makes your staff unhappy. Customers soon notice the changes and stay away from your restaurant. You're ruined.

- You have come to the end of this activity.
  BAD LUCK!

70

You don't sell up, but as a result your working relationship suffers. You didn't realize how much your partner wanted to sell. It has damaged your working relationship and the restaurant as a result. You don't remain open for long.

- You have come to the end of this activity.
  BAD LUCK!

5

The bistro is ready to open. Your partner feels that you should spend the last of your money on a big opening night party for family and friends who have helped. You would prefer to start generating revenue and have paying customers in.

- Have a big party for family and friends. go to 21
- Have an opening party for paying customers. go to 43

16

You didn't take the opportunity to open a chain. However, the investors you were going to link with have offered a very high price for your restaurant. Are you going to sell or not?

- Sell up for half a million pounds and give something else a go. This restaurant business is pretty hard work. go to 66
- Don't sell even though your partner wants to. You have come a long way since your first idea. go to 70

68

Business is OK just being open in the evening. You're getting more calls from local companies asking whether they can bring in clients for lunch. You can't bear turning money away, so decide to open for lunch-times.

- You decide to open for lunch-times as well. go to 53

15

You refuse their demands and gain a lot of respect. You prove through your management that the running of the restaurants should be left to you and your partner. You make a lot of money for the investors and yourselves.

- You have come to the end of this activity.
  WELL DONE!

21

Great party! Everyone had a wonderful time. So good in fact that they drank a lot more of your opening supplies of drink than you expected. You don't have the money to replace all of the stocks immediately. How are you going to open without sufficient stocks of alcohol to offer the customers?

- You could become a Bring Your Own restaurant where the customers bring alcoholic drinks in themselves. go to 36
- There is a lot of profit on drink and you don't want to lose this. You know where you can get some cheap drink to tide things over until you can afford more. go to 50

4

This is extremely unpopular. Customers are furious when you ask them to give up the table at the end of the meal. It's giving you a very bad name. You think it might ruin you eventually and decide to do something different.

- You'll lose all your customers if you persist with this plan. You decide to try charging a bottle opening fee. go to 60

36

It proves to be extremely popular with your customers. The problem is they bring an awful lot of drink with them and stay for a long time. You're not making enough money from them to keep the business profitable.

- You could restrict the amount of time people are allowed to stay. Lots of restaurants have a number of 'sittings' in a night – so can you. go to 4
- Charge a bottle opening fee for the drink that they bring in. At least then you'll be making some money from it. go to 60

43

Your party for customers was very successful! They love the place. A number of people tell you to open at lunch-time as well as the evening. You'll make money, but you'll also need more staff. Is it worth it?

- You decide to open at lunch-time as well as the evening. *go to* **53**
- You think you'll just stick to being open in the evening. *go to* **68**

10

Your business is now highly profitable and relations with the companies are excellent. The regulars ask for special table booking rights above all other people as they eat in your restaurant so frequently.

- You think its a good idea. After all, they are the best customers. *go to* **30**
- You decide not to agree with them as it will tie you in with these companies too closely. *go to* **62**

60

The bottle opening charge makes money but it still does not cover the loss from not selling drinks. You decide to offer live entertainment but you have to decide what type of entertainment.

- You decide to put on regular live music – that's always a popular event. *go to* **46**
- You've heard people talking about a restaurant that does live comedy while people eat. Sounds like a good idea. *go to* **7**

30

It goes very well for a while. Your special relationship with the local companies is very good for business. Unfortunately recession hits, and the first savings companies make are in entertainment. You are soon looking at an empty restaurant and need to attract some more customers.

- You go looking for other companies. You're a specialized business restaurant now, and need to maintain a similar profit margin. *go to* **49**
- You cut prices drastically in an attempt to get your old customers back through the door. *go to* **3**

53

Lunch-time trade is good, business people buy the expensive food and wine to impress clients. They also tip well. You could easily increase prices on everything and start making very expensive dishes. You know they'll sell very well.

- You introduce your new and more expensive menu and drinks list. *go to* **10**
- You worry about losing your normal customers. You stick with the original menu. *go to* **27**

3

Luckily for you everyone still appreciates a bargain! People return to your restaurant and the low prices in the recession prove to be very popular. Even through the bad times your restaurant remains successful. You've been through a lot but you've proven that you can run a restaurant in any circumstances.

- You have come to the end of this activity.
  WELL DONE!

62

Recession hits! What a good job you didn't tie up too closely with those businesses! You've still lost a large percentage of your turnover though. How are you going to keep the restaurant going in a recession?

- There must be companies still making money in the area. You've specialized for businesses so that's who you will attract. *go to* **49**
- You cut prices drastically in an attempt to get your old customers back through the door. *go to* **3**

45

It's a good idea. The food is still very good but people can't eat as much. They even think it's better value than before because they're so full. You now have a permanently busy restaurant that you and your partner enjoy running. You're a great success!

- You have come to the end of this activity.
  WELL DONE!

49

So many companies have closed down that there is no business lunch market at all. Your highly specialized restaurant is doomed until the economy picks up markedly. The local people do not have much sympathy for you as you forgot them when better profits came along. You have to close down.

- You have come to the end of this activity.
  BAD LUCK!

19

You scrap the buffet, and lunch-time trade soon disappears. You are convinced people will change their minds, so you do nothing to reverse the trend. By the time you realize they aren't coming back, you've lost too much money and are forced to close.

- You have come to the end of this activity.
  BAD LUCK!

40

The all-you-can-eat buffet is very popular, and people in the area soon start putting on weight at your expense. This is the problem! It's so popular and people so greedy that the buffet is a large drain on your profit. Something needs to change.

- Scrap the idea. It's done the job of making the place popular. You don't need it now. *go to* **19**
- Change the food you offer and include a lot more filling recipes to make people eat less. *go to* **45**

27

You keep your normal menu without specializing. It does not bring in enough daytime revenue so you need to consider other options.

- You can't resist specializing for businesses at lunch-time. The prospects look too good. *go to* **10**
- You introduce an all-you-can-eat lunch-time buffet. These are always popular and bound to increase business. *go to* **40**

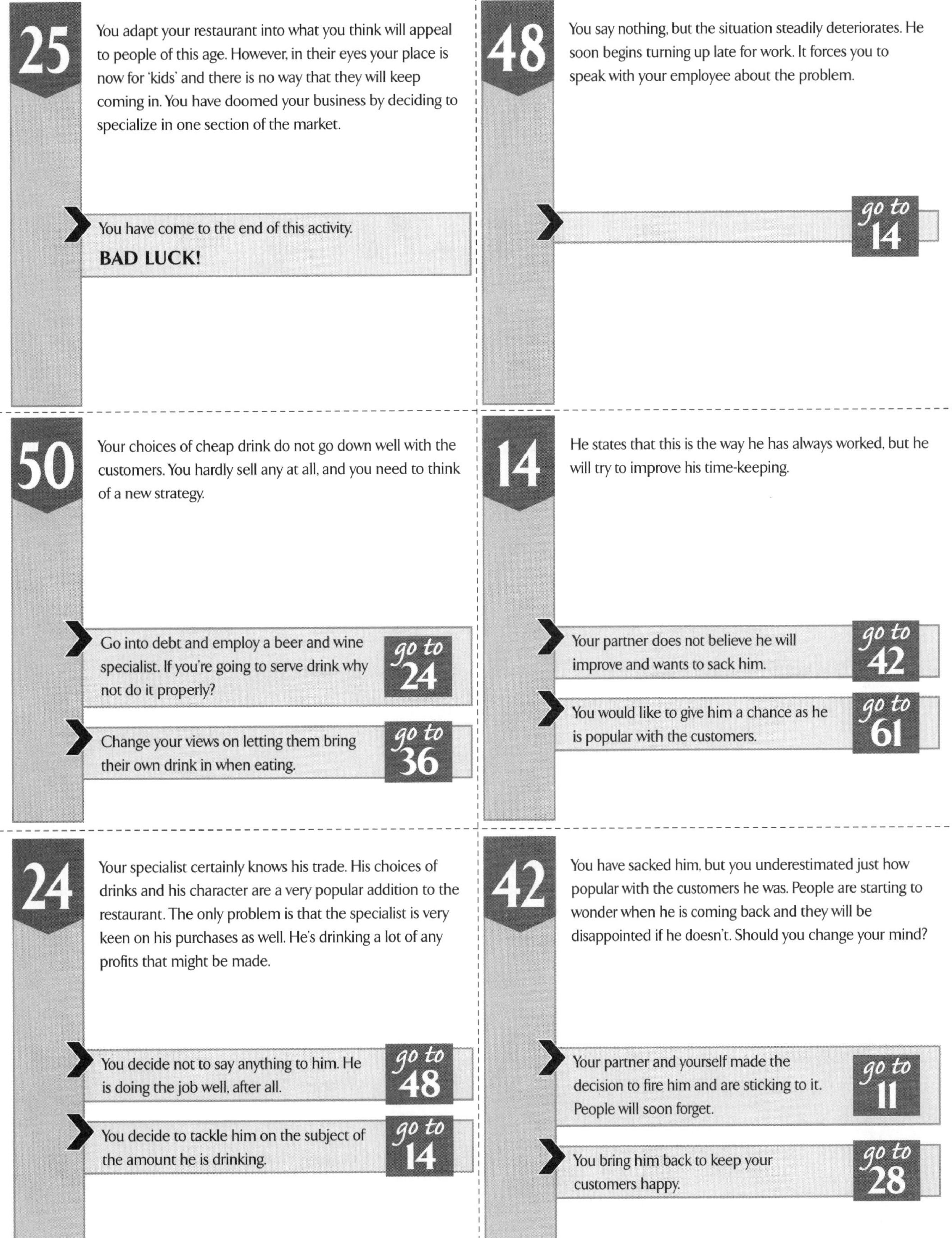

25

You adapt your restaurant into what you think will appeal to people of this age. However, in their eyes your place is now for 'kids' and there is no way that they will keep coming in. You have doomed your business by deciding to specialize in one section of the market.

> You have come to the end of this activity.
> **BAD LUCK!**

48

You say nothing, but the situation steadily deteriorates. He soon begins turning up late for work. It forces you to speak with your employee about the problem.

> *go to* **14**

50

Your choices of cheap drink do not go down well with the customers. You hardly sell any at all, and you need to think of a new strategy.

> Go into debt and employ a beer and wine specialist. If you're going to serve drink why not do it properly? *go to* **24**

> Change your views on letting them bring their own drink in when eating. *go to* **36**

14

He states that this is the way he has always worked, but he will try to improve his time-keeping.

> Your partner does not believe he will improve and wants to sack him. *go to* **42**

> You would like to give him a chance as he is popular with the customers. *go to* **61**

24

Your specialist certainly knows his trade. His choices of drinks and his character are a very popular addition to the restaurant. The only problem is that the specialist is very keen on his purchases as well. He's drinking a lot of any profits that might be made.

> You decide not to say anything to him. He is doing the job well, after all. *go to* **48**

> You decide to tackle him on the subject of the amount he is drinking. *go to* **14**

42

You have sacked him, but you underestimated just how popular with the customers he was. People are starting to wonder when he is coming back and they will be disappointed if he doesn't. Should you change your mind?

> Your partner and yourself made the decision to fire him and are sticking to it. People will soon forget. *go to* **11**

> You bring him back to keep your customers happy. *go to* **28**

61

You keep him on, but he is still not very dependable. He believes he would be much better if he had extra responsibility and a profit share of the wine takings. This would be a risky move.

- You decide to take the risk with him and give him a more important role in the restaurant. *go to* **12**
- There's no way you can give him more responsibility. Who knows what could happen? *go to* **72**

28

Being given the sack was a sobering experience for him. He is a changed person on return and makes an extremely valuable member of the team. You've made your restaurant a success!

- You have come to the end of this activity. **WELL DONE!**

72

With no extra responsibilities his drinking problem gets worse. You are just thinking about warning him again when there is an accident with a flaming brandy and the restaurant is burnt down. Everyone is safe but you have not got a business any more.

- You have come to the end of this activity. **BAD LUCK!**

58

You stuck with what you are good at, which is appealing to young people who don't have anywhere else to go. You've got a guaranteed business for many years if each new generation follows the one before. They're also a lot easier to please than older people. Your restaurant remains a success for many years.

- You have come to the end of this activity. **WELL DONE!**

12

It's a gamble, but it pays off. The added responsibility leads to a whole new attitude from your drinks expert. You now have a very good team and a profitable restaurant, a success.

- You have come to the end of this activity. **WELL DONE!**

46

The live music experiment is working, but you need to specialize with one type of music. People are confused about what sort of restaurant you are running.

- You could specialize in jazz music. You're not keen on it, but the band you had in was liked by the customers. *go to* **13**
- Or you could have some music you can really dance to! You're still young, as are a lot of the customers. *go to* **9**

9

You don't sell much food at the gigs but you don't need to. Everyone gets through such large amounts of soft drinks that you're making vast amounts of money and having a great time as well. You're the proud owners of a Rock Café and loving every second of it.

> You have come to the end of this activity.
> **WELL DONE!**

7

Your most popular acts use some very bad language. This offends some of your customers. You tell them that comedy is only at weekends but they seem very upset by it.

> Change the comedians to some safer ones who will not upset anyone. *go to* **41**

> Stick with the acts you have. They might be rude but they are very popular with most people. *go to* **52**

13

You and your partner have so little idea about jazz music that you hire some truly awful bands. This means that people actually stay away. This, together with the cost of the bands, damages your profitability so much you're forced to close.

> You have come to the end of this activity.
> **BAD LUCK!**

41

Your new comedians are certainly inoffensive, they are also not very funny. People are actually staying away from the bistro and you do not make enough money to keep the place in business. You tried your best but simply could not make it a success.

> You have come to the end of this activity.
> **BAD LUCK!**

33

You run into trouble very quickly. As well as paying the large interest payments there is only one of you to do the work. That means it will be twice as long before you open and are able to start repaying the bank.

> The prospect of setting up with a partner who will pay off the bank with his share and help set up is too attractive. You change your mind and go in with him/her. *go to* **22**

52

Rude but funny, the comedians are very popular and ensure that you have regular packed nights in the bistro. You have now covered the revenue from not selling alcohol, and you have a very successful and busy restaurant.

> You have come to the end of this activity.
> **WELL DONE!**

Unit 5 **Listening and speaking** (SB page 56)

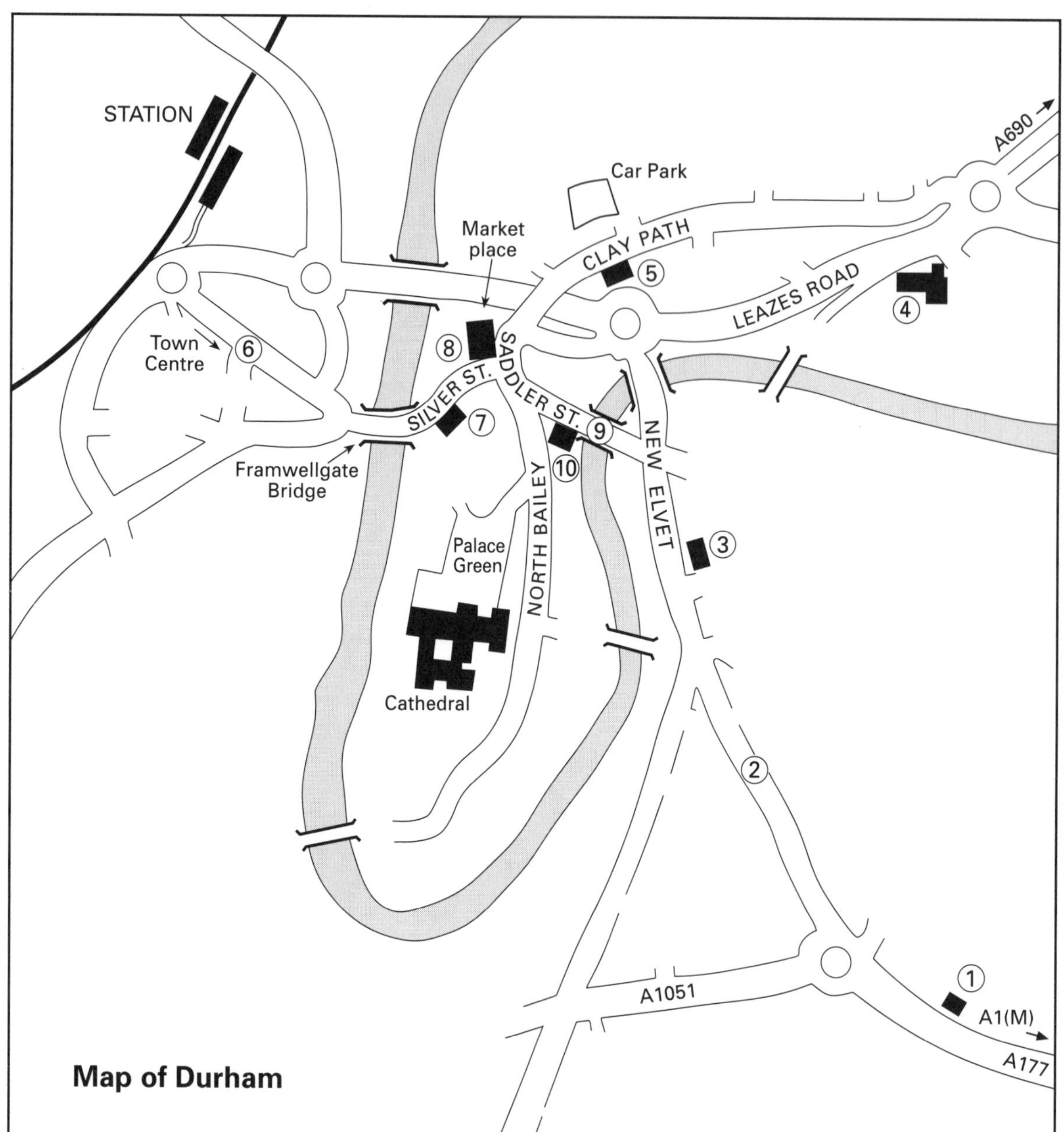

Questions for Group A

1 What's this building? ________________

2 What's this road? ________________

3 What's this building? ________________

4 What's this building? ________________

5 What's this? ________________

Questions for Group B

6 What's this road? ________________

7 What's this shop? ________________

8 What's this building? ________________

9 What's this bridge? ________________

10 What's this? ________________

Unit 5 **PostScript** (SB page 57)

Beginning a phone conversation	
Answering the phone	Hello. 267890. Hello. Simpson's Travel Agents. Hello. The Regent Hotel. Kathy speaking. How can I help you?
Introducing yourself	Hello, James. This is Sarah Jackson. Hi, Sarah. It's Alan, Alan Cunningham. (Is that Mr Brown?) Speaking.
Asking who is speaking	Is that Sarah? Who's calling? (This is Keith Jones.)
Asking how someone is	How are things? How's the family? How's everything?
Saying how you are	Not too bad, thanks. We're surviving. Pretty good, thanks.
Asking about someone's work	What are you up to? Have you got a lot on at the moment? How are things at work?
Talking about work	I've got a lot on. Things are looking up. I mustn't complain.
Ending a phone conversation	
Signalling that you want to end	So, Barry. It was good to talk to you. Anyway, Barry ... Right, Barry. I must fly. I'm late for a meeting.
Confirming arrangements at the end of a phone call	So you'll give me a ring when you're back, right? And you'll send me a copy of the report? It'll be in the post tonight. I'll see you on the fourteenth in the bar of The County.

Unit 6 **Practice 4 Describing** (SB page 61)

Sentences to expand

A lady was sitting in her garden.
Peter has a huge house in the country.
Ann Croft, the actress, was seen having lunch in a restaurant.
The general inspected the soldiers.
The cowboy rode off into the sunset.
The holiday was a total disaster.
I found a wallet in the street.
I finally got to bed at 4 a.m.
Peter Barnes, the pop star, had a party for five hundred people.
New York is one of the most exciting cities in the world.

Unit 5 **PostScript** (SB page 57)

Role cards for telephones

Student A1

You are James from the listening activity about *The reunion* on page 56 of the Student's Book.

You are married with two girls, and you work in a travel agent's.

You are going to phone Alan, who is an old university friend. Alan now runs a small engineering company in the Midlands. He isn't married. He likes football very much. He supports Sheffield United. You also like football. You support Sunderland.

Alan thinks you're going to meet at the Lotus Garden Restaurant on the fourteenth, so you need to tell him that it has closed. You also need to tell him that you're going to meet at the Kwai Lam at about 7.15. He'll probably need to know where this restaurant is.

Student B1

You are Alan from the listening activity about *The reunion* on page 56 of the Student's Book.

You run a small engineering company in the Midlands. You aren't married. You are a big football fan. You support Sheffield United, who are doing well at the moment.

Your old university friend, James, is going to phone you. James works in a travel agent's in Sunderland, in the north of England. You haven't spoken to each other for a while.

Remember that you are meeting up with him and Sarah on the fourteenth. You're going to have a meal in the Lotus Garden Restaurant in Durham, where you all went to university about ten years ago.

Remember! You answer the phone. Begin by giving your phone number.

Student A2

You are a student of English. You are going to stay with a host family, Mr and Mrs Brown, who live in London, for a month while you study at International House. An agency has organized your stay with the Browns.

You are going to phone Mr and Mrs Brown to introduce yourself, and to give details of when you're arriving . Decide how you're travelling (By plane? By Eurostar?), what day you're travelling, and what time you expect to arrive.

End by saying something like 'I'm very excited about coming to London', or 'I'm really looking forward to meeting you'.

Student B2

You are Mr or Mrs Brown. You are English, and you live in London. Both Heathrow Airport and Waterloo Station, where the Eurostar train arrives, are pretty close to your house.

You are going to be a host family to a foreign student, who is coming to London for a month to study English. He/she is going to phone you to say hello, and to give details of his/her travel arrangements. You could offer to meet him/her.

Remember! You answer the phone. Begin by giving your phone number.

Student A3

You are going to phone a taxi firm to book a taxi to take you to the airport. Decide where you're going, on what date, and at what time. Which airport are you going from? Which terminal? What time does the plane leave? What time do you need to check in? How long does it take to get to the airport from your house? Will the traffic hold you up?

Student B3

You work for Tony's Taxis. Someone is going to ring to book a taxi. You need to get the following information.

What day? What time? What's the address? What's the name of the person? Where are they going?

You will need to decide a time to pick up, as you know what the traffic can be like at different times of day.

Remember! You answer the phone. Begin by saying 'Tony's Taxis. (Pat) speaking. How can I help you?'

Student A4

You are James from the listening activity about *The reunion* on page 56 of the Student's Book.

You are married with two girls, and you work in a travel agent's.

You are going to phone your friend Martin, who lives in Durham, about fifteen miles away. He runs a bookshop. He isn't married. He's mad about dogs – he breeds German Shepherds, which he takes to dog shows. His favourite dog is called Wizzer.

You want to ask Martin if you can stay the night at his house on the night of Friday the fourteenth, because you are meeting up with two old university friends, Alan and Sarah, in Durham, and you want to be able to spend time with them.

Student B4

You are Martin. You are a friend of James from the listening activity about *The reunion* on page 56 of the Student's Book. James works in a travel agent's in Sunderland, and he is married with two girls.

You live in Durham, about fifteen miles away from where James lives. You run a bookshop. You aren't married, but you adore dogs! You breed German Shepherds, and you take them to dog shows. Your favourite dog is called Wizzer.

James is going to ask you a favour. Maybe you can oblige, but maybe you're busy that night!

Remember! You answer the phone. Begin by giving your phone number.

Student A5

You want to book two seats to see a film, so you phone the cinema.

You want to see *Fear of the Dark* next Friday, either early in the evening or at about nine o'clock-ish.

You need to ask what time the film starts, how much the tickets are, and whether there's a booking fee.

Have your credit card details ready.

Student B5

You work for the Odeon Cinema. You take bookings, and give details of when films are showing.

Someone is going to phone you, asking for details about the film *Fear of the Dark*. Decide what time it starts in the evening. Presumably there are at least two showings per evening.

How much are the tickets? Is there one price, or several different ones? Is there a booking fee?

You need to get the person's credit card details.

Remember! You answer the phone. Begin by saying 'Odeon Cinemas. (Pat) speaking. How can I help you?'

Student A6

You are going to phone your local hairdresser to make an appointment to have your hair done.

You know the person who takes the bookings quite well, so you could have a little chat first. It's Monday today, so you could ask about the weekend. Or you could chat about the weather, which has changed very suddenly! Your mother has been ill recently, but she's getting better now.

Decide when you want an appointment for, what day and what time. What do you want to have done to your hair?

Student B6

You work for Jason's Hair Salon. You take bookings over the phone.

Someone is going to ring who you know quite well, so before you get details of the booking you could have a little chat first. It's Monday morning, so you could ask about the weekend that's just gone by. You could ask the person about his/her mother, who has been ill recently.

Finally, get details of the booking. What day? What time? Would the person like any particular hairdresser?

Remember! You answer the phone. Begin by saying 'Jason's Hair Salon. (Pat) speaking. How can I help you?'

Unit 9 **Practice 1** (SB page 89)

Student A

1 a … (***Who / write?***) the stories of *Dracula*.
b The stories are set in Transylvania.

2 a The ceiling of the Sistine Chapel in Rome was painted by Michelangelo.
b The frescoes depict … (***What?***).

3 a …'s son (***Whose?***) had an apple shot off his head by his father.
b He shot it off with a crossbow and arrow.

4 a The Eiffel Tower was built to celebrate the Centennial Exposition in 1889.
b It is … metres high (***How?***).

5 a Einstein wrote to President Roosevelt in 1939 to … (***What … for?***).
b After the war, he campaigned for nuclear disarmament.

6 a Nelson Mandela was sent to prison for twenty-eight years.
b … (***Who / release?***) him in 1990.

7 a Concorde was developed by France and Britain.
b It travels at … (***How fast?***).

8 a … (***Which war?***) was sparked off by an incident in Sarajevo in June 1914.
b Archduke Ferdinand, the heir to the Austro-Hungarian throne, was assassinated.

9 a The statue of Christ the Redeemer stands on a mountain overlooking Rio de Janeiro.
b It is situated on … (***Which mountain?***).

10 a … (***Which plants?***) produce opium.
b It has been used for centuries in medicine for the relief of pain.

Student B

1 a Bram Stoker, an Irish novelist, wrote the stories of *Dracula*.
b They are set in … (***Which country?***).

2 a … (***Which ceiling / paint?***) by Michelangelo.
b The frescoes depict *The Last Judgment*, and a series of scenes and people from the Old Testament.

3 a William Tell's son had an apple shot off his head by his father.
b He shot it off with a … (***What … with?***).

4 a The Eiffel Tower was built to … (***Why?***) in 1889.
b It is 300 metres high, and it was the highest building in the world until 1930.

5 a Einstein wrote to President Roosevelt in 1939 to warn him that an atomic bomb could soon be built.
b After the war, he campaigned for … (***What?***).

6 a Nelson Mandela was sent to prison for … (***How long … for?***) years.
b President de Klerk released him in 1990.

7 a Concorde was developed by … (***Which countries?***).
b It travels at 2,179 kilometres an hour, over twice the speed of sound.

8 a World War I was sparked off by an incident in Sarajevo in June 1914.
b Archduke Ferdinand, the heir to the Austro-Hungarian throne, … (***What happened?***).

9 a … (***Whose statue / stand?***) on a mountain overlooking Rio de Janeiro.
b It is situated on Mount Corcovado, 2,310 feet high.

10 a Poppies produce opium.
b It has been used for centuries … (***What … for?***).

Unit 9 **Reading** (SB page 92)

Find a word in the texts with a similar meaning to the following.

Introduction worried, troubled

Text 1 keeping alive worked out

Text 2 huge blocks filling up

Text 3 fight characteristics certain

Text 4 of the present time

Text 5 received from an ancestor, especially your mother or father

Text 6 time to get better a lack of something you need and want

Text 7 cause to start passed from one person to another, especially an illness

Text 8 travelling very quickly

Text 9 general opinion

Text 10 vary exists without being seen

Unit 9 **Writing** (SB page 96)

Write in a conjunction from the list on page 96 of the Student's Book.

time

a I didn't know what love was _____ I met you.

b _____ I hear this song, I think of my first boyfriend.

c _____ she saw what the hairdresser had done to her hair, she burst out crying.

d Joe, come home __________ you can. We've been burgled!

e _____ I was having breakfast, the phone rang.

f I've made a lot of friends _____ I started at this school.

g _____ we'd eaten, we did the washing-up.

h I didn't like George at first, but _____ time passed I grew to love him more and more.

reason

i I didn't have any money, _____ I went to the bank.

j I'm tired __________ I didn't sleep well last night.

k _____ you all know, I'm retiring next year.

l I looked round for a chair, but _____ there wasn't one, I sat on the floor.

result

m I was _____ tired _____ I fell asleep in front of the television.

n We had _____ a big meal at lunchtime _____ I didn't want anything in the evening.

purpose

o I'll give you my key, __________ you can let yourself in whenever you want.

p Take your umbrella __________ it rains.

condition

q _____ I'm going to be late, I'll give you a ring.

r __________ I know where my children are, I don't worry about them.

s You'll fail your exam __________ you do some work.

contrast

t I tried to carry the bag, _____ I wasn't strong enough.

u The two boys like each other, __________ they're always fighting and hitting each other.

v __________ I can understand French, I can't speak it.

Homelessness

I **Chris, can you tell us why it was that you ended up homeless?**

C Well, I 'ad a house wiv a woman that I … er took on, wiv 'er kids and I 'ad a job 'n' all, workin' at the Royal Mail Post Office … erm I dunno about … what … er two, two years it was into the relationship and all of a sudden, like, she just wanted out, so … er I tried to patch fings up which really didn't work, yer know, so I ended up going back to the woods, well, yer know where I was before … .

I **Back to the woods?**

C Yeah.

I **How d'you mean? Literally to the woods?**

C Yeah. I used to live out in the woods.

I **Did you?**

C Yeah.

I **What … er … you mean … living rough or in a tent, or how?**

C Just in a 'bivvy' bag, Goretex 'bivvy' bag[1], 'n sleeping bag and stuff, in the woods, for a while, lighting fires 'n havin' my grub[2] out there, yer know. There's just summink about the woods … yer free out there … you, yer can't do it round the towns 'cos there … you know … … erm … yer too at risk in towns, too many people … yer know … too much … too much hassle[3] in towns. Best fing to do is get out and, and get … get where yer feel safe, so I feel safe in the woods all the time yer know … erm …

I **So why aren't you in the woods now?**

C 'Cos I 'ad a breakdown out there and I went to the doctor's 'n' that and he give me some tablets for that, and I ended up comin' here[4] … was the best solution … yer know … to … er get meself back on me feet … sort of thing … yer know.

I **But … so living in the wood, although as you say … it was … you know, you were free, free from the hassles and so on, I mean … it's not the ideal way of life for you?**

C … Erm … . no and yes. It was my job once … (upon) a time.

I **Living in the woods?**

C I was a survival instructor, teaching the army and stuff.

I **So you like the woods?**

C … the woods, the mountains is fine for me. Coming into towns I find very stressful … erm, … I'm here now but each time, here now, I'm still fightin'. I've be here six months, so each day now I'm still fighting to stay here, which is hard for me, … erm I'd be safe out there, yer know, instead of here but … erm all I'm trying to do is get me act togever[5] and start again really. It's … it's hard work.

I **What's it mean to you not to have a home?**

C Devastating, really. I miss the family feeling or the family comfort, not … not the television but having a woman there to care for, and someone to talk to. You get very lonely. I mean, in here you've got friends 'n' 'at … but I admit I get very lonely … when you're on your own, 'n' it takes its toll[6] because if you're used to that way of life, it's hard to comprehend what it's all about … yer know the worst fing is, when yer fink about that which hurts most, is to see people holding hands going down the street with their wife and kids and you've had that once and you've lost it, and you'd like that again but it's going to take time to get that back … yer know so … erm I find it really hard, actually.

I **And what's it like when you're actually on the road?**

C When yer roamin' round the country yer see so many of yer people like yerself … erm on the street, sleepin' in doorways, parks, benches, yer know, and … erm yeah, yer kind of get used to it after a while, it takes about a week to get used to being on the road but then it takes about seven … seven to eight months trying to get used to getting back into society again. I find it hard anyway, even now.

Glossary

1. **a Goretex 'bivvy' bag** a bivouac bag = kind of weather-proof cover for a sleeping bag. 'Goretex' is a brand name.
2. **grub** food (informal)
3. **hassle** trouble (informal)
4. **I ended up comin' here** in the end he came here (Oliver's home for the homeless)
5. **to get me (my) act together** to get myself organized
6. **it takes its toll** it causes damage

Unit 12 **Language in context** (SB page 119)

Fill the gaps with one of the words in the box.

a	an	the	his	all	this
its	every	their	(nothing = zero article)		

Michelangelo (1475–1564) was one of (a) ______ most inspired creators in (b) ______ history of (c) ______ art. As (d) ______ sculptor, (e) ______ architect, a painter, and a poet, he had (f) ______ tremendous influence on (g) ______ his contemporaries.

He was born near Arezzo, but it was Florence that he considered to be (h) ______ home town. What he loved above all was (i) ______ city's art, architecture, and culture.

Initially he concentrated on (j) ______ sculpture. In 1501 he began to carve (k) ______ figure of David from (l) ______ huge block of marble. This was finished in 1504, when he was 29. David is shown with (m) ______ sling on (n) ______ shoulder, looking into (o) ______ distance.

Later, Michelangelo was asked by (p) ______ Pope Julius II to paint (q) ______ ceiling of the Sistine Chapel. (r) ______ day for four years, from 1508 till 1512, he worked on (s) ______ task, lying on (t) ______ back at the top of high scaffolding, his neck stiff, with (u) ______ paint trickling onto his face.

He designed many buildings, but it was his work at St Peter's Basilica that represented (v) ______ greatest achievement as (w) ______ architect. His dome became the model for domes all over the Western world. What is difficult to appreciate nowadays is (x) ______ revolutionary design.

There is a small group of artists such as Shakespeare and Beethoven who, through (y) ______ work, have been able to express the deepest experiences of humanity. Michelangelo belongs to (z) ______ group.

Fill the gaps with one of the words in the box.

a	an	the	his	all	this
its	every	their	(nothing = zero article)		

Michelangelo (1475–1564) was one of (a) ______ most inspired creators in (b) ______ history of (c) ______ art. As (d) ______ sculptor, (e) ______ architect, a painter, and a poet, he had (f) ______ tremendous influence on (g) ______ his contemporaries.

He was born near Arezzo, but it was Florence that he considered to be (h) ______ home town. What he loved above all was (i) ______ city's art, architecture, and culture.

Initially he concentrated on (j) ______ sculpture. In 1501 he began to carve (k) ______ figure of David from (l) ______ huge block of marble. This was finished in 1504, when he was 29. David is shown with (m) ______ sling on (n) ______ shoulder, looking into (o) ______ distance.

Later, Michelangelo was asked by (p) ______ Pope Julius II to paint (q) ______ ceiling of the Sistine Chapel. (r) ______ day for four years, from 1508 till 1512, he worked on (s) ______ task, lying on (t) ______ back at the top of high scaffolding, his neck stiff, with (u) ______ paint trickling onto his face.

He designed many buildings, but it was his work at St Peter's Basilica that represented (v) ______ greatest achievement as (w) ______ architect. His dome became the model for domes all over the Western world. What is difficult to appreciate nowadays is (x) ______ revolutionary design.

There is a small group of artists such as Shakespeare and Beethoven who, through (y) ______ work, have been able to express the deepest experiences of humanity. Michelangelo belongs to (z) ______ group.

Stop and check 1

Units 1–4

Tenses

This is a letter from Joanna, who is staying with a family in New York, to her parents in England. Put the verb in brackets in the correct tense.

New York
Sunday 22nd

Dear Mum and Dad

I can't believe I 1 __________ (be) in New York for three months now. Time 2 __________ (pass) far too quickly. So much has happened since I last 3 ______ (write) to you that I 4 __________ (not know) where to begin.

I 5 __________ (start) by telling you of my little adventure. Last Saturday I 6 ______ (go) shopping in the local shopping mall. I 7 __________ (look) for some new jeans for the party I was going to that evening when suddenly I 8 __________ (realize) that my purse 9 __________ (steal). The police 10 __________ (call) immediately, but I couldn't answer their questions because I 11 __________ (cry) so much. I 12 __________ (look) in my bag for a tissue when – guess what? – I 13 ______ (find) my purse! It 14 __________ (get) hidden underneath all the other stuff. I 15 ______ (feel) such a fool!

Anyway, the party that evening wasn't much good, which was a shame as I 16 __________ (look) forward to it all week. When I 17 __________ (arrive), all the food 18 __________ (eat). The friends I hoped to meet 19 __________ (go) home already. After half an hour we 20 __________ (tell) we were making too much noise, so we 21 __________ (have to) turn off the music. I decided to leave at about 11.00. I 22 __________ (give) a lift home by a guy called Peter, who you'd really like. When I got home, I 23 __________ (starve)!

Mrs Goldstein 24 __________ (say) for weeks that she wants to take me to the Statue of Liberty, so tomorrow we 25 __________ (see) it. They're a very kind family, and I 26 ______ (feel) at home here. They 27 __________ (teach) me to speak with an American accent, so when I speak to you on the phone you 28 __________ (not recognize) me!

The course I 29 __________ (do) in psychology is interesting. The college 30 __________ (situate) on the edge of Central Park, so I often 31 ______ (have) my lunch there as the canteen in the college 32 __________ (decorate) at the moment. My teachers are great. One of them 33 __________ (write) a book which 34 __________ (translate) into five languages! I 35 __________ (not read) it yet, but it's on my list. She 36 __________ (study) how children learn their first language for years and years, and I 37 ______ (think) she's quite well-known.

Dad, please could you send me some money? I only 38 ______ (have) $10 to last me till I 39 __________ (pay) next week. I 40 __________ (save) up for my return fare home, so you can't be cross with me!

Please write soon with all the news from England. Give my love to the dog.

Lots of love
Joanna

	40

Present Perfect

Underline the correct verb form.

1 'Where's Pete?' 'He's *gone / been* to Peru.'
2 Sorry to keep you. *Have you waited / Have you been waiting* long?
3 'How *have you cut / did you cut* yourself?' 'It was an accident.'
4 *I've never seen / I've never been seeing* a funnier film. You must see it.
5 *I've had / I've been having* driving lessons for ten months.
6 *I haven't passed / I haven't been passed* my test yet.
7 How long *have you had / have you been having* your car?
8 *Has the car serviced / Has the car been serviced* regularly?
9 My father *worked / has worked* in the same job until the day he retired.
10 'Why are you so muddy?' '*I've worked / I've been working* in the garden.'

	10

Narrative tenses

Put the verb in **bold** in the correct tense, Past Simple or Continuous, or Past Perfect Simple or Continuous. There are both active and passive tenses.

do

1 What ______ you ______ with my hairbrush when you'd finished with it?
2 There was a lot of noise in your room last night.
What ______ you ______?
3 Sally's garden was a mess. She ______ nothing in it for years, and it was like a jungle.
4 'My office has been redecorated!' 'Yes. It ______ while you were away.'

make

5 I took my car to the garage yesterday because it ______ some funny noises.
6 Tim was depressed. He ______ redundant three months before, and he couldn't pay his bills.
7 My grandfather ______ all his money from selling second-hand cars.

rain

8 The roads were dangerous because it ______.
9 'Did you have a good holiday?' 'No. It ______ every day.'
10 We couldn't play tennis because it ______.

	10

Some and *any*

Put *some* or *any* into each gap.

1 Could I have ______thing to eat?
2 She replied without ______ hesitation.
3 Shouldn't you do ______ revision for your exam?
4 She made hardly ______ mistakes.
5 Can we go ______where quiet?

	5

Quantifiers

Fill in the gaps in the following sentences with an appropiate word from the box. In some cases more than one word is possible.

fewer	all	some	everyone
many	no	much	a huge amount
a little	lots	none	

1 There is too ______ traffic on the roads in London.
2 We've been to Greece ______ of times.
3 Let me give you ______ advice.
4 We have ______ money in the bank, but not enough to buy luxuries.
5 He must earn ______ of money. He's got five cars and three houses.
6 'Can I have a meat pie please?' 'I'm afraid there are ______ left.'
7 ______ people go to church these days compared to fifty years ago.
8 ______ my friends came to my party.
9 The party was brilliant. ______ had a good time.
10 Jane's so serious. She has absolutely ______ sense of humour.

	10

Vocabulary

1 Match a word in **A** with its opposite in **B**.

A	B
fiction	carefree
fantastic	set off
success	broke
worried	broad
peaceful	failure
arrive	software
narrow	fact
hardware	ashamed
well off	noisy
proud	dreadful

	10

2 Complete the words from Units 1–4 of New Headway Upper-Intermediate. The first letters are given to help you.

1 Rooms or offices that are *a*__________ - *c*__________ have a system that makes the air cool even in hot weather.

2 The letters and adverts you get in the post that you didn't ask for. *j*__________ *m*__________

3 When you've eaten something that upsets your stomach, you can suffer from sickness and *d*__________. You go to the toilet a lot.

4 If you can't read or write properly, you're *i*__________.

5 If you have been attacked and robbed in the street, you have been *m*__________.

6 If you're unhappy because you're missing your family, you're *h*__________.

7 The paper you sign if you agree to do something is a *c*__________.

8 The result of the football match was 3–0. three *n*__________

9 Ginger, curry powder, and chilli are all examples of *s*__________.

10 A dustman takes away your *r*__________.

11 If you buy something cheap, you get a *b*__________.

12 The things you buy on holiday to remind you of the place you've been to. *s*__________

13 Sixty seconds or very small! *m*__________

14 If you cry, these come out of your eyes. *t*__________

15 Another word for toilet. *l*__________

	15

Total		100

Stop and check 2

Units 5–8

General revision

Look at the letter from Joanna's parents to Joanna. Underline the correct version.

Sunday 12

Dear Joanna

(1) *We love getting / We'd love to get* your letters. They're always full of so much **(2)** *exciting / excited* news. We believe the story about your lost purse. We **(3)** *totally / distinctly* remember the same thing happening to your car keys a few months before you left. You **(4)** *can't have / might have* looked very carefully in your bag before **(5)** *to phone / phoning* the police. Did you really need **(6)** *buying / to buy* a new pair of jeans? You **(7)** *must / should* be spending all your money on clothes. You'll be **(8)** *absolutely / very* hard up if you **(9)** *won't be / aren't* careful. We can't afford **(10)** *keeping / to keep* sending you money all the time. Anyway I'll stop **(11)** *moaning / to moan* now, or you **(12)** *won't be writing / won't write* to us again!

(13) *You are / You'll be* pleased to hear that Sally passed all her exams, **(14)** *that / which* means she'll be leaving next month **(15)** *for to start / to start* her course at Oxford. She finished **(16)** *to work / working* at the local bookshop last week, but **(17)** *she'll be working / she works* there again during the Christmas holidays. **(18)** *She must have saved / She's had to save* as much as possible to take to college with her. We just don't know if she has enough money. We'll have to **(19)** *give and take / wait and see.*

The house **(20)** *is going to feel / will be feeling* very empty with you and Sally away. I expect your father and I **(21)** *will just get used to / will have just got used to* the **(22)** *peace and quiet / quiet and peace* when you two are back!

It's Grandma and Grandad's wedding anniversary in two weeks. **(23)** *They'll have been married / They're going to be married* for 50 years. **(24)** *There's going to be / There will be* a big party at the village hall, and all the family have been invited. Please remember **(25)** *to send / sending* a card. They'll be so pleased **(26)** *to hear / hearing* from you. Grandma has been very busy **(27)** *making / to make* all the arrangements. She'll be **(28)** *very / absolutely* exhausted when **(29)** *it's / it'll be* all over. She's 74, and **(30)** *sooner or later / more or less* she'll realize that she can't go running around like someone half her age.

Do you remember **(31)** *to meet / meeting* Sheila and Bob, **(32)** *that / who* we got to know on holiday last year? Well, **(33)** *they're coming / they come* to visit us next weekend. Dad painted the spare room especially, but he **(34)** *didn't need to bother / needn't have bothered*, as they've decided to stay at a hotel **(35)** *that / what* is just down the road. We haven't decided where **(36)** *to take / we took* them yet. We **(37)** *shall / might* go for a drive in the country.

I **(38)** *must / have to* say goodbye now. Dad went to London today, but he **(39)** *must / should* be back any minute now. We can't wait **(40)** *seeing / to see* you again.

Lots of love and kisses.
Mum and Dad

	40

Future forms

Put the verb in brackets in the correct tense. Sometimes there is more than one possibility.

When Sally [1] ______ (go) to college next month, she [2] __________ (find) everything a little strange at first. She'll probably be a bit lonely until she [3] __________ (make) a few friends. She [4] __________ (go) to Oxford by train. It [5] __________ (leave) at 12.00, so she should be there by 3.00. She [6] ____________ (study) economics, because she's always been interested in business. She [7] ____________ (have) lectures with the famous Professor Edmond, who is the Head of Department. I hope she [8] ______ (like) him.

She [9] ____________ (have) a big party with all her friends before she goes. We've said that we'll visit her in Oxford as soon as she [10] __________ (settle) in.

	10

Participles and verb patterns

Complete the words with *-ed* or *-ing*.

1 a bor______ book
2 a tir______ journey
3 a furnish______ flat
4 an unexpect______ storm
5 an exhaust______ walk

Put the verb in brackets in the correct form.

6 There's no point in __________ (ask) me. I haven't a clue.
7 Can you tell me how __________ (get) to the station?
8 I think that __________ (live) in a big city is exciting.
9 The story was so sad that it made me __________ (cry).
10 You must try __________ (understand) my point of view.

	10

Relative clauses

Fill the gaps with a word from the box.

that	who	(nothing)	whose	which
why	what	whatever	where	

1 We are very proud of our son, James, ______'s an accountant.
2 James has just decided to get married, ______ came as a bit of a shock.
3 His fiancée, ______ parents live in Leeds, is organizing the wedding.
4 The church ______ they're getting married is tiny.
5 We don't know ______ they want such a small wedding.
6 The thing ______ bothers us is deciding who to invite.
7 Of course, we'll do __________ they want to help.
8 We'll have to ask them ______ they want as a wedding present.
9 The present ______ we'd like to buy them is a new car.
10 The car ______ they have at the moment is ancient.

	10

Modal verbs

Underline the correct part of the sentence.

1 You *might / ought / must* see that new film. It's fantastic!
2 I'm sorry I'm late. I *should have gone / must have gone / had to go* to the doctor's.
3 Pam was very upset when you told her she was fat. You *mustn't / wouldn't / shouldn't* have said that.
4 'Where's Pippa?' 'She *shall / can / might* be in the kitchen.'
5 How *did you manage to / could you* save £1,000 so quickly?
6 Peter was mugged yesterday. He *should have been / must have been / had to be* terrified!
7 Laura's worked very hard for her exams. She *must / would / should* do well.
8 'I got 100% in my test!' 'Did you? It *shouldn't / can't / might not* have been very difficult.'
9 These pills will make you feel sleepy, so you *don't have to / needn't / mustn't* drive.
10 *Must / May / Will* I ask you a question? How old are you?

	10

Vocabulary

1 Match a word in **A** with its synonym in **B**.

A	B
keen	admit
dull	odd
weird	fix
stubborn	handy
confess	enthusiastic
terrified	obstinate
useful	boring
mend	scared

2 Choose the right answer.

1 There are ________________ to being rich. Personally, I'd rather be comfortably well off.
odds and ends   pros and cons   all or nothing

2 In any relationship you have to be prepared to ________________.
wait and see   grin and bear it   give and take

3 Politicians are ______________ not to be trusted.
by and large   back to front   up and down

4 You look miserable. What's ___________ you?
down to   off with   up with

5 The score is 4–3, but the match isn't _____ yet. There's another five minutes.
off   over   up

6 My children always get _____ doing the washing-up by saying they've got homework.
into   out at   out of

7 It took her a long time to get _____ the death of her father.
over   through   off

3 Complete the sentences with an adjective from the box.

filthy	starving	delighted	hilarious	gorgeous

1 'Sorry I'm a bit dirty.' 'Actually, you're __________.'
2 'Wasn't the film funny?' 'Mm. It was __________.'
3 'George is very nice, isn't he?' 'Oh, yes. I think he's __________.'
4 'You must be pleased with your son's progress.' 'Indeed. We're __________.'
5 'Have something to eat. You must be hungry.' 'I'm absolutely __________.'

	20

Total		100

Stop and check 3

Units 9–12

This is a letter from Sally, who is a student in Oxford, to her sister Joanna, who is working in the USA. She has recently moved from New York City to New Jersey.

Put *one* word only into each gap. (Negatives such as *isn't*, *didn't* count as one word.)

Sunday 7th, 3.00pm

Dear Joanna

I know I promised to write at least 1 _____ a month, but I just 2 _____ had the time. You have no idea 3 _____ busy I've been. Oxford is 4 _____ fantastic place. 5 _____ I like most about it is that it's so cosmopolitan, as well as having loads of history. I've already made lots of friends. I wish you 6 _____ meet them.

What's New Jersey 7 _____ ? You will write and tell me all about it, 8 _____ you? Mum says you liked New York better. She says if you 9 _____ lived in New York when you were first in the USA, you 10 _____ be enjoying life more in New Jersey now. It's just the contrast. Anyway, you don't live very far from New York, 11 _____ you? You'll still be able to go there at weekends, if you can afford 12 _____ . You 13 _____ possibly be as hard-up as I am. I'm absolutely 14 _____ . Most of my money 15 _____ on books and writing paper.

Have you made many friends 16 _____ ? Americans usually like an English accent, 17 _____ they? I'm sure it can help 18 _____ the ice when you first meet people.

I have 19 _____ interesting piece of news! Do you remember when we were little and we 20 _____ to go to Auntie Margaret's in Manchester 21 _____ Christmas? And do you remember Ben, 22 _____ horrible little boy who lived next door? He 23 _____ always stealing our sweets. Well, he's here in Oxford, studying politics, and he's really nice! I can't believe that we didn't 24 _____ to like him when we were kids. He's so interesting. We've got so much in common, often we 25 _____ just sit and talk for hours. 26 _____ it funny how life turns out? 27 _____ we'll go to the cinema but not often, it's too expensive, so he just 28 _____ round to my flat for the evening and we work and chat. The 29 _____ that I like best about him is his sense of humour, he makes me laugh.

I have to go, Ben'll be here soon. Take care 'big sis' and write when you can. I want to know 30 _____ about life in the USA!

Love
Sally

	30

Questions

Complete the following questions so that the answers sound natural.

1 ' _____ on holiday?' 'Twice a year.'

2 ' _____ afraid _____ ?' 'Snakes and spiders.'

3 'She liked the film, _____ ?' 'I think so.'

4 'You _____ like Indian food, _____ ?' 'Well, I didn't use to like it, but I love it now.'

5 ' _____ to smoke?' 'Yes, I did, but I gave up two years ago.'

6 ' _____ won £1,000,000?' 'I'd buy a luxury yacht.'

7 'What _____ if _____ passed all your exams?' 'I'd have had to take them all again!'

8 'Have the police any idea _____ your car?' 'No they haven't, but at least they found it.'

9 ' _____ in that new Italian restaurant?' 'Delicious! We're going again next Saturday.'

10 ' _____ dictionary _____ ?' 'It's mine.'

11 ' _____ this lovely birthday card _____ ?' 'My Aunt Marjorie. She never forgets.'

12 'Do you know _____ television _____ and who _____ ?' 'In 1925, by a man called John Logie Baird.'

	12

Wishes and conditionals

Match the first part of the sentence with the second part.

A	B
1 If I get up early,	**a** I would get there on time. **b** I should get there on time. **c** I'll have got there on time.
2 If I hadn't parked on a yellow line,	**a** I would have got a ticket. **b** I would be getting a ticket. **c** I wouldn't have got a ticket.
3 I wish	**a** I could buy a house in the country. **b** I would buy a house in the country. **c** I'd have bought a house in the country.
4 If I'd seen him,	**a** I'd tell him. **b** I could have told him. **c** I'd be able to tell him.
5 If only	**a** I'd have studied German. **b** I'd studied German. **c** I'd study German.
6 If I'd had more time,	**a** I'd have been able to help. **b** I'd be able to help. **c** I should have helped.
7 I wish	**a** I wouldn't have lost my temper. **b** I hadn't have lost my temper. **c** I hadn't lost my temper.
8 If I'm late again,	**a** I could lose my job. **b** I'd lose my job. **c** I'll be losing my job.
9 If this lesson doesn't end soon,	**a** I fall asleep. **b** I'll fall asleep. **c** I'd fall asleep.
10 If he hadn't finished the race,	**a** he'd never have forgiven himself. **b** he'd never forgive himself. **c** he could never forgive himself.
11 I wish	**a** you'd be here. **b** you were here. **c** you'll be here.
12 If only	**a** I wouldn't have to go. **b** I couldn't have to go. **c** I didn't have to go.

☐ 12

Vocabulary

1 Complete the sentences with a word from the box. You need an antonym for the words in italics.

huge	tender	priceless
simple	plump	distraught
curly	cruel	failure
soft	easy	teetotal
fake	temporary	occasionally

1 I thought the painting was *worthless*, but it turned out to be __________.

2 I can't believe that *tiny* puppy will grow into a _____ great dog!

3 When I last saw Susie she was a _____ little girl. Now she's a beautiful, tall, *slim* woman.

4 You deserve your *success* after all those years of __________.

5 We don't eat out *often*, only __________.

6 Your steak looks really __________. Mine's so *tough* I can't chew it.

7 It wasn't an _____ thing to decide. In fact it was a very *tough* decision to make.

8 I can't sleep on *hard* pillows, they must be _____.

9 You said this was a __________ problem, but it's really *hard*.

10 He was an *alcoholic* for years before he became __________.

11 That's not a *genuine* Van Gogh. It's a _____.

12 I was *delighted* when my brother left home but my mother was __________.

13 I wish I had _____ hair like my sister. Mine is absolutely *straight*.

14 I'm tired of part-time __________ jobs. I want a full-time, *permanent* one.

15 You should always be *kind* to animals. I don't understand how people can be _____ to them.

☐ 15

2 Which word is the 'odd one out' in each group? Underline it.

1 bankrupt hard up penniless broke
2 stingy generous mean tight
3 in the red in debt in the black overdrawn
4 lick blink wave (v) ache
5 waste spend save rent
6 miss catch take lose
7 friend wore piece sea
8 well off expensive extravagant privileged
9 regularly infrequently rarely seldom
10 cross race match bomb

	10

Revision

Underline the correct alternative in the following text.

The people's princess

THE PRINCESS OF WALES, or Princess Di (**1**) *as / like* she was affectionately called, was the most photographed woman in the world. (**2**) *From / Since* her tragic death in 1997 at the age of 36 she has become an icon of compassion, humanity, and fashion.

When Diana was born in 1961, her parents were hugely disappointed. They had longed for (**3**) *a / the* son. As a result of (**4**) *this / which*, Diana, for the (**5**) *all / whole* of her life, (**6**) *despite / in spite* her privileged background, suffered (**7**) *from / of* the feeling of being (**8**) *an / one* unloved daughter. However, (**9**) *a / the* thing (**10**) *that / what* most affected her was her parents' divorce, when she was six years old. Her reaction was to (**11**) *come / go* into deep depression.

Diana, her brother, and two sisters were brought up by their father, The Earl Spencer. He was at the time the Queen's adjutant, and he (**12**) *used / would* often do administrative (**13**) *work / works* in Buckingham Palace. Consequently, Diana grew up in the company of the Queen's children and was used to (**14**) *play / playing* with the two youngest princes, Andrew and Edward.

(**15**) *Firstly / At first,* Charles seemed to be more interested in her elder sister, Jane, who was much closer to him in age. It (**16**) *was / wasn't* until much later that he began to notice Diana. (**17**) *In the end / At the end* she was invited to a barbecue in July 1980 as Charles' dinner partner. Afterwards, he invited her to a concert at the Royal Albert Hall.

In that same year Charles (**18**) *introduced / was introduced* the beautiful, shy Diana (**19**) *to / by* his mother and the wedding followed in 1981. Diana's wish had (**20**) *come / become* true. If only her marriage (**21**) *had marked / would have marked* the end of her unhappy childhood. However, fate was to turn against her many more times in her short life.

	21

Total		100

Progress test 1 Units 1–6

Exercise 1 Tenses

Put the verb in brackets in the correct tense, active or passive. Sometimes more than one tense is correct.

Example

I *saw* (see) him yesterday when he *was being driven* (drive) to work.

A FLIGHT FULL OF SURPRISES

Jane and Andy 1 __________ (wait) at the airport in Cape Town to catch their plane back to London. They 2 __________ (be) on honeymoon in South Africa for four weeks and they 3 __________ (feel) very relaxed and happy. They 4 ________________ (not wait) long when their flight 5 __________ (announce) over the tannoy:

'Flight BA 207 to London, Heathrow 6 __________ (leave) in one hour. Will passengers please go to Gate 4 and wait there to board?'.

As they 7 __________ (make) their way to Gate 4, Jane and Andy 8 __________ (hear) another announcement: 'Flight D 234 to New York 9 ______________ (delay) due to a technical fault. Will passengers please go to Gate 5 and wait there for further information.'

'Oh dear!' said Jane. 'I 10 _____ (hope) people 11 __________ (not get) confused. What 12 __________ (happen) if someone 13 _____ (get) on the wrong flight?'

14 '__________ (not be) silly,' said Andy. 'That's impossible. This is an international airport. All boarding cards 15 __________ (check) before anyone 16 __________ (allow) to board the plane.'

They arrived at Gate 4. Two hours later they still 17 __________ (not board) their plane, and no explanation 18 __________ (give). Eventually there was an announcement: 'We are sorry for the delay. Will all passengers please have their boarding cards ready? Flights BA 207 to London and D 234 for New York are both now ready to depart'.

'At last!' said Jane. 'We 19 ________________ (wait) at this airport for nearly five hours by the time our plane 20 _____ (take) off!'

There were only two flight attendants checking boarding cards and ushering passengers on to their respective flights. But they worked very quickly and soon Jane and Andy 21 __________ (sit) comfortably in their seats, fastening their seat belts.

'Good evening, ladies and gentlemen,' said the pilot, 'and welcome to flight D 234 to New York.'

Jane and Andy both 22 _____ (leap) to their feet and ran to the front of the plane. Fortunately the pilot 23 ______________ (not start) the engines and Jane and Andy 24 __________ (lead) from Flight D 234 to Flight BA 207 by a very anxious air steward. They fastened their seat belts for a second time.

'Phew! I 25 __________ (have) enough surprises for one day,' said Andy. 'This 26 __________ (not be) a very relaxing end to our holiday, has it? We need another holiday! Where 27 _____ we _____ (go) next year?'

'Well,' said Jane, 'as we 28 __________ (have) a baby by then, maybe we should just stay at home.'

'Pardon? What did you say?' whispered Andy.

	28

Exercise 2 **Active and passive**

Change the sentences from active to passive, or passive to active.

Example
They announced a delay.
A delay *was announced* .

1 They have made 200 workers redundant.
200 workers ______________________ .

2 Has anyone fed the cat?
Has the cat ______________________ .

3 She could not be persuaded to give up smoking.
Nobody ______________________ .

4 My purse has been stolen.
Someone ______________________ .

5 They couldn't move it.
It ______________________ .

6 Is someone giving you a lift?
Are you ______________________ .

7 The house will have to be sold.
We ______________________ .

8 I was told the train would be 10 minutes late.
The guard ______________________ .

9 Someone wants you on the phone.
You ______________________ .

10 No computer is needed for this Open University course. You ______________________ .

11 The police are watching him closely.
He ______________________ .

12 I was told to wait outside.
The secretary ______________________ .

☐ 12

Exercise 3 **Correct the sentences**

Example
I lived here since 1996.
I've lived *here since 1996.*

1 I'll see the dentist on Friday morning at 10 o'clock.
______________________ .

2 Our cat has been missed since five days.
______________________ .

3 At last! I've been finding my contact lens.
______________________ .

4 As soon as I opened the front door it was obvious that the house was burgled.
______________________ .

5 I hadn't got on very well with my father when I was young, but I do now.
______________________ .

6 I hadn't worked for very long when I was interrupted.
______________________ .

7 Who's smoked? Can't you read? There's a 'No Smoking' sign in here.
______________________ .

8 I'll be finishing this book by tonight.
______________________ .

9 He's written a novel for the past ten years.
______________________ .

10 Don't come at 7.00. We'll have supper then.
______________________ .

☐ 10

Exercise 4 **Relative clauses**

Put in a relative pronoun (*what*, *who*, *which*, *where*, *whose*, or *that*). If the pronoun is optional, write nothing.

Examples
The town *where* I grew up has changed a lot.
The town — I grew up in has changed a lot.

1 The hotel ______ we're staying in is miles away from the beach.

2 I'm working for a company ______ main branch is in Manchester.

3 That factory, ______ employs 500 people, makes computers.

4 That's the woman ______ didn't turn up at her own wedding!

5 That new computer is just ______ we need in this office.

6 Is that the button ______ you pressed?

7 My wife, ______ work takes her away from home a lot, has decided she needs an assistant.

8 My car's at the garage, ______ means we'll have to walk.

9 The team ______ wins will get £1,000.

10 The town ______ I was born has completely changed.

[ ] 10

Exercise 5 **Quantifiers**

Substitute *very little*, *a little*, *very few*, or *a few* for the words underlined.

Example
Could I have some biscuits?
Could I have a few biscuits?

1 There are some things I want to discuss with you.

____

____.

2 I've had hardly any sleep since the baby was born.

____

____.

3 'Did the injection hurt?' 'A bit.'

____.

4 I've had practically nothing to do with him since he was a small child.

____

____.

5 A lot of people have tried, but almost none of them have succeeded.

____

____.

Underline the correct words.

6 She *some time/sometimes* comes round to see me on Saturday mornings.

7 Could you come and see me *some time/sometimes* tomorrow.

8 I called out the class register. *Everyone/Every one* was there.

9 *Everyone/Every one* of my prize roses had been damaged in the thunderstorm.

10 Has *anyone/any one* here been to Australia?

[ ] 10

Exercise 6 **Compound words**

Fill each gap with a compound made from a word in **A** and a word in **B**.

A		**B**	
life	home	packers	phone
food	wild	like	life
back	mobile	sick	pocket
search	package	holiday	selling
best	pick	poisoning	party

1 I often felt ____________ when I was living in Nepal. I missed my family a lot, especially when I was very ill with ____________.

2 Two ____________ from Australia have gone missing on a mountain in Scotland. The rescue services have sent a ____________ to find them.

3 We've got a real bargain! A ____________ to East Africa for only £300. We're hoping to see lots of ____________ in the game parks.

4 The characters in Tom Ruddock's novels are so ____________, it isn't surprising that he's a ____________ author.

5 Stop that man! He's a ____________! He's just stolen my wallet. Has anybody got a ____________ to call the police?

[ ] 5

Exercise 7 **Suffixes and prefixes**

Change the form of the words in brackets to complete the sentence.

Examples
What's that *funny* noise? (fun)
Max never keeps his promises. He is very *unreliable* . (rely)

1 Have I told you about the most __________ moment in my life? (embarrass)

2 Do you know if this mushroom is __________? (poison)

3 The rate of __________ amongst the poor is still quite high, despite all the __________ in education. (literate) (improve)

4 Jane was so __________ that she didn't get the job. (disappoint)

5 I want to complain. Your sales assistants were very __________. They couldn't give me any of the information I needed. (help)

6 I'm afraid most of the points you have made in your essay are __________. (relevant)

7 The extent of the damage after the storm was terrible, quite __________ in fact. (believe)

8 What you need is a really __________ holiday! (relax)

9 Parents should always take __________ for their children's bad behaviour. (responsible)

10 It's __________ talking to him. He won't listen to a word you say. (use)

11 My brother was __________ for two hours after he fell off his bike. (conscious)

12 We are sorry to inform you that your application has been __________. (success)

13 This wet weather is so __________. (depress)

14 He was accused of __________ to the company, and asked to resign from his job. (loyal)

15 Do you have a good __________ with your mother-in-law? (relation)

	15

Exercise 8 ***Take, put, and be***

Complete these sentences with *take*, *put*, or *be* in the correct form.

1 I'm sorry. You can't ______ photographs inside the church.

2 I rang last night, but your flatmate said you ______ out.

3 I __________ on so much weight recently. I'll have to go on a diet.

4 Please __________ (not) offence, but I don't think that colour suits you.

5 My uncle ______ into collecting toy soldiers. He has hundreds of them.

6 I wasn't invited to Jack's party, and I felt really ______ out.

7 What ______ up with you? You look awful.

8 We had to ______ a stop to his spending so much money. He had huge debts.

9 She loves __________ part in school debates. I think she'll be politician when she grows up.

10 If you ______ my advice, you'll get an early night tonight.

	10

Total		100

Progress test 2 Units 7–12

Exercise 1

Read the text quickly. Put *one* word only into each gap.

The bride who married the best man

Casey O'Doherty, from [1] _____ village of Kileter in County Tyrone, Ireland, was [2] _____ the moon when his childhood sweetheart, Connie O'Toole, agreed [3] _____ marry him in the village church. He immediately [4] __________ his best friend Christie Muldoon to be his best man.

Casey, Connie, and Christie [5] _____ all grown up together in Kileter. They had all been pupils at the small village school, where they weren't [6] __________ to sit next to each other because they were [7] __________ laughing and talking. As teenagers, they [8] _____ to go to the local disco on Saturday nights, and in summer they [9] _____ spend days together, sitting [10] _____ the river, [11] __________ plans for the brilliant futures they were looking [12] __________ to.

On hot days they'd [13] __________ their bikes to the coast and spend the day on the beach. They were [14] __________ seen out of each other's company and [15] __________ known locally as 'the three Cs'.

On the day of his wedding, Casey was very nervous and hungover after a stag party with his friends the night before. [16] __________, he and Christie [17] __________ to the church [18] __________ time and stood side by side, waiting for Connie to arrive. The music started and [19] __________ was Christie, not Casey, who turned to watch the bride coming down the aisle. She looked more beautiful than he ever remembered [20] __________ her before. Casey was still feeling sick and dizzy. He closed his eyes and wished that he [21] __________ had so much to drink. The ceremony began and old Father O'Reilly, seeing Christie look so lovingly at the bride, put all the questions to him – and Christie answered. Suddenly Casey woke up and [22] __________ to stop the ceremony, but it was too late. Christie and Connie were married, and happy to be so.

Christie said later: 'I know we [23] __________ have done this, but when the priest turned to me, I started [24] __________ the questions because Casey didn't speak, and then something passed between Connie and me and we both realized this was [25] _____ we wanted! If only it [26] __________ happened like this. We know that we've [27] __________ Casey's heart, and we will never be completely happy [28] _____ he forgives us.'

Casey said: 'This can't [29] _____ happened. I [30] _____ be dreaming! I've lost a wife and my two best friends.'

	30

Exercise 2 Verb patterns and modals

Underline the correct answer.

1. How did you stop *biting / to bite* your nails?
2. *May / Can* you help me carry my suitcase?
3. I saw Timmy *break / breaking* the window.
4. We *don't have to / mustn't* get up early tomorrow because it's Sunday.
5. She's not at all used to *do / doing* the housework.
6. You *must / might* be feeling really excited about your holiday.
7. I'd like *to have / having* travelled the world before I grow old.
8. I'll never forget *to meet / meeting* you. It was the most important day of my life.
9. The house doesn't need *to be decorated / being decorated.*
10. Ted didn't succeed *in getting / to get* the job.
11. My father *can / should* be able to give you a lift.
12. How much homework are you made *do / to do* every day?

	12

Exercise 3 **Present to past**

Put these sentences into the past.

1 I must do my homework quickly tonight.

_______________ last night.

2 He usually walks to work.

____

but he doesn't any more.

3 She should see a doctor immediately.

_______________ ages ago.

4 I'll answer the phone. It could be for me.

I answered the phone because _______________

_______________.

5 I'm going to be late but I can't help it. The car won't start.

I was late but _______________

_______________.

6 That car's red. It can't be John's.

That car was red. _______________

_______________.

7 I wish I lived near the sea , but I don't.

_______________ when I was a child, but _______________.

8 Look at you! If your father saw you wearing that, he'd be absolutely furious.

You were lucky! _______________.

8

Exercise 4 **Questions and negatives**

Look at the chart.

	Harry Bewick	Helen Walford
born	1965	1937
married	Betty, 1990	Charlie, 1955 (died, March 1986)
job	advertising executive	nurse, now retired
children	1 son, Tom	3 daughters, 7 grandchildren
hobbies	golf	swimming, twice a week
newspaper	*The Times*	—
fears	heights	spiders
pets	—	two black cats and a Labrador
work abroad	worked in the USA,1995-97	—

Use the information in the chart to write an appropriate question about Harry or Helen.

1 _______________?
Since 1990.

2 _______________ 1986?
Her husband, Charlie, died.

3 _______________?
In March.

4 Do you know _______________?
Yes, he has. He has a son.

5 Have you got any idea _______________
_______________?
Seven.

6 _______________?
Twice a week.

7 _______________?
The Times.

8 _______________?
Heights.

9 Do you know _______________?
Yes. Spiders.

10 Can you tell me _______________?
Because he doesn't like animals.

11 _______________?
A Labrador.

12 _______________ the USA?
Harry did.

Complete these sentences about Harry and Helen.

13 Harry _______________ daughters.

14 Helen _______________ abroad.

15 Helen _______________ a nurse, but _______________ any longer.

15

Exercise 5 **Regret and emphasis**

Rewrite the following sentences to mean the same using the prompts given.

Example
Why didn't I speak to him?
I wish *I'd (had) spoken to him*.

1 I'm sorry I lost my temper.

If only _______________.

2 We don't have enough money to buy that car.

If _______________.

3 I shouldn't have told you.

I wish I ______________________________.

4 I was stuck in a traffic jam. I missed the beginning of the concert.

If ______________________________.

5 You must stop wasting money.

It's time you ______________________________.

6 Why did you tell everybody?

I'd rather you ______________________________.

7 I love Dave's sense of humour.

What I love ______________________________.

8 I admire the way you never get angry.

The thing I ______________________________.

9 I need a full-time job, not a part-time one.

It's ______________________________.

10 Someone discovered Antarctica in 1820. People are still exploring it.

Antarctica ______________________________ and

it ______________________.

	10

Exercise 6 **Choosing the right word**

Complete the sentences. Choose the correct word.

1 I __________ understand your problem.
seriously fully distinctly strongly

2 I'm not just hard up. I'm __________ penniless.
extremely absolutely very badly

3 What a bargain! He only paid £100 for that painting and it's absolutely __________.
valuable expensive worthless priceless

4 This steak is really __________. I can't eat it.
tough hard rich strong

5 My teacher is always __________ at me.
criticizing going getting coming

6 I've never got ______ with my youngest sister.
on out over up

7 On my salary it's difficult to make ends ______.
touch meet together up

8 I'm spending a month in France because I want to __________ up my French.
take put brush pick

9 I'm living with my aunt for the time __________.
now being lately passing

10 Pop stars often have really __________ lifestyles.
rich extravagant generous excited

11 You look __________. What have you been getting up to?
innocent guilty down-and-out risky

12 I love big cities __________ all the drawbacks.
although however whereas despite

13 The Balzac Boys have just had another ______ hit with their latest record.
pop smash crash jackpot

14 Did you __________ see the thief?
clearly well actually surely

15 I had some time to __________ before the meeting, so I had a coffee.
waste kill lose spend

16 I'll remember in a minute. His name is on the __________ of my tongue.
tip end edge point

17 I don't enjoy __________ business with him.
doing making having any

18 I've only got ______ pair of hands. Hang on!
the a one my

19 We're going to ________ a car in Rome.
higher hire rent pay for

20 Housework must have taken ages to do before all these labour-saving __________ were invented.
discoveries instruments tools gadgets

	20

Exercise 7 ***get, come,* and *go***

Complete these sentences with *get*, *come*, or *go* in the correct form.

1 Look at Sally! You can tell she's embarrassed. She __________ bright red!

2 I'm worried because I think my English __________ worse not better!

3 Our football team ______ first in the league.

4 Most of my salary ______ on the rent for my flat.

5 The time __________ soon for us to say goodbye.

	5

Total		100

Answer keys

Stop and check 1 Units 1–4

Tenses

1 've been
2 has passed
3 wrote
4 don't know
5 'll start
6 went
7 was looking
8 realized
9 had been stolen
10 were called
11 was crying
12 was looking/looked
13 found
14 had got
15 felt
16 had been looking/was looking
17 arrived
18 had been eaten/was eaten
19 had gone
20 were told
21 had to
22 was given
23 was starving
24 has been saying
25 're going to see/'re seeing
26 feel
27 are teaching/have been teaching
28 won't recognize
29 'm doing/'ve been doing
30 is situated
31 have
32 is being decorated
33 has written
34 has been translated
35 haven't read
36 has been studying
37 think
38 have
39 am paid/get paid
40 'm saving/have been saving

Total 40

Present Perfect

1 gone
2 Have you been waiting
3 did you cut
4 I've never seen
5 I've been having
6 I haven't passed
7 have you had
8 Has the car been serviced
9 worked
10 I've been working

Total 10

Narrative tenses

1 did you do
2 were you doing
3 had done
4 was done
5 had been making/was making
6 had been made
7 made
8 had been raining/was raining
9 rained
10 was raining

Total 10

Some and *any*

1 something
2 any
3 some
4 any
5 somewhere

Total 5

Quantifiers

1 much
2 lots
3 some
4 a little
5 a huge amount
6 none
7 Fewer
8 All
9 Everyone
10 no

Total 10

Vocabulary

Exercise 1

fiction	fact
fantastic	dreadful
success	failure
worried	carefree
peaceful	noisy
arrive	set off
narrow	broad
hardware	software
well-off	broke
proud	ashamed

Total 10

Exercise 2

1 air-conditioned
2 junk mail
3 diarrhoea
4 illiterate
5 mugged
6 homesick
7 contract
8 nil
9 spices
10 refuse/rubbish
11 bargain
12 souvenirs
13 minute
14 tears
15 loo/lavatory

Total 15

Stop and check 2 Units 5–8

General revision

1 We love getting
2 exciting
3 distinctly
4 can't have
5 phoning
6 to buy
7 must
8 very
9 aren't
10 to keep
11 moaning
12 won't write
13 You'll be
14 which
15 to start
16 working
17 she'll be working
18 She's had to save
19 wait and see
20 is going to feel
21 will have just got used to
22 peace and quiet
23 They'll have been married
24 There's going to be
25 to send
26 to hear
27 making
28 absolutely
29 it's
30 sooner or later
31 meeting
32 who
33 they're coming
34 needn't have bothered
35 that
36 to take
37 might
38 must
39 should
40 to see

Total 40

Future forms

1 goes
2 'll find
3 makes/has made
4 's going
5 leaves
6 's going to study/'s studying/'ll be studying
7 'll be having
8 likes/'ll like
9 's having/'s going to have
10 has settled

Total 10

Relative clauses

1 who
2 which
3 whose
4 where
5 why
6 that
7 whatever
8 what
9 (nothing)
10 (nothing)

Total 10

Participles and verb patterns

1 boring
2 tiring
3 furnished
4 unexpected
5 exhausting
6 asking
7 to get
8 living
9 cry
10 to understand

Total 10

Modal verbs

1 must
2 had to go
3 shouldn't
4 might
5 did you manage to
6 must have been
7 should
8 can't
9 mustn't
10 May

Total 10

Vocabulary

Exercise 1

keen	enthusiastic
dull	boring
weird	odd
stubborn	obstinate
confess	admit
terrified	scared
useful	handy
mend	fix

Exercise 2

1 pros and cons
2 give and take
3 by and large
4 up with
5 over
6 out of
7 over

Exercise 3

1 filthy
2 hilarious
3 gorgeous
4 delighted
5 starving

Total 20

Stop and check 3 Units 9–12

General revision

1 once/twice
2 haven't
3 how
4 a
5 What
6 could
7 like
8 won't
9 hadn't
10 would
11 do
12 to
13 can't
14 broke/penniless
15 goes
16 yet
17 don't
18 break
19 one/an
20 used
21 every/at
22 that/a
23 was
24 use
25 'll
26 Isn't
27 Occasionally
28 comes
29 thing
30 all

Total 30

Questions

1 How often do you go
2 What are you afraid of?
3 didn't she
4 don't like do you
5 Did you use
6 What would you do if you
7 would you have had to do/what would have happened if you hadn't
8 who stole/what happened to
9 What's the food like
10 Whose dictionary is that/this?
11 Who did you get this from
12 when television was invented by

Total 12

Wishes and conditionals

1 b	4 b	7 c	10 a
2 c	5 b	8 a	11 b
3 a	6 a	9 b	12 c

Total 12

Vocabulary

Exercise 1

1 priceless
2 huge
3 plump
4 failure
5 occasionally
6 tender
7 easy
8 soft
9 simple
10 teetotal
11 fake
12 distraught
13 curly
14 temporary
15 cruel

Total 15

Exercise 2

1 hard-up, because the other words mean you have no money at all
2 generous
3 in the black
4 ache, because the other verbs are things you can do with parts of your body
5 rent, because the other verbs apply to money and time
6 lose, because the other verbs apply to forms of transport
7 friend, because the others are homophones
8 expensive, because the other adjectives refer to a person
9 regularly, because it is positive
10 bomb, because the others are homonyms

Total 10

Revision

1 as
2 Since
3 a
4 this
5 whole
6 despite
7 from
8 an
9 the
10 that
11 go
12 would
13 work
14 playing
15 At first
16 wasn't
17 In the end
18 introduced
19 to
20 come
21 had marked

Total 21

Progress test 1 Units 1–6

Exercise 1

1 were waiting
2 had been
3 were feeling/felt
4 hadn't been waiting/hadn't waited
5 was announced
6 leaves/will leave/will be leaving
7 were making
8 heard
9 has been delayed/is delayed
10 hope
11 don't get/won't get
12 would happen
13 got
14 Don't be
15 are checked
16 is allowed
17 hadn't boarded
18 had been given
19 will have been waiting
20 takes/has taken
21 were sitting
22 leapt
23 hadn't started
24 were led
25 have had
26 hasn't been
27 shall we go/are we going
28 will have

Total 28

Exercise 2

1 have been made
2 been fed
3 could persuade her
4 has stolen my purse
5 couldn't be moved
6 being given a lift
7 will have to sell
8 told me the train
9 are wanted
10 don't need a computer
11 is being watched
12 told me to wait

Total 12

Exercise 3

1 I'm seeing / I'm going to see
2 has been missing for
3 I've found
4 the house had been burgled
5 I didn't get on
6 hadn't been working
7 Who's been smoking?
8 I'll have finished
9 He's been writing
10 We'll be having

Total 10

Exercise 4

1	(nothing)	6	(nothing)
2	whose	7	whose
3	which	8	which
4	who	9	that / which
5	what	10	where

Total 10

Exercise 5

1	a few	6	sometimes
2	very little	7	some time
3	a little	8	Everyone
4	very little	9	Every one
5	very few	10	anyone

Total 10

Exercise 6

1	homesick	food poisoning
2	backpackers	search party
3	package holiday	wildlife
4	lifelike	best-selling
5	pickpocket	mobile phone

Total 5

Exercise 7

1 embarrassing
2 poisonous
3 illiteracy improvements
4 disappointed
5 unhelpful
6 irrelevant
7 unbelievable
8 relaxing
9 responsibility
10 useless
11 unconscious
12 unsuccessful
13 depressing
14 disloyalty
15 relationship

Total 15

Exercise 8

1	take	6	put
2	were	7	is
3	have put	8	put
4	don't take	9	taking
5	is	10	take

Total 10

Progress test 2 Units 7–12

Exercise 1

1	the	16	Nevertheless
2	over	17	got
3	to	18	on
4	asked / invited	19	it
5	had	20	seeing
6	allowed	21	hadn't
7	always	22	tried
8	used	23	shouldn't
9	would	24	answering
10	by	25	what
11	making	26	hadn't
12	forward	27	broken
13	ride	28	until / unless
14	never	29	have
15	were	30	must

Total 30

Exercise 2

1	biting	7	to have
2	Can	8	meeting
3	break	9	to be decorated
4	don't have to	10	in getting
5	doing	11	should
6	must	12	to do

Total 12

Exercise 3

1 had to do
2 used to walk
3 should have seen
4 it could have been
5 I couldn't help it because the car wouldn't start
6 couldn't have been
7 I wish I had lived but I didn't
8 had seen you he'd have been

Total 8

Exercise 4

1 How long has Harry been married?
2 What happened to Helen in 1986?
3 What month did her husband die in?
4 if Harry has / has got any children?
5 how many grandchildren she has?
6 How often does she go swimming?
7 Which / what paper does he read?
8 What's he afraid of?
9 if she's afraid of anything?
10 why he doesn't have any pets?
11 What sort of dog has she got?
12 Who worked in
13 hasn't got / doesn't have any
14 has never worked
15 used to work as / she doesn't / isn't

Total 15

Exercise 5

1 I hadn't lost
2 If only we had
3 hadn't told you
4 I hadn't been
I wouldn't have missed
5 stopped wasting
6 hadn't told
7 about Dave is his sense of humour
8 admire about you is the fact / way that
9 a full-time job I need, not a
10 was discovered
is still being explored

Total 10

Exercise 6

1	fully	11	guilty
2	absolutely	12	despite
3	priceless	13	smash
4	tough	14	actually
5	getting	15	kill
6	on	16	tip
7	meet	17	doing
8	brush	18	one
9	being	19	hire / rent
10	extravagant	20	gadgets

Total 20

Exercise 7

1 has gone
2 is getting
3 came
4 goes
5 will come

Total 5

Wordlist

Here is a list of words that appear unit by unit in *New Headway Upper-Intermediate*. Photocopy the list for each unit, and give it out as you go through the book.

There are different ways of using the lists.

- Give students the list when you *begin* the unit. They can write in translations as you go through.
- Give out the list at the *end* of the unit. This will serve as revision and consolidation.

Most of the new words are here, but if we feel a word isn't very useful or common, we have omitted it. Some words are repeated if they appear in a later unit.

Abbreviations

adj = adjective
adv = adverb
Am = American
conj = conjunction
id = idiom
inf = informal
n = noun
pl n = plural noun
pp = past participle
prep = preposition
(r) = an 'r' heard when the word is followed by a vowel sound
sb = somebody
sth = something
v = verb

Unit 1

alligator *n* /'ælɪgeɪtə(r)/
appeal (= ask for) *v* /ə'pi:l/
armed *pp* /ɑ:md/
baboon *n* /bə'bu:n/
backhand (tennis) *n* /'bækhænd/
ball (= dance) *n* /bɔ:l/
be sick (= vomit) *v* /ˌbi 'sɪk/
bear (= animal) *n* /beə(r)/
blizzard *n* /'blɪzəd/
book token *n* /'bʊk ˌtəʊkn/
bookmaker *n* /'bʊkˌmeɪkə(r)/
bracelet *n* /'breɪslɪt/
bum *(inf) n* /bʌm/
bunk-bed *n* /'bʌŋk ˌbed/
carefree *adj* /'keəfri:/
convert *v* /kən'vɜ:t/
crash out *(inf) v* /ˌkræʃ 'aʊt/
culture shock *n* /'kʌltʃə ˌʃɒk/
cute *adj* /kju:t/
department (at university) *n* /dɪ'pɑ:tmənt/
fan (to keep cool) *n* /fæn/
fir *n* /fɜ:(r)/
food poisoning *n* /'fu:d ˌpɔɪznɪŋ/
fresher (at university) *n* /'freʃə(r)/
frost *n* /frɒst/
gorgeous *adj* /'gɔ:dʒəs/
hail *n, v* /heɪl/
hike *v* /haɪk/
hold up (= rob) *v* /ˌhəʊld 'ʌp/
home-made *adj* /ˌhəʊm 'meɪd/
homeless *adj* /'həʊmləs/
homesick *adj* /'həʊmsɪk/
hook *n, v* /hʊk/
house-proud *adj* /'haʊs ˌpraʊd/
house-trained *adj* /'haʊs ˌtreɪnd/
house-warming party *n* /'haʊs ˌwɔ:mɪŋ ˌpɑ:ti/
hug *n, v* /hʌg/
jeweller *n* /'dʒʊələ(r)/
junk food *n* /'dʒʌŋk ˌfu:d/
knackered *(inf) adj* /'nækəd/
lavatory *n* /'lævətri/
lifelong *adj* /'laɪflɒŋ/
lifestyle *n* /'laɪfstaɪl/
light bulb *n* /'laɪt ˌbʌlb/
light-headed *adj* /ˌlaɪt 'hedɪd/
loads (= lots) *(inf) pl n* /ləʊdz/
log fire *n* /ˌlɒg 'faɪə(r)/
loo *(inf) n* /lu:/
made redundant *pp* /ˌmeɪd rɪ'dʌndənt/
malaria *n* /mə'leərɪə/
match point (tennis) *n* /ˌmætʃ 'pɔɪnt/
paw (of an animal) *n* /pɔ:/
pony-trekking *n* /'pəʊni ˌtrekɪŋ/
precious *adj* /'preʃəs/
pride *n* /praɪd/
raindrop *n* /'reɪndrɒp/
release *n, v* /rɪ'li:s/
remote controlled *adj* /rɪˌməʊt kən'trəʊld/
scare *n, v* /skeə(r)/
search *n, v* /sɜ:tʃ/
set (tennis) *n* /set/
shotgun *n* /'ʃɒtgʌn/
software *n* /'sɒftweə(r)/
speed boat *n* /'spi:d ˌbəʊt/
stable (for a horse) *n* /'steɪbl/
steamy *adj* /'sti:mi/
sticky *adj* /'stɪki/
time consuming *adj* /'taɪm kənˌsju:mɪŋ/
tutorial *n* /tju:'tɔ:riəl/
well off *adj* /ˌwel 'ɒf/
whitewater rafting *n* /'waɪtwɔ:tə ˌrɑ:ftɪŋ/
widespread *adj* /'waɪdspred/

Unit 2

abandon *v* /ə'bændən/
academic *adj* /ˌækə'demɪk/
achievement *n* /ə'tʃi:vmənt/
appalling *adj* /ə'pɔ:lɪŋ/
award *n, v* /ə'wɔ:d/
backpacker *n* /'bækpækə(r)/
backpacking trip *n* /'bækpækɪŋ ˌtrɪp/
bacteria *n* /bæk'tɪəriə/
barely *adv* /'beəli/
beehive *n* /'bi:haɪv/
bet *v* /bet/
breath *n* /breθ/
broadcast *v* /'brɔ:dkɑ:st/
broaden *v* /'brɔ:dn/
bury *v* /'beri/
cable car *n* /'keɪbl ˌkɑ:(r)/
camcorder *n* /'kæmˌkɔ:də(r)/
camel *n* /'kæml/
candle *n* /'kændl/
canoe *n* /kə'nu:/
carve *v* /kɑ:v/
cave *n* /keɪv/
cedar tree *n* /'si:də ˌtri:/
chisel *n, v* /'tʃɪzl/
click *v* /klɪk/
coastline *n* /'kəʊstlaɪn/
compelling *adj* /kəm'pelɪŋ/
conquer *v* /'kɒŋkə(r)/
consumer goods *pl n* /kən'sju:mə ˌgʊdz/
cruel *adj* /krʊəl/
cuisine *n* /kwɪ'zi:n/
decade *n* /'dekeɪd/
delicate *adj* /'delɪkət/
demonstration *n* /ˌdemən'streɪʃn/
diarrhoea *n* /ˌdaɪə'rɪə/
display *n, v* /dɪs'pleɪ/
estimated *pp* /'estɪˌmeɪtɪd/
expand *v* /ɪk'spænd/
expedition *n* /ˌekspə'dɪʃn/
explorer *n* /ɪk'splɔ:rə(r)/
exquisite *adj* /ɪk'skwɪzɪt/
extinction *n* /ɪk'stɪŋkʃn/
faulty *adj* /'fɔ:lti/
fit *adj* /fɪt/
found (= establish) *v* /faʊnd/
fumes *pl n* /fju:mz/
ghetto *n* /'getəʊ/
glider *n* /'glaɪdə(r)/
go trekking *v* /ˌgəʊ 'trekɪŋ/
grave (danger) *adj* /greɪv/
imprison *v* /ɪm'prɪzn/
indifferent (= mediocre) *adj* /ɪn'dɪfrənt/
inhabitant *n* /ɪn'hæbɪtənt/
inscription *n* /ɪn'skrɪpʃn/
jumbo jet *n* /ˌdʒʌmbəʊ 'dʒet/
landscape *n* /'lændskeɪp/
lavender *n* /'lævɪndə(r)/
lemur *n* /'li:mə/
librarian *n* /laɪ'breəriən/
local *n, adj* /'ləʊkl/
misinformation *n* /ˌmɪsɪnfə'meɪʃn/
mission *n* /'mɪʃn/
mosquito *n* /mɒs'ki:təʊ/
mug *v* /mʌg/
naval *adj* /'neɪvl/
oath *n* /əʊθ/
outer space *n* /ˌaʊtə 'speɪs/
package holiday *n* /'pækɪdʒ ˌhɒlədeɪ/
peak *n* /pi:k/
permit *n* /'pɜ:mɪt/
permit *v* /pə'mɪt/
plaster (for a cut finger) *n* /'plɑ:stə(r)/
powder *n* /'paʊdə(r)/
prehistoric *adj* /ˌpri:hɪ'stɒrɪk/
presume *v* /prɪ'zju:m/
privileged *adj* /'prɪvəlɪdʒd/
put in charge of *v* /ˌpʊt ɪn 'tʃɑ:dʒ əv/
put off *v* /ˌpʊt 'ɒf/
put on make-up *v* /ˌpʊt ɒn 'meɪk ʌp/
put pressure on sb *v* /ˌpʊt 'preʃər ɒn .../
put sb down (= criticize) *v* /ˌpʊt ... 'daʊn/
put sb up *v* /ˌpʊt ... 'ʌp/
put up with *v* /ˌpʊt 'ʌp wɪð/
region *n* /'ri:dʒn/
remains *pl n* /rɪ'meɪnz/
remarkable *adj* /rɪ'mɑ:kəbl/
remote *adj* /rɪ'məʊt/
replica *n* /'replɪkə/
reveal *v* /rɪ'vi:l/
ruins *pl n* /'ru:ɪnz/
scratch *v* /skrætʃ/
scuba dive *v* /'sku:bə ˌdaɪv/
share *n* /ʃeə(r)/
site *n* /saɪt/
source *n* /sɔ:s/
souvenir *n* /ˌsu:və'nɪə(r)/
spiritual *adj* /'spɪrɪtʃʊəl/
spring up (= appear suddenly) *v* /ˌsprɪŋ 'ʌp/
sting *v* /stɪŋ/
swell *v* /swel/
take a risk *v* /ˌteɪk ə 'rɪsk/
take for granted *v* /ˌteɪk fə 'grɑ:ntɪd/
take no notice *v* /ˌteɪk nəʊ 'nəʊtɪs/
take off (= become successful) *v* /ˌteɪk 'ɒf/
take over *v* /ˌteɪk 'əʊvə(r)/
take part *v* /ˌteɪk 'pɑ:t/
take place *v* /ˌteɪk 'pleɪs/
take responsibility for *v* /ˌteɪk rɪˌspɒnsə'bɪləti/
take things easy *v* /ˌteɪk ˌθɪŋz 'i:zi/
theme park *n* /'θi:m ˌpɑ:k/
tiresome *adj* /'taɪəsəm/
tomb *n* /tu:m/
tourist spot *n* /'tʊərɪst ˌspɒt/
tramp *v* /træmp/
travel bug *(inf) n* /'trævl ˌbʌg/
treasured *adj* /'treʒəd/
triplets *pl n* /'trɪpləts/
turtle *n* /'tɜ:tl/
undeveloped *adj* /ʌndɪ'veləpt/
unique *adj* /ju:'ni:k/
utterly *adv* /'ʌtəli/
vanish *v* /'vænɪʃ/
vile *adj* /vaɪl/
violent *adj* /'vaɪələnt/
vivid *adj* /'vɪvɪd/
warfare *n* /'wɔ:feə(r)/
whir *v* /wɜ:(r)/
wire *n, v* /'waɪə(r)/

Unit 3

accustomed to *pp* /ə'kʌstəmd tə/
acute (observation) *adj* /ə'kju:t/
aggressive *adj* /ə'gresɪv/
aisle *n* /aɪl/
anew *adv* /ə'nju:/
antenatal *adj* /ˌæntɪ'neɪtl/
auction *n, v* /'ɔ:kʃn/
auctioneer *n* /ˌɔ:kʃə'nɪə(r)/
baffling *adj* /'bæflɪŋ/
bar *v* /bɑ:(r)/
based on *pp* /'beɪsd ɒn/
beachwear *n* /'bi:tʃweə(r)/
befuddled *adj* /bɪ'fʌdəld/
beggar *n* /'begə(r)/
belligerent *adj* /bɪ'lɪdʒərənt/
bitterness *n* /'bɪtənəs/
bow *v* /baʊ/
break out (= start fighting) *v* /ˌbreɪk 'aʊt/
broke (= no money) *adj* /brəʊk/
cabin staff *n* /'kæbɪn ˌstɑ:f/
celebrate *v* /'seləbreɪt/
chap *(inf) n* /tʃæp/
chilling (very frightening) *adj* /'tʃɪlɪŋ/
cider *n* /'saɪdə(r)/
commit suicide *v* /kəˌmɪt 'su:ɪsaɪd/
community *n* /kə'mju:nəti/
competition *n* /ˌkɒmpə'tɪʃn/
consciousness *n* /'kɒnʃəsnəs/
consequence *n* /'kɒnsɪkwəns/
convicted *pp* /kən'vɪktɪd/
cramped *adj* /kræmpt/
crisp *adj* /krɪsp/
deliberately *adv* /dɪ'lɪbrətli/
denims *pl n* /'denɪmz/
deserted *adj* /dɪ'zɜ:tɪd/
designer jeans *pl n* /dɪˌzaɪnə 'dʒi:nz/
disloyal *adj* /dɪs'lɔɪəl/
disloyalty *n* /dɪs'lɔɪəlti/
disrespectful *adj* /ˌdɪsrɪ'spektfl/
disuse *n* /dɪs'ju:s/
(What a) **drag!** (= How awful!) *(inf) n* /dræg/
drip *n, v* /drɪp/
drunken stupor *n* /ˌdrʌŋkən 'stju:pə(r)/
encounter *n, v* /ɪŋ'kaʊntə(r)/
fair *n* /feə(r)/
fellow *(inf) n* /'feləʊ/
fist *n* /fɪst/
flashback *n* /'flæʃbæk/
flight attendant *n* /'flaɪt əˌtendənt/
fling *v* /flɪŋ/
food poisoning *n* /'fu:d ˌpɔɪznɪŋ/
foresee *v* /fɔ:'si:/
frustration *n* /frʌ'streɪʃn/
gang *n* /gæŋ/
get rid of *v* /ˌget 'rɪd əv/
gipsy *n* /'dʒɪpsi/
gloomy *adj* /'glu:mi/
gravestone *n* /'greɪvstəʊn/
guinea *n* /'gɪni/
harshly *adv* /'hɑ:ʃli/
helpless *adj* /'helpləs/
helplessness *n* /'helpləsnəs/
hysterical *adj* /hɪ'sterɪkl/
identical *adj* /aɪ'dentɪkl/
ill-tempered *adj* /ˌɪl 'tempəd/
illiteracy *n* /ɪ'lɪtərəsi/
illiterate *adj* /ɪ'lɪtərət/
immature *adj* /ˌɪmə'tjʊə(r)/
immaturity *n* /ˌɪmə'tjʊərəti/
immeasurable *adj* /ɪ'meʒərəbl/
implore *v* /ɪm'plɔ:(r)/
impolite *adj* /ɪmpə'laɪt/
indifference *n* /ɪn'dɪfrəns/
insensitive *adj* /ɪn'sensətɪv/
insight *n* /'ɪnsaɪt/
insult *n* /'ɪnsʌlt/
insult *v* /ɪn'sʌlt/
investigate *v* /ɪn'vestɪgeɪt/
irrelevance *n* /ɪ'reləvəns/
irrelevant *adj* /ɪ'reləvənt/
irresponsible *adj* /ɪrɪ'spɒnsəbl/
kind-hearted *adj* /ˌkaɪnd 'hɑ:tɪd/
leak *n, v* /li:k/
literacy *n* /'lɪtərəsi/
long-haul flight *n* /ˌlɒŋ hɔ:l 'flaɪt/
long-suffering *adj* /ˌlɒŋ 'sʌfərɪŋ/
loyalty *n* /'lɔɪəlti/
mare *n* /meə(r)/
mask *n* /mɑ:sk/
maturity *n* /mə'tjʊərəti/
measurable *adj* /'meʒərəbl/
mind! (= watch out!) *v* /maɪnd/
misuse *v* /ˌmɪs'ju:z/
mobile phone *n* /ˌməʊbaɪl 'fəʊn/
murmur *n, v* /'mɜ:mə(r)/
nonsense *n* /'nɒnsəns/
notorious *adj* /nəʊ'tɔ:riəs/
off balance *adj* /ˌɒf 'bæləns/
optimistic *adj* /ˌɒptɪ'mɪstɪk/
overcook *v* /ˌəʊvə'kʊk/
overhead compartment *n* /ˌəʊvəhed kəm'pɑ:tmənt/
pessimistic *adj* /ˌpesɪ'mɪstɪk/
pinpoint *v* /'pɪnpɔɪnt/
pitiable *adj* /'pɪtiəbl/
post-mortem *n* /ˌpəʊst 'mɔ:təm/
prolific *adj* /prə'lɪfɪk/
reckless *adj* /'rekləs/
relevance *n* /'reləvəns/
reliability *n* /rɪˌlaɪə'bɪləti/
remark *n, v* /rɪ'mɑ:k/
respectful *adj* /rɪ'spektfl/
riveted *pp* /'rɪvətɪd/
security guard *n* /sɪ'kjʊərəti ˌgɑ:d/
self-conscious *adj* /ˌself 'kɒnʃəs/
self-pitying *adj* /ˌself 'pɪtiɪŋ/
senseless *adj* /'sensləs/
sensitivity *n* /ˌsensə'tɪvəti/
skip (pages in a book) *v* /skɪp/
sober *adj* /'səʊbə(r)/
spectator *n* /spek'teɪtə(r)/
stonemason *n* /'stəʊnmeɪsn/
stumble across (= find by chance) *v* /'stʌmbl əˌkrɒs/
submarine *n* /ˌsʌbmə'ri:n/
swing doors *pl n* /ˌswɪŋ 'dɔ:z/
synopsis *n* /sɪ'nɒpsɪs/
take shelter *v* /ˌteɪk 'ʃeltə(r)/
thoughtful *adj* /'θɔ:tfl/
thoughtless *adj* /'θɔ:tləs/
threatened *pp* /'θretənd/
thriller *n* /'θrɪlə(r)/
torn *adj* /tɔ:n/
treat *n, v* /tri:t/
uncaring *adj* /ˌʌn'keərɪŋ/
unconscious *adj* /ˌʌn'kɒnʃəs/
undercook *v* /ˌʌndə'kʊk/
unfold *v* /ˌʌn'fəʊld/
unkind *adj* /ˌʌn'kaɪnd/
unobserved *pp* /ˌʌnəb'zervd/
unreliable *adj* /ˌʌnrɪ'laɪəbl/
usefulness *n* /'ju:sfəlnəs/
useless *adj* /'ju:sləs/
uselessness *n* /'ju:sləsnəs/
weighty *adj* /'weɪti/
well off/better off *adj* /ˌwel 'ɒf/, /ˌbetər 'ɒf/

Unit 4

appalling *adj* /ə'pɔ:lɪŋ/
armour *n* /'ɑ:mə(r)/
attempt *n* /ə'tempt/
bail *n* /beɪl/
bargain *n* /'bɑ:gɪn/
(I don't) **blame** (you) *v* /bleɪm/
(I can't be) **bothered** *v* /'bɒðəd/
(be) **bound** (to happen) (= sure) *adj* /baʊnd/
boycott *v* /'bɔɪkɒt/
budget *n* /'bʌdʒɪt/
canteen *n* /kæn'ti:n/
caravan trade *n* /'kærəvæn ˌtreɪd/
(I don't) **care** *v* /keə(r)/
cargo *n* /'kɑ:gəʊ/
chain (of shops) *n* /tʃeɪn/
cocoa *n* /'kəʊkəʊ/
competitive *adj* /kəm'petətɪv/
contract *n* /'kɒntrækt/
contract *v* /kən'trækt/
copper *n* /'kɒpə(r)/
corn *n* /kɔ:n/
currency *n* /'kʌrənsi/
desert *v* /dɪ'zɜ:t/
designer clothes *pl n* /dɪˌzaɪnə 'kləʊðz/
discount *n* /'dɪskaʊnt/
diversity *n* /ˌdaɪ'vɜ:səti/
doomed *pp* /du:md/
dustman *n* /'dʌstmən/
expand *v* /ɪk'spænd/
fast food restaurant *n* /ˌfɑ:st 'fu:d ˌrestrɒnt/
fig *n* /fɪg/
fire (an employee) *v* /'faɪə(r)/
flint *n* /flɪnt/
gamble *n, v* /'gæmbl/
gig (= music concert) *n* /gɪg/
glassware *n* /'glɑ:sweə(r)/
goods *pl n* /gʊdz/
grain *n* /greɪn/
guaranteed *pp* /gærən'ti:d/
hang on (= wait) *v* /ˌhæŋ 'ɒn/
health freak *(inf) n* /'helθ ˌfri:k/
homogeneous *adj* /ˌhɒmə'dʒi:niəs/
hunt *n, v* /hʌnt/
inedible *adj* /ɪn'edɪbl/
invalid *adj* /ɪn'vælɪd/
invalid *n* /'ɪnvəlɪd/
investor *n* /ɪn'vestə(r)/
jammed (photocopier) *adj* /dʒæmd/
kid (= joke) *v* /kɪd/
lawsuit *n* /'lɔ:su:t/
lead (metal) *n* /led/
lead *n, v* /li:d/
leaflet *n* /'li:flət/
live (concert) *adj* /laɪv/
livelihood *n* /'laɪvlihʊd/
luxury *n* /'lʌkʃəri/
manufacturer *n* /ˌmænjʊ'fæktʃərə(r)/
market *n, v* /'mɑ:kɪt/
merchant *n* /'mɜ:tʃənt/
(I don't) **mind** *v* /maɪnd/
minute *adj* /maɪ'nju:t/
necessity *n* /nə'sesəti/
never mind! *(id)* /'nevə ˌmaɪnd/
niche *n* /ni:ʃ, nɪtʃ /
night shift *n* /'naɪt ˌʃɪft/
object *n* /'ɒbdʒɪkt/
object *v* /əb'dʒekt/
offend *v* /ə'fend/
olive oil *n* /ˌɒlɪv 'ɔɪl/
pattern *n* /'pætn/
penetrate *v* /'penɪtreɪt/
penniless *adj* /'penɪləs/
permit *n* /'pɜ:mɪt/
permit *v* /pə'mɪt/
phone card *n* /'fəʊn ˌkɑ:d/
point (= reason) *n* /pɔɪnt/
pottery *n* /'pɒtəri/
poverty *n* /'pɒvəti/
present *v* /prɪ'zent/
primitive *adj* /'prɪmətɪv/
profit margin *n* /'prɒfɪt ˌmɑ:dʒɪn/
profitablity *n* /ˌprɒfɪtə'bɪləti/
protest *n* /'prəʊtest/
protest *v* /prə'test/
recession *n* /rɪ'seʃn/
record *n* /'rekɔ:d/
record *v* /rɪ'kɔ:d/
refund *n* /'ri:fʌnd/
refund *v* /ˌri:'fʌnd/
refuse (= rubbish) *n* /'refju:s/
refuse *v* /rɪ'fju:z/
renovate *v* /'renəveɪt/
rival *n* /'raɪvl/
row (= argue) *n, v* /raʊ/
row (a boat) *v* /rəʊ/
run (a business) *v* /rʌn/
sack (an employee) *v* /sæk/
(for goodness') **sake** *(id)* /seɪk/
silk *n* /sɪlk/
slave *n* /sleɪv/
sobering *adj* /'səʊbərɪŋ/
soft drink *n* /ˌsɒft 'drɪŋk/
spice *n* /spaɪs/
stallholder *n* /'stɔ:lˌhəʊldə(r)/
stand a chance *(id)* /ˌstænd ə 'tʃɑ:ns/
stock (= supply) *n* /stɒk/
stunt (advertising) *n* /stʌnt/
supplier *n* /sə'plaɪə(r)/
survey *n* /'sɜ:veɪ/
survey *v* /sə'veɪ/
tactfully *adv* /'tæktfəli/
tear (= a hole) *n, v* /teə(r)/
tear (in your eye) *n* /tɪə(r)/
textiles *pl n* /'tekstaɪlz/
tin *n* /tɪn/
tip (for a waiter) *n, v* /tɪp/
trade *n, v* /treɪd/
trainers *pl n* /'treɪnəz/
turnover *n* /'tɜ:nəʊvə(r)/
underestimate *v* /ˌʌndər'estɪmeɪt/
upmarket *adj* /ˌʌp'mɑ:kɪt/
wind (your watch) *v* /waɪnd/

Unit 5

affection *n* /ə'fekʃn/
antibiotics *pl n* /ˌæntɪbaɪ'ɒtɪks/
be for (= in favour of) *v* /ˌbi 'fɔ:(r)/
be off (= not fresh) *v* /ˌbi: 'ɒf/
be over (= at an end) *v* /ˌbi: 'əʊvə(r)/
be snowed under *v* /ˌbi ˌsnəʊd 'ʌndə(r)/
be up to *v* /ˌbi: 'ʌp tu:/
bliss *n* /blɪs/
budget *n, v* /'bʌdʒɪt/
by and large *(id)* /ˌbaɪ ən 'lɑ:dʒ/
calculating *adj* /'kælkjʊleɪtɪŋ/
cautious *adj* /'kɔ:ʃəs/
ceremony *n* /'serɪməni/
chaotic *adj* /keɪ'ɒtɪk/
compromise *n, v* /'kɒmprəmaɪz/
concern *n* /kən'sɜ:n/
confirm *v* /kən'fɜ:m/
courtship *n* /'kɔ:tʃɪp/
cruising speed *n* /'kru:zɪŋ ˌspi:d/
cure *n, v* /kjʊə(r)/
curiously *adv* /'kjʊəriəsli/
customer services *pl n* /ˌkʌstəmə 'sɜ:vɪsɪz/
declare *v* /dɪ'kleə(r)/
deepen *v* /'di:pən/
disturb *v* /dɪ'stɜ:b/
divorce rate *n* /dɪ'vɔ:s ˌreɪt/
dramatically *adv* /drə'mætɪkəli/
drop sb a line *v* /ˌdrɒp ... ə 'laɪn/
emergency *n* /ɪ'mɜ:dʒənsi/
ensure *v* /ɪn'ʃɔ:(r)/
enterprise *n* /'entəpraɪz/
facilities *pl n* /fə'sɪlətiz/
fancy (= want) *(inf) v* /'fænsi/
fee *n* /fi:/
finalize *v* /'faɪnəlaɪz/
fine *n* /faɪn/
flexible *adj* /'fleksɪbl/
fondness *n* /'fɒndnəs/
fuel guage *n* /'fjʊəl ˌgeɪdʒ/
fuel tank *n* /'fjʊəl ˌtæŋk/
fulfil *v* /ˌfʊl'fɪl/
fundamental *adj* /ˌfʌndə'mentl/
get-together *n* /'get təˌgeðə(r)/
ginger *n* /'dʒɪndʒə(r)/
give and take *(id)* /ˌgɪv ən 'teɪk/
gland *n* /glænd/
grin and bear it *(id)* /ˌgrɪn ən 'beər ɪt/
hippy *n* /'hɪpi/
in common *(id)* /ɪn 'kɒmən/
inclusive *adj* /ɪn'klu:sɪv/
ingredient *n* /ɪn'gri:diənt/
ins and outs *pl n* /ˌɪnz ən 'aʊts/
intensity *n* /ɪn'tensəti/
itemize *v* /'aɪtəmaɪz/
junkie *n* /'dʒʌnki/
leadership *n* /'li:dəʃɪp/
look up (= improve) *v* /ˌlʊk 'ʌp/
lousy (= bad) *adj* /'laʊzi/
marine *n* /mə'ri:n/
mate (= friend) *(inf) n* /meɪt/
mediation *n* /ˌmi:di'eɪʃn/
more or less *(id)* /ˌmɔ:r ɔ: 'les/
mutual *adj* /'mju:tʃʊəl/
now and then *(id)* /ˌnaʊ ən 'ðen/
odds and ends *pl n* /ˌɒdz ən 'endz/
ponderously *adv* /'pɒndərəsli/
prenuptial *adj* /pri:'nʌptʃl/
presume *v* /prɪ'zju:m/
pristine *adj* /'prɪsti:n/
probe *v* /prəʊb/
prospect *n* /'prɒspekt/
raise your voice *v* /ˌreɪz jɔ: 'vɔɪs/
reassure *v* /ˌrɪ:ə'ʃʊə(r)/
regulate *v* /'regjʊləɪt/
reservation *n* /ˌrezə'veɪʃn/
reunion *n* /ˌri:'ju:niən
ridiculous *adj* /rɪ'dɪkjʊləs/
roundabout (for traffic) *n* /'raʊndəbaʊt/
run the house *v* /ˌrʌn ðə 'haʊs/
safe and sound *(id)* /ˌseɪf ən 'saʊnd/
savings *pl n* /'seɪvɪŋz/
saviour *n* /'seɪvjə(r)/
score *n, v* /skɔ:(r)/
sick and tired *(inf) adj* /ˌsɪk ən 'taɪəd/
slowly but surely *(id)* /ˌsləʊli bət 'ʃʊəli/
small talk *n* /'smɔ:l ˌtɔ:k/
solar-powered *adj* /ˌsəʊlə 'paʊəd/
sooner or later *(id)* /ˌsu:nər ɔ: 'leɪtə(r)/
split up *v* /ˌsplɪt 'ʌp/
spontaneity *n* /ˌspɒntə'neɪəti/
spontaneous *adj* /ˌspɒn'teɪniəs/
standstill *n* /'stændstɪl/
swollen *pp* /'swəʊlən/
tap *n* /tæp/
telly (= television) *n* /'teli/
temporarily *adv* /ˌtempə'reərəli/
tense *v, adj* /tens/
tide *n* /taɪd/
touch and go *(id)* /ˌtʌtʃ ən 'gəʊ/
ultimate *adj* /'ʌltɪmət/
unacceptable *adj* /ˌʌnək'septəbl/
unconditional *adj* /ˌʌnkən'dɪʃənl/
union *n* /'ju:niən/
unleaded fuel *n* /ˌʌnledɪd 'fjʊəl/
vital *adj* /'vaɪtəl/
wedding vows *pl n* /'wedɪŋ ˌvaʊz/
weird *adj* /wɪəd/
witness *n, v* /'wɪtnəs/
yoga *n* /'jəʊgə/

Unit 6

abound *v* /ə'baʊnd/
ahead *adv* /ə'hed/
atheism *n* /'eɪθiɪzm/
attach *v* /ə'tætʃ/
back-up (= support) *n* /'bæk ˌʌp/
black box /ˌblæk 'bɒks/
bloke *(inf) n* /bləʊk/
breed *v* /bri:d/
cattle *pl n* /'kætl/
claim *n, v* /kleɪm/
click *n, v* /klɪk/
cockpit *n* /'kɒkpɪt/
cold-blooded *adj* /ˌkəʊld 'blʌdɪd/
comply *v* /kəm'plaɪ/
conduct *v* /kən'dʌkt/
convinced *adj* /kən'vɪnst/
crew *n* /kru:/
crumpled *adj* /'krʌmpəld/
dash around *v* /ˌdæʃ ə'raʊnd/
daunting task *n* /ˌdɔ:ntɪŋ 'tɑ:sk/
deer *n* /dɪə(r)/
delighted *adj* /dɪ'laɪtɪd/
depressed *adj* /dɪ'prest/
depressing *adj* /dɪ'presɪŋ/
derive *v* /dɪ'raɪv/
disappointing *adj* /ˌdɪsə'pɔɪntɪŋ/
disappointed *adj* /ˌdɪsə'pɔɪntɪd/
display *v* /dɪs'pleɪ/
ditch (a boyfriend/girlfriend) *(inf) v* /dɪtʃ/
diversion *n* /daɪ'vɜ:ʃn/
dose *n* /dəʊs/
duck *n* /dʌk/
dull *adj* /dʌl/
eccentric *n, adj* /ɪk'sentrɪk/
elderly *adj* /'eldəli/
encode *v* /ɪn'kəʊd/
entire *adj* /ɪn'taɪə(r)/
exceed *v* /ɪk'si:d/
fancy (a boy/girl) *v* /'fænsi/
fascinated *adj* /'fæsɪneɪtɪd/
fascinating *adj* /'fæsɪneɪtɪŋ/
feat *n* /fi:t/
fluffy *adj* /'flʌfi/
fluorescent *adj* /ˌflʊə'resənt/
frog *n* /frɒg/
fuselage *n* /'fju:zəlɑ:ʒ/
gadgetry *n* /'gædʒətri/
handy *adj* /'hændi/
hardware *n* /'hɑ:dweə(r)/
icon (computer) *n* /'aɪkɒn/
impact *n* /'ɪmpækt/
indestructible *adj* /ˌɪndɪ'strʌktəbl/
infantry *n* /'ɪnfəntri/
inquisitive *adj* /ɪn'kwɪzətɪv/
insane *adj* /ɪn'seɪn/
insert *v* /ɪn'sɜ:t/
invincibility *n* /ɪnˌvɪnsə'bɪləti/
legendary *adj* /'ledʒəndəri/
nerd *(inf) n* /nɜ:d/
non-conformist *adj* /ˌnɒn kən'fɔ:mɪst/
obstinate *adj* /'ɒbstɪnət/
output *n* /'aʊtpʊt/
outskirts *pl n* /'aʊtskɜ:ts/
overlook *v* /ˌəʊvə'lʊk/
penguin *n* /'pengwɪn/
pickpocket *n* /'pɪkˌpɒkɪt/
preach *v* /pri:tʃ/
prominent *adj* /'prɒmɪnənt/
prosecute *v* /'prɒsɪkju:t/
public conveniences /ˌpʌblɪk kən'vi:niənsɪz/
rear *n* /rɪə(r)/
recruit *n, v* /rɪ'kru:t/
reject *v* /rɪ'dʒekt/
remarkable *adj* /rɪ'mɑ:kəbl/
risky *adj* /'rɪski/
scanner *n* /'skænə(r)/
scared stiff *(inf) adj* /ˌskeəd 'stɪf/
seal *n, v* /si:l/
smart card *n* /'smɑ:t ˌkɑ:d/
store *n, v* /stɔ:(r)/
strain *n, v* /streɪn/
striking *adj* /'straɪkɪŋ/
stubborn *adj* /'stʌbən/
swap *v* /swɒp/
talented *adj* /'tæləntɪd/
tray *n* /treɪ/
trespasser *n* /'trespəsə(r)/
tycoon *n* /taɪ'ku:n/
vacancies (at a hotel) *pl n* /'veɪkənsɪz/
venture *v* /'ventʃə(r)/
virtual *adj* /'vɜ:tʃʊəl/
visible *adj* /'vɪzəbl/
wander *v* /'wɒndə(r)/
whale *n* /weɪl/
withstand *v* /wɪð'stænd/

Unit 7

air raid shelter *n* /ˈeə ˌreɪd ˌʃeltə(r)/
album *n* /ˈælbəm/
ambiguous *adj* /æmˈbɪgju:əs/
appliance *n* /əˈplaɪəns/
board (a plane) *v* /bɔ:d/
bypass *n* /ˈbaɪpɑ:s/
checkout girl *n* /ˈtʃekaʊt ˌgɜ:l/
comprise *v* /kəmˈpraɪz/
conceivable *adj* /kənˈsi:vəbl/
convenient *adj* /kənˈvi:niənt/
deep freeze *n* /ˌdi:p ˈfri:z/
develop (a film) *v* /dɪˈveləp/
discourage *v* /dɪsˈkʌrɪdʒ/
dishwasher *n* /ˈdɪʃˌwɒʃə(r)/
doubtless *adv* /ˈdaʊtləs/
dreaded *pp* /ˈdredɪd/
drowned *pp* /draʊnd/
experiment *n* /ɪkˈsperɪmənt/
food processor *n* /ˈfu:d ˌprəʊsesə(r)/
gadget *n* /ˈgædʒɪt/
gaze *v* /geɪz/
get at (the truth) *v* /ˈget ət/
get at sb (= criticize) *v* /ˈget ət .../
get off (= not punished) *v* /ˌget ˈɒf/
get off with sb (at a party) *v* /ˌget ˈɒf wɪð .../
get out of (doing sth) *v* /ˌget ˈaʊt əv/
get over (= recover) *v* /ˌget ˈəʊvə(r)/
get over (a point in discussion) *v* /ˌget ˈəʊvə(r)/
(can't) **get over** (= very surprised at) *v* /ˌget ˈəʊvə(r)/
get through (= pass an exam) *v* /ˌget ˈθru:/
get through (= spend) *v* /ˌget ˈθru:/
get through (on the phone) *v* /ˌget ˈθru:/
get under way *v* /ˌget ˌʌndə ˈweɪ/
get up to (= reach) *v* /ˌget ˈʌp tə/
get up to (sth naughty) *v* /ˌget ˈʌp tə/
gym kit *n* /ˈdʒɪm ˌkɪt/
hamster *n* /ˈhæmstə(r)/
hold-up (traffic) *n* /ˈhəʊld ˌʌp/
in spite of *(id)* /ɪn ˈspaɪt əv/
inconsistent *adj* /ˌɪnkənˈsɪstənt/
jacuzzi *n* /dʒəˈku:zi/
labour-saving *adj* /ˈleɪbə ˌseɪvɪŋ/
long for sth *v* /ˈlɒŋ fə(r) .../
milkshake *n* /ˈmɪlkʃeɪk/
mixed feelings *pl n* /ˌmɪkst ˈfi:lɪŋz/
microwave oven *n* /ˌmaɪkrəʊweɪv ˈʌvn/
moody *adj* /ˈmu:di/
nap *n* /næp/
nevertheless *conj* /ˌnevəðəˈles/
olden days *pl n* /ˈəʊldən ˌdeɪz/
pop out *v* /ˌpɒp ˈaʊt/
power shower *n* /ˈpaʊə ˌʃaʊə(r)/
promote *v* /prəˈməʊt/
props *pl n* /prɒps/
puncture *n* /ˈpʌŋktʃə(r)/
push-button *adj* /ˈpʊʃ ˌbʌtn/
quit *v* /kwɪt/
rationed *pp* /ˈræʃənd/
razor *n* /ˈreɪzə(r)/
release (a record) *v* /rɪˈli:s/
remind *v* /rɪˈmaɪnd/
screen *n* /skri:n/
siren *n* /ˈsaɪrən/
slam (= criticize strongly) *v* /slæm/
spa bath *n* /ˈspɑ: ˌbɑ:θ/
stack *n, v* /stæk/
sullen *adj* /ˈsʌlən/
sway *v* /sweɪ/
tidal wave *n* /ˈtaɪdl ˌweɪv/
tin opener *n* /ˈtɪn ˌəʊpnə(r)/
tremble *v* /ˈtrembl/
trouser press *n* /ˈtraʊzə ˌpres/
tumble drier *n* /ˌtʌmbl ˈdraɪə(r)/
vacuum cleaner *n* /ˈvækju:m ˌkli:nə(r)/
vigorously *adv* /ˈvɪgərəsli/
wee-wee *(inf) n* /ˈwi: ˌwi:/
whereas *conj* /ˈweərəz/
wrap *v* /ræp/

Unit 8

according to *prep* /ə'kɔ:dɪŋ tə/
adaptation *n* /ˌædæp'teɪʃn/
anonymously *adv* /ə'nɒnɪməsli/
attachment *n* /ə'tætʃmənt/
award *n* /ə'wɔ:d/
back stage *n* /ˌbæk 'steɪdʒ/
bedridden *adj* /'bedˌrɪdn/
betray *v* /bɪ'treɪ/
blasphemous *adj* /'blæsfəməs/
brave *adj* /breɪv/
bright (= intelligent) *adj* /braɪt/
brilliant *adj* /'brɪliənt/
bungee-jumper *n* /'bʌndʒi ˌdʒʌmpə(r)/
chapel *n* /'tʃæpl/
christen *v* /'krɪsn/
clergyman *n* /'klɜ:dʒimən/
compose *v* /kəm'pəʊz/
congregation *n* /ˌkɒŋgrɪ'geɪʃn/
contemplate *v* /'kɒntəmpleɪt/
convincingly *adv* /kən'vɪnsɪŋli/
crack a joke /ˌkræk ə 'dʒəʊk/
crucifixion *n* /ˌkru:sɪ'fɪkʃn/
distinctly *adj* /dɪ'stɪŋktli/
do justice to *(id)* /ˌdu: 'dʒʌstɪs tə/
draft *n, v* /drɑ:ft/
dreadful *adj* /'dredfl/
elevator (*Am* = lift in Brit Eng) *n* /'eləveɪdə(r)/
enduring *adj* /ɪn'djʊərɪŋ/
examine *v* /ɪg'zæmɪn/
exhausted *adj* /ɪg'zɔ:stɪd/
fan club *n* /'fæn ˌklʌb/
fan *n* /fæn/
filthy *adj* /'fɪlθi/
flu (= influenza) *n* /flu:/
fully *adv* /'fʊli/
glamorous *adj* /'glæmərəs/
go on strike *v* /ˌgəʊ ɒn 'straɪk/
governess *n* /'gʌvənəs/
grumble *v* /'grʌmbl/
guy *(inf) n* /gaɪ/
hammer (= criticize) *v* /'hæmə(r)/
haunted *pp* /'hɔ:ntɪd/
hero *n* /'hɪərəʊ/
heroine *n* /'herəʊɪn/
hilarious *adj* /hɪ'leəriəs/
hit the roof *(id)* /ˌhɪt ðə 'ru:f/
hurl *v* /hɜ:l/
inequality *n* /ɪnɪ'kwɒləti/
influence *n, v* /'ɪnflʊəns/
intrigued *pp* /ɪn'tri:gd/
keen (on) *adj* /ki:n/
kidney *n* /'kɪdni/
knackered *(inf) adj* /'nækəd/
ledge *n* /ledʒ/
loaded (= very rich) *(inf) adj* /'ləʊdɪd/
loads of *(inf) adv* /'ləʊdz əv/
lyrics *pl n* /'lɪrɪks/
magical *adj* /'mædʒɪkl/
mate *n, v* /meɪt/
matrimony *n* /'mætrɪməni/
medical practice *n* /'medɪkl ˌpræktɪs/
muscles *pl n* /'mʌsəlz/
narrowness *n* /'nærəʊnəs/
originally *adv* /ə'rɪdʒɪnəli/
Oscar-winning *adj* /'ɒskə ˌwɪnɪŋ/
overcome *v* /ˌəʊvə'kʌm/
parachute *n* /'pærəʃu:t/
peckish *adj* /'pekɪʃ/
penniless *adj* /'penɪləs/
perform *v* /pə'fɔ:m/
portray *v* /pɔ:'treɪ/
poster *n* /'pəʊstə(r)/
priceless *adj* /'praɪsləs/
prize *n* /praɪz/
propensity *n* /prə'pensəti/
proposal *n* /prə'pəʊzl/
protest *v* /prə'test/
rambling (old house) *adj* /'ræmblɪŋ/
reaction *n* /rɪ'ækʃn/
recognizable *adj* /ˌrekəg'naɪzəbl/
(break a) **record** *n* /'rekɔ:d/
rectory *n* /'rektəri/
rescue *v* /'reskju:/
revise *v* /rɪ'vaɪz/
risky *adj* /'rɪski/
rival *n, v* /'raɪvl/
role *n* /rəʊl/
rural *adj* /'rʊərəl/
satirize *v* /'sætəraɪz/
screen *v* /skri:n/
screenplay *n* /'skri:npleɪ/
simplistic *adj* /sɪm'plɪstɪk/
sketch *n, v* /sketʃ/
slightly *adv* /'slaɪtli/
smash hit *n* /ˌsmæʃ 'hɪt/
smashed (= drunk) *(inf) adj* /smæʃt/
sole (only one) *adj* /səʊl/
spectacular *adj* /ˌspek'tækjʊlə(r)/
spinster *n* /'spɪnstə(r)/
starving *adj* /'stɑ:vɪŋ/
taboo *n* /tə'bu:/
talented *adj* /'tæləntɪd/
tipsy *(inf) adj* /'tɪpsi/
tulip *n* /'tju:lɪp/
valuable *adj* /'væljʊəbl/
version *n* /'vɜ:ʃn/
viewer *n* /'vju:ə(r)/
vile *adj* /vaɪl/
vulnerability *n* /ˌvʌlnərə'bɪləti/
waste (= become weak) *v* /weɪst/
worship *v* /'wɜ:ʃɪp/
yearn *v* /jɜ:n/
youthful *adj* /'ju:θfl/

Unit 9

agnostic *n, adj* /æg'nɒstɪk/
agoraphobic *n, adj* /ˌægrə'fəʊbɪk/
aisle *n* /aɪl/
ajar *adv* /ə'dʒɑː(r)/
alien *n* /'eɪliən/
anti-social *adj* /ˌænti 'səʊʃl/
atheist *n* /'eɪθiɪst/
babysit *v* /'beɪbisɪt/
bark (a dog) *n, v* /bɑːk/
basement *n* /'beɪsmənt/
bathe *v* /beɪð/
best man (at a wedding) *n* /ˌbest 'mæn/
bitter (taste) *adj* /'bɪtə(r)/
bridesmaid *n* /'braɪdzmeɪd/
caffeine *n* /'kæfiːn/
campainer *n* /kæm'peɪnə(r)/
casualty *n* /'kæʒʊəlti/
ceiling *n* /'siːlɪŋ/
challenge *n, v* /'tʃælɪndʒ/
chat *n, v* /tʃæt/
chest of drawers *n* /ˌtʃest əv 'drɔːz/
chunk *n* /tʃʌŋk/
claustrophobic *n, adj* /ˌklɒstrə'fəʊbɪk/
cloth *n* /klɒθ/
comet *n* /'kɒmɪt/
concerned *adj* /kən'sɜːnd/
condense *v* /kən'dens/
consensus *n* /kən'sensəs/
cork *n* /kɔːk/
cowardly *adj* /'kaʊədli/
crossbow *n* /'krɒsbəʊ/
crossword *n* /'krɒswɜːd/
dare *n, v* /deə(r)/
depict *v* /dɪ'pɪkt/
destiny *n* /'destəni/
deteriorate *v* /dɪ'tɪərɪəreɪt/
dinosaur *n* /'daɪnəsɔː(r)/
disarmament *n* /ˌdɪs'ɑːməmənt/
distraught *adj* /dɪ'strɔːt/
downtown *n, adj* /'daʊnˌtaʊn/
drive (to a house) *n* /draɪv/
dyslexic *adj* /dɪs'leksɪk/
estate agent *n* /ɪ'steɪt ˌeɪdʒənt/
fake *adj* /feɪk/
feature *n* /'fiːtʃə(r)/
figure (= think) *v* /'fɪgə(r)/
fresco *n* /'freskəʊ/
genetics *pl n* /dʒə'netɪks/
go through (= continue) *v* /ˌgəʊ 'θruː/
hallucination *n* /həˌluːsɪ'neɪʃn/
ice (a cake) *v* /aɪs/
incident *n* /'ɪnsɪdənt/
infectious *adj* /ɪn'fekʃəs/
insomniac *n* /ɪn'sɒmniæk/
ivory *n, adj* /'aɪvəri/
leave sb in the lurch *(id)* /ˌliːv ... ɪn ðə 'lɜːtʃ/
lurk *v* /lɜːk/
mammal *n* /'mæml/
mankind *n* /mæn'kaɪnd/
matter (in the universe) *n* /'mætə(r)/
misery *n* /'mɪzəri/
nut *n* /nʌt/
odd (sock) *adj* /ɒd/
overcast *adj* /ˌəʊvə'kɑːst/
oversleep *v* /ˌəʊvə'sliːp/
panic attack *n* /'pænɪk əˌtæk/
parsnip *n* /'pɑːsnɪp/
pluck up courage *(id)* /ˌplʌk ʌp 'kʌrɪdʒ/
praise *n, v* /preɪz/
recuperation *n* /rɪˌkuːpə'reɪʃn/
rehearsal *n* /rɪ'hɜːsl/
release (from prison) *v* /rɪ'liːs/
reptile *n* /'reptaɪl/
rid *v* /rɪd/
salesman *n* /'seɪlzmən/
shameful *adj* /'ʃeɪmfl/
spark off (a war) *v* /ˌspɑːk 'ɒf/
stationery *n* /'steɪʃənri/
sustain *v* /sə'steɪn/
teetotal *adj* /ˌtiː'təʊtl/
temporary *adj* /'tempərəri/
thrust *v* /θrʌst/
tough (= difficult) *adj* /tʌf/
trigger (= start) *n, v* /'trɪgə(r)/
trip over *v* /ˌtrɪp 'əʊvə(r)/
vague *adj* /veɪg/
vapour *n* /'veɪpə(r)/
vegan *n* /'viːgən/
visa *n* /'viːzə/
warm-blooded *adj* /ˌwɔːm 'blʌdɪd/
white lie *n* /ˌwaɪt 'laɪ/
workaholic *n* /ˌwɜːkə'hɒlɪk/
wound *n* /wuːnd/
zoom off *(inf)* *v* /ˌzuːm 'ɒf/

Unit 10

(nervous) **breakdown** *n* /ˈbreɪkdaʊn/
alcoholic *n, adj* /ˌælkəˈhɒlɪk/
aristocrat *n* /ˈærɪstəˌkræt/
available *adj* /əˈveɪləbl/
bankrupt *adj* /ˈbæŋkrʌpt/
barmaid *n* /ˈbɑːmeɪd/
basically *adv* /ˈbeɪsɪkli/
baulk (at) *v* /bɔːk/
beat (= hit) *v* /biːt/
bench *n* /bentʃ/
boar *n* /bɔː(r)/
boast *v* /bəʊst/
boil *v* /bɔɪl/
bouquet *n* /bʊˈkeɪ/
brand new *adj* /ˌbrænd ˈnjuː/
bucket *n* /ˈbʌkɪt/
bunch of flowers *n* /ˌbʌntʃ əv ˈflaʊəz/
burst into tears *v* /ˌbɜːst ˌɪntə ˈtɪəz/
cabbage *n* /ˈkæbɪdʒ/
charity *n* /ˈtʃærəti/
chimney *n* /ˈtʃɪmni/
chop *v* /tʃɒp/
cobbled *adj* /ˈkɒbəld/
colleague *n* /ˈkɒliːg/
collection *n* /kəˈlekʃn/
commuter *n* /kəˈmjuːtə(r)/
constantly *adv* /ˈkɒnstəntli/
course (of a meal) *n* /kɔːs/
deposit *v* /dɪˈpɒzɪt/
devastating *adj* /ˈdevəˌsteɪtɪŋ/
do a roaring trade *(id)* /ˌduː ə ˈrɔːrɪŋ ˌtreɪd/
dodge (= avoid) *v* /dɒdʒ/
donate *v* /dəʊˈneɪt/
down-and-out *adj* /ˌdaʊn ən ˈaʊt/
drop in (= visit) *v* /ˌdrɒp ˈɪn/
dusk *n* /dʌsk/
earthquake *n* /ˈɜːθkweɪk/
expenditure *n* /ɪkˈspendɪtʃə(r)/
extravagant *adj* /ɪkˈstrævəgənt/
feast *n* /fiːst/
fence (with swords) *v* /fens/
filth *n* /fɪlθ/
funeral parlour *n* /ˈfjuːnərəl ˌpɑːlə(r)/
garment *n* /ˈgɑːmənt/
gather *v* /ˈgæðə(r)/
generation *n* /ˌdʒenəˈreɪʃn/
get your act together *(id)* /ˌget jɔːr ˈækt təˌgeðə(r)/
go rambling *v* /ˌgəʊ ˈræmblɪŋ/
gobble *v* /ˈgɒbl/
gradually *adj* /ˈgrædʒʊəli/
grim *adj* /grɪm/
grub (= food) *(inf) n* /grʌb/
hard up *adj* /ˌhɑːd ˈʌp/
hassle *(inf) n, v* /ˈhæsl/
iceberg *n* /ˈaɪsbɜːg/
in bulk *(id)* /ˌɪn ˈbʌlk/
in the black *(id)* /ˌɪn ðə ˈblæk/
income *n* /ˈɪnkʌm/
indulge *v* /ɪnˈdʌldʒ/
infinite *adj* /ˈɪnfɪnət/
inherit *v* /ɪnˈherɪt/
joust *v* /dʒaʊst/
kettle *n* /ˈketl/
lap of luxury *(id)* /ˌlæp əv ˈlʌkʃəri/
lark (= bird) *n* /lɑːk/
lifespan *n* /ˈlaɪfspæn/
literally *adv* /ˈlɪtərəli/
live on a shoestring *(id)* /ˌlɪv ɒn ə ˈʃuːstrɪŋ/
live rough *(id)* /ˌlɪv ˈrʌf/
long-term *adj* /ˈlɒŋ ˌtɜːm/
lost a quid and found a fiver *(id)* /ˌlɒst ə ˌkwɪd ən ˌfaʊnd ə ˈfaɪvə(r)/
made of money *(id)* /ˈmeɪd əv ˌmʌni/
make ends meet *(id)* /ˌmeɪk endz ˈmiːt/
malt whisky *n* /ˌmɒlt ˈwɪski/
mansion *n* /ˈmænʃn/
meanness *n* /ˈmiːnnəs/
miser *n* /ˈmaɪzə(r)/
mislay *v* /mɪsˈleɪ/
monarch *n* /ˈmɒnək/
monastry *n* /ˈmɒnəstri/
monolingual *adj* /ˌmɒnəˈlɪŋgwəl/
mutter *v* /ˈmʌtə(r)/
nauseating *adj* /ˈnɔːzieɪtɪŋ/
network *n* /ˈnetwɜːk/
overcrowded *adj* /ˌəʊvəˈkraʊdɪd/
overdrawn *pp* /ˌəʊvəˈdrɔːn/
packed lunch *n* /ˌpækt ˈlʌntʃ/
passer-by *n* /ˌpɑːsə ˈbaɪ/
patch up *v* /ˌpætʃ ˈʌp/
penny pincher *n* /ˈpeni ˌpɪntʃə(r)/
pensioner *n* /ˈpenʃənə(r)/
plague *n* /pleɪg/
playwright *n* /ˈpleɪraɪt/
pocket money *n* /ˈpɒkɪt ˌmʌni/
pond *n* /pɒnd/
precious *adj* /ˈpreʃəs/
principle *n* /ˈprɪnsəpl/
rarely *adv* /ˈreəli/
recycle *v* /ˌriːˈsaɪkl/
reformed *pp* /rɪˈfɔːmd/
regularly *adv* /ˈregjʊləli/
repairs *pl n* /rɪˈpeəz/
roam *v* /rəʊm/
rolling in money *(id)* /ˈrəʊlɪŋ ɪn ˌmʌni/
rotten *adj* /ˈrɒtn/
sewer *n* /ˈsuːə(r)/
skinflint *n* /ˈskɪnflɪnt/
sleeping bag *n* /ˈsliːpɪŋ ˌbæg/
smart *adj* /smɑːt/
social leper *n* /ˌsəʊʃl ˈlepə(r)/
sour *adj* /ˈsaʊə(r)
spendthrift *n* /ˈspendθrɪft/
spiral *n* /ˈspaɪrəl/
stash (away money) *(inf) v* /stæʃ/
state benefit *n* /ˌsteɪt ˈbenəfɪt/
stingy *adj* /ˈstɪndʒi/
support *v* /səˈpɔːt/
survival *n* /səˈvaɪvl/
tablet *n* /ˈtæblət/
tag (= label) *n* /tæg/
taxman *n* /ˈtæksmæn/
thrifty *adj* /ˈθrɪfti/
thrive *v* /θraɪv/
tight-fisted *adj* /ˌtaɪt ˈfɪstɪd/
tighten your belt *(id)* /ˌtaɪtn jɔː ˈbelt/
tights *pl n* /taɪts/
treat *n* /triːt/
turnip *n* /ˈtɜːnɪp/
underprivileged *adj* /ˌʌndəˈprɪvəlɪdʒd/
upholstery *n* /ʌpˈhəʊlstəri/
vary *v* /ˈveəri/
vast *adj* /vɑːst/
venison *n* /ˈvenɪsn/
victim *n* /ˈvɪktɪm/
wishing well *n* /ˈwɪʃɪŋ ˌwel/
withdraw *v* /wɪðˈdrɔː/
worthless *adj* /ˈwɜːθləs/
wrapping paper *n* /ˈræpɪŋ ˌpeɪpə(r)/

Unit 11

accusingly *adv* /ə'kju:zɪŋli/
bald *adj* /bɔ:ld/
be a far cry from *(id)* /ˌbi: ə 'fɑ: ˌkraɪ frəm/
be at a loose end *(id)* /ˌbi: ət ə ˌlu:s 'end/
bedsit *n* /'bedsɪt/
bleak *adj* /bli:k/
blink *v* /blɪŋk/
break sb's heart *(id)* /ˌbreɪk ... 'hɑ:t/
break the ice *(id)* /ˌbreɪk ði: 'aɪs/
broad *adj* /brɔ:d/
broken-hearted *adj* /ˌbrəʊkn 'hɑ:tɪd/
compartment (of a bag) *n* /kəm'pɑ:tmənt/
damp *adj* /dæmp/
date sb *v* /deɪt ... /
deserve *v* /dɪ'zɜ:v/
dispassionate *adj* /dɪs'pæʃənət/
distraught *adj* /dɪ'strɔ:t/
distressing *adj* /dɪ'stresɪŋ/
envy *n, v* /'envi/
exotic *adj* /ɪg'zɒtɪk/
fall head over heels in love *(id)* /ˌfɔ:l ˌhed əʊvə ˌhi:lz in 'lʌv/
flatmate *n* /'flætmeɪt/
focus *n, v* /'fəʊkəs/
gesture *n* /'dʒestʃə(r)/
get cold feet *(id)* /ˌget ˌkəʊld 'fi:t/
go down the drain *(id)* /ˌgəʊ ˌdaʊn ðə 'dreɪn/
go through the roof *(id)* /ˌgəʊ ˌθru: ðə 'ru:f/
go up in the world *(id)* /ˌgəʊ 'ʌp ɪn ðə ˌwɜ:ld/
grab *v* /græb/
groan *v* /grəʊn/
have an affair *v* /ˌhæv ən ə'feə(r)/
have butterflies in your stomach *(id)* /ˌhæv ˌbʌtəflaɪz ɪn jɔ: 'stʌmək/
have time to kill *(id)* /ˌhæv ˌtaɪm tə 'kɪl/
have your head in the sand *(id)* /ˌhæv jɔ: ˌhed ɪn ðə 'sænd/
hit the jackpot *(id)* /ˌhɪt ðə 'dʒækpɒt/
hum and haw *(id)* /ˌhʌm ən 'hɔ:/
icily *adv* /'aɪsəli/
ideally *adv* /aɪ'di:əli/
indiscretion *n* /ˌɪndɪ'skreʃn/
interrupt *v* /ˌɪntə'rʌpt/
layabout *n* /'leɪəbaʊt/
loathe *v* /ləʊð/
lose touch *(id)* /ˌlu:z 'tʌtʃ/
lousy (= bad) *(inf) adj* /'laʊzi/
massive *adj* /'mæsɪv/
moan *n, v* /məʊn/
mousey-brown *adj* /ˌmaʊsi 'braʊn/
napkin *n* /'næpkɪn/
not be a patch on *(id)* /ˌnɒt bi: ə 'pætʃ ɒn/
offspring *n* /'ɒfsprɪŋ/
on the tip of my tongue *(id)* /ɒn ðə ˌtɪp əv maɪ 'tʌŋ/
over the moon *(id)* /ˌəʊvə ðə 'mu:n/
oversleep *v* /ˌəʊvə'sli:p/
permanent *adj* /'pɜ:mənənt/
pluck up courage *(id)* /ˌplʌk ʌp 'kʌrɪdʒ/
plump *adj* /plʌmp/
quick-tempered *adj* /ˌkwɪk 'tempəd/
quicken *v* /'kwɪkn/
self-portrait *n* /ˌself 'pɔ:treɪt/
short-sighted *adj* /ˌʃɔ:t 'saɪtɪd/
sigh *n, v* /saɪ/
single-mindedly *adv* /ˌsɪŋgl 'maɪndɪdli/
sister-in-law *n* /'sɪstər ɪn ˌlɔ:/
sleeve *n* /sli:v/
splutter *v* /'splʌtə(r)/
stepmother *n* /'stepmʌðə(r)/
storm out *v* /ˌstɔ:m 'aʊt/
stove *n* /stəʊv/
succession *n* /sək'seʃn/
temporary *adj* /'tempərəri/
that rings a bell *(id)* /ˌðæt rɪŋz ə 'bel/
treatment *n* /'tri:tmənt/
tuck *v* /tʌk/
unruly *adj* /ˌʌn'ru:li/
verge *n* /vɜ:dʒ/
waves (of hair) *n* /weɪvz/
zipped *pp* /zɪpt/

Unit 12

account (= report) *n* /ə'kaʊnt/
account (in the bank) *n* /ə'kaʊnt/
achievement *n* /ə'tʃi:vmənt/
actually *adv* /'æktʃʊəli/
after all *(id)* /ˌɑ:ftər 'ɔ:l/
all the same *(id)* /ˌɔ:l ðə 'seɪm/
anecdote *n* /'ænɪkdəʊt/
apartheid *n* /ə'pɑ:taɪt/
apparently *adv* /ə'pærəntli/
attempt *n* /ə'tempt/
barbed-wire fence *n* /ˌbɑ:bd ˌwaɪə 'fens/
basically *adv* /'beɪsɪkli/
benefit *n, v* /'benəfɪt/
bet *n, v* /bet/
blast *n, v* /blɑ:st/
bonus *n* /'bəʊnəs/
bore (= make a hole) *v* /bɔ:(r)/
burglary *n* /'bɜ:gləri/
call it quits *(id)* /ˌkɔ:l ɪt 'kwɪts/
censor *v* /'sensə(r)/
charismatic *adj* /ˌkærɪz'mætɪk/
childbirth *n* /'tʃaɪldbɜ:θ/
collapse *n* /kə'læps/
concentrate *v* /'kɒnsəntreɪt/
congestion (on roads) *n* /kən'dʒestʃn/
conscience *n* /'kɒnʃəns/
contemporary *n* /kən'tempərəri/
creator *n* /krieɪtə(r)/
cross (= angry) *adj* /krɒs/
deadly *adj* /'dedli/
declare *v* /dɪ'kleə(r)/
definitely *adv* /'defɪnətli/
deliberately *adv* /dɪ'lɪbərətli/
design *n, v* /dɪ'zaɪn/
devastating *adj* /'devəsteɪtɪŋ/
device *n* /dɪ'vaɪs/
dingy (dark, dirty) *adj* /'dɪndʒi/
dismiss *v* /dɪs'mɪs/
dome *n* /dəʊm/
draw (a picture) *v* /drɔ:/
drift (= move aimlessly) *v* /drɪft/
dusty *adj* /'dʌsti/
equal *v* /'i:kwəl/
expire *v* /ɪk'spaɪə(r)/
expose *v* /ɪk'spəʊz/
fateful *adj* /'feɪtfl/
filling station *n* /'fɪlɪŋ ˌsteɪʃn/
fit (= healthy) *adj* /fɪt/
foothill *n* /'fʊthɪl/
guess *n, v* /ges/
honestly *adv* /'ɒnəstli/
icon (= person) *n* /'aɪkɒn/
imminent *adj* /'ɪmɪnənt/
imprecise *adj* /ˌɪmprɪ'saɪs/
indication *n* /ˌɪndɪ'keɪʃn/
inspired *adj* /ɪn'spaɪəd/
instinctive *adj* /ɪn'stɪŋktɪv/
interact *v* /ˌɪntə'rækt/
jog *v* /dʒɒg/
left-wing *adj* /ˌleft 'wɪŋ/
lick *v* /lɪk/
lifejacket *n* /'laɪfdʒækɪt/
long for sth *v* /'lɒŋ fə(r) ... /
luminosity *n* /ˌlu:mɪ'nɒsəti/
marble *n* /'mɑ:bl/
mark (= correct) *v* /mɑ:k/
model *n* /'mɒdl/
nickname *n* /'nɪkneɪm/
obviously *adv* /'ɒbviəsli/
outspoken *adj* /ˌaʊt'spəʊkən/
pacifism *n* /'pæsɪfɪzm/
parking ticket *n* /'pɑ:kɪŋ ˌtɪkɪt/
pelvis *n* /'pelvɪs/
penicillin *n* /ˌpenɪ'sɪlɪn/
personally *adv* /'pɜ:sənəli/
perspective *n* /pə'spektɪv/
(the) **Pill** (contraceptive) *n* /pɪl/
pounce *v* /paʊns/
profound *adj* /prə'faʊnd/
protégé *n* /'prɒtəʒeɪ/
race (of people) *n* /reɪs/
race around (= rush) *v* /ˌreɪs ə'raʊnd/
rebel *v* /rɪ'bel/
reflective *adj* /rɪ'flektɪv/
ripe for change *(id)* /ˌraɪp fə 'tʃeɪndʒ/
rule out *v* /ˌru:l 'aʊt/
scaffolding *n* /'skæfəʊldɪŋ/
scale *n* /skeɪl/
sceptic *n* /'skeptɪk/
sculptor *n* /'skʌlptə(r)/
second thoughts *(id)* /ˌsekənd 'θɔ:ts/
seminal event *n* /ˌsemɪnl ɪ'vent/
sentence (sb to prison) *v* /'sentəns/
shark *n* /ʃɑ:k/
shopping mall *n* /'ʃɒpɪŋ ˌmɔ:l/
sling *n* /slɪŋ/
still *adj, adv* /stɪl/
stuff (sth in a bag) *v* /stʌf/
stun *v* /stʌn/
sum (of money) *n* /sʌm/
sum up *v* /ˌsʌm 'ʌp/
summon *v* /'sʌmən/
surely *adv* /'ʃʊəli/
switch *v* /swɪtʃ/
sworn to secrecy *pp* /ˌswɔ:n tə 'si:krəsi/
tail *v* /teɪl/
task *n* /tɑ:sk/
thatched roof *n* /ˌθætʃt 'ru:f/
trial *n* /'traɪəl/
trickle *n, v* /'trɪkl/
undetected *pp* /ˌʌndɪ'tektɪd/
urge *v* /ɜ:dʒ/
villain *n* /'vɪlən/
VIP *n* /ˌvi: aɪ 'pi:/
watchtower *n* /'wɒtʃˌtaʊə(r)/
weapon *n* /'wepən/